Assessment Reform in Educ

EDUCATION IN THE ASIA-PACIFIC REGION: ISSUES, CONCERNS AND PROSPECTS

Volume 14

Rita Berry · Bob Adamson
Editors

Assessment Reform in Education

Policy and Practice

Springer

Editors
Rita Berry
Hong Kong Institute of Education
Tai Po
Hong Kong
rsyberry@ied.edu.hk

Bob Adamson
Hong Kong Institute of Education
Tai Po
Hong Kong
badamson@ied.edu.hk

ISBN 978-94-007-0728-3 e-ISBN 978-94-007-0729-0
DOI 10.1007/978-94-007-0729-0
Springer Dordrecht Heidelberg London New York

Library of Congress Control Number: 2011923080

Printed on acid-free paper

Springer is part of Springer Science+Business Media (www.springer.com)

Foreword

This is an important and insightful book on a topic of great importance, which is attracting increasing attention worldwide: that of the reform of methods of educational and learning assessment. Knowledge and skills shape the future lives of learners, so it is important that learning assessment is accurate, reliable and fair.

Recent decades have seen significant developments in the field of educational assessment. New approaches to the assessment of student learning achievement have been accompanied by the increasing prominence of educational assessment as a policy issue. In particular, there has been a growth in modes of assessment that promote, as well as measure, standards and quality. These developments have profound implications for individual learners, institutions and educational systems.

Educational assessment refers to the process of gathering accurate and reliable information on the knowledge, skills, attitudes and beliefs of learners. Assessment can focus on the individual learner, a group of learners, a learning institution such as a school, or the educational system as a whole. Assessment is a form of educational research since it is concerned with obtaining reliable, verifiable information on the learning outcomes of those being assessed.

In a report (2000) by the Hong Kong Curriculum Development Council entitled *Learning to Learn: The Way Forward in Curriculum Development,* the general directions for curriculum development and student assessment in Hong Kong to fulfil the vision of enabling students to attain all-round development and life-long learning, were set out. The Report recommended that there should be a change in assessment practices and that schools should put more emphasis on assessment for learning, a process in which teachers seek to identify and diagnose student learning problems, and provide quality feedback for students on how to improve their work.

The CDC report notes that: 'The concept of assessment for learning is not new. It is underpinned by the confidence and belief that every student is unique and possess the ability to learn, and that we should develop their multiple intelligences and potentials. To promote better learning, assessment is conducted as an integral part of the curriculum, learning and teaching, and feedback cycle. The curriculum has set out what students should learn in terms of the learning targets/objectives (e.g. knowledge, skills, values and attitudes). Assessment, a practice of collecting evidence of student learning, should be so designed that it assesses what students are expected to learn (i.e. learning targets and content) and the learning processes that lead there. Different modes of assessment are to be used whenever appropriate for a comprehensive understanding of student learning in various aspects. Feedback can then be given to students and teachers to form basis on decisions as to what to do to improve learning and teaching.'

The ways in which learners are assessed have a major influence on most aspects of how an education system is designed, organised and implemented including teaching methods and teacher behaviour. In terms of logical sequencing the ways in which learners are assessed should flow on naturally from the well considered aims, expected outcomes and the content of what is being taught. The core purpose of assessment involves determining the extent to which the aims and expected outcomes of learning have actually been achieved, and in so doing seeks to provide reliable information that helps promote effective learning. However in reality it is often the case that the methods of assessment strongly influence pedagogy and key aspects of teacher behaviour so that assessment becomes the tail wagging the dog. This is particularly the case where, for example, assessment is externally imposed, by outsiders who are not personally or directly involved with the teaching enterprise in particular education institutions and systems. The impact of the ways in which learners are assessed is so profound that it can be argued that those who control the ways in which learners are assessment actually control most aspects of the education enterprise.

Student assessment is of profound importance, not just to individual learners and their families, but also to nations as a whole. Take for example the case of PISA scores, which assess how far students near the end of compulsory education have acquired some of the knowledge and skills that are essential for full participation in society. In all cycles, the domains of reading, mathematical and scientific literacy are covered not merely in terms of mastery of the school curriculum, but in terms of important knowledge and skills needed in adult life.

PISA scores have resulted in the education systems of different countries being ranked and rated in a hierarchy with regard to the learning outcomes of students. For a country to receive a low PISA score relative to other countries results in much soul searching on the part of politicians and the society at large, since PISA is seen as being an accurate and objective way of assessing the educational outcomes of students, and so the quality and effectiveness of education systems as a whole. It is for these types of reasons that the reform of learning assessment is so contentious in many countries.

What is apparent from this valuable and comprehensive volume, which examines cutting edge issues, concerns and prospects regarding the reform of learning assessment, with an explicitly international focus, is the complex nature of assessment. Learning assessment often fulfils very different functions for different stakeholders, be they teachers, administrators, parents, employers, policy makers or individual learners themselves. These various stakeholders often have diverse and very different expectations and requirements of assessment.

This book is a refreshing contribution to the field of assessment reform. By drawing on the perspectives of researchers, policy makers and education practitioners from various parts of the world, the book provides a multitude of perspectives on assessment reform, from different cultural and educational orientations. The book provides a useful historical overview of changes in learning assessment including major influences and ideas that have shaped changing patterns of assessment over time.

The book examines major issues and concerns regarding assessment reform, including the impact of assessment reform on teacher behaviour and the empowerment (or marginalisation) of teachers, and the impact of assessment on learning outcomes.

It is because assessment has such a far ranging impact on the overall functions of education systems (with many influential values being embedded in the assessment exercise) that learning assessment reform is of considerable importance to the overall education reform process. In fact, those who argue for a need to re-engineer education for change also claim that this is only possible if assessment systems are reformed, with many of the taken-for granted values and beliefs upon assess is based being carefully scrutinised and re-evaluated.

This book by Rita Berry and Bob Adamson is an important and timely addition to our Springer Book Series on ***Education in the Asia-Pacific Region: Issues, Concerns and Challenges***. As such it has much to offer that will be of considerable value to readers, and so deserves to be widely read.

Tai Po, Hong Kong
Tokyo, Japan
November 2010

Rupert Maclean
Ryo Watanabe

Acknowledgments

Many people have helped us with this book project. In particular, we would like to thank Professor Rupert Maclean and Ryo Watanabe, the series editors, for their encouragement and for writing the foreword. We are grateful to the anonymous reviewers for their constructive comments on the chapters. A special word of thanks goes to our research assistants, Mr Wilson Chung Ka Wai and Mr Pecco Yin Qinsi, who never failed in support throughout this book project. We would also like to acknowledge the enabling role of the Hong Kong Institute of Education and the funding support from the Faculty of Education Studies. Our greatest appreciation must go to Rita's husband and Bob's family for their moral support and encouragement.

Contents

Contributors

Bob Adamson Department of International Education and Lifelong Learning, Hong Kong Institute of Education, Tai Po, Hong Kong, badamson@ied.edu.hk

Rita Berry Department of Curriculum and Instruction, Hong Kong Institute of Education, Tai Po, Hong Kong, rsyberry@ied.edu.hk

Paul Black Department of Education and Professional Studies, School of Social Science and Public Policy, Franklin-Wilkins Building, Waterloo Road, London, UK, paul.black@kcl.ac.uk

Alice Chow Department of English, Hong Kong Institute of Education, Tai Po, Hong Kong, alice@ied.edu.hk

Richard Daugherty School of Social Sciences, Cardiff University, Wales, UK, daughertyr@Cardiff.ac.uk

Kathryn Ecclestone School of Education, University of Birmingham, Birmingham, UK, k.ecclestone@bham.ac.uk

Jim Flaitz Educational Foundations and Leadership Department, College of Education at the University of Louisiana at Lafayette, Lafayette, LA, USA, jflaitz@louisiana.edu

John Gardner School of Education at Queen's University, Belfast, Northern Ireland, UK, j.gardner@qub.ac.uk

Eleanore Hargreaves Institute of Education, University of London, London, UK, E.Hargreaves@ioe.ac.uk

Wynne Harlen Graduate School of Education, University of Bristol, Bristol, England, UK, wynne@torphin.freeserve.co.uk

Louise Hayward School of Education, Glasgow University, Glasgow, Scotland, UK, l.hayward@educ.gla.ac.uk

Mary James Faculty of Education, University of Cambridge, Cambridge, UK, mej1002@cam.ac.uk

Val Klenowski Queensland University of Technology, Brisbane, QLD, Australia, val.klenowski@qut.edu.au

Pamela Leung Department of Chinese, Hong Kong Institute of Education, Tai Po, Hong Kong, pleung@ied.edu.hk

Yu-Jen Lu Graduate Institute of Science Education, National Taiwan Normal University, Taipei, Taiwan, hitachi6@gmail.com

Paul Newton Assessment Research and Development Group, Cambridge Assessment Network Division, Cambridge Assessment, 1 Hills Road, Cambridge, UK, Newton.P@cambridgeassessment.org.uk

David Scott Institute of Education, University of London, 20, Bedford Way, London WCIH OAL, UK, d.scott@ioe.ac.uk

Gordon Stobart Institute of Education, University of London, London, England, UK, g.stobart@ioe.ac.uk

Hak Ping Tam Graduate Institute of Science Education, National Taiwan Normal University, Taipei, Taiwan, t45003@ntnu.edu.tw

Kelvin Tan Policy and Leadership Studies Department, National Institute of Education, Singapore, Kelvin.tan@nie.edu.sg

List of Abbreviations

ACME	Advisory Committee on Mathematics Education
ACT	American College Testing
ARIA	Analysis and Review of Innovations in Assessment
AYP	annual yearly progress
AaL	Assessment as learning
AfL	Assessment for learning
AifL	Assessment is for Learning
AoL	Assessment of learning
ASLO	Assessment of Significant Learning Outcomes
ARG	Assessment Reform Group
ASF	Assessment Systems for the Future
ACE	Australian Certificate of Education
ACER	Australian Council for Educational Research
ACARA	Australian Curriculum, Assessment and Reporting Authority
BCA	Basic Competency Assessment
BERA	British Educational Research Association
CA	continual assessment
CCEA	Council for the Curriculum, Examinations and Assessment
CID	Curriculum and Instruction Development
CDC	Curriculum Development Council
DARG	Daugherty Assessment Review Group
DCSF	Department for Children, Schools and Families
DfE	Department for Education
DfES	Department for Education and Skills
ESRC	Economic and Social Research Council
EOC	end-of-course
EUMIE	European Masters in Inclusive Education
EU	European Union
GCSE	General Certificate of Secondary Education
HKSAR	Hong Kong Special Administrative Region
IEA	International Association for the Evaluation of Educational Achievement

JAFA	Jersey Actioning Formative Assessment
KOSAP	King's-Oxfordshire Summative Assessment Project
LHTL	learning how to learn
LOTG	Learning Outcomes Thematic Group
L2L	learning to learn
MEETYA	Ministerial Council for Employment, Education, Training and Youth Affairs
MOE	Ministry of Education
NAPLAN	National Assessment Program – Literacy and Numeracy
NTAC	National Technical Advisory Council
NVQs	National Vocational Qualifications
OECD	Organization for Economic Cooperation and Development
PRC	People's Republic of China
PNS	Primary National Strategy
PISA	Programme for International Student Assessment
PIRLS	Progress in International Reading Literacy Study
QCA	Qualifications and Curriculum Authority
QCDA	Qualifications and Curriculum Development Agency
QAA	Quality Assurance Agency
QCATs	Queensland Comparable Assessment Tasks
QCAR	Queensland Curriculum, Assessment and Reporting
QSA	Queensland Studies Authority
SAT	Scholastic Assessment Test
SBA	School-based Assessment
SQA	Scottish Qualifications Authority
SSA	Scottish Survey of Achievement
SNS	Secondary National Strategy
SA	semestral assessment
SLTs	single level tests
SES	supplemental educational support
TOC	Target-Oriented Curriculum
TGAT	Task Group on Assessment and Testing
TLLM	Teach Less, Learn More
TLRP	Teaching and Learning Research Programme
TSA	Territory–wide System Assessment
TSLN	Thinking Schools Learning Nation
Ts	Thinking Skills
TIMSS	Trends in International Mathematics and Science Study
UCET-NI	Universities' Council for the Education of Teachers – Northern Ireland

List of Figures

List of Tables

About the Authors

Editor

Rita Berry is an Associate Professor in the Department of Curriculum and Instruction, Hong Kong Institute of Education. She obtained her doctoral title from the University of Exeter UK but her teaching qualifications (main stream and slow learners) were obtained in Hong Kong. Dr Berry has extensive experience in teaching and has worked in schools and universities in the UK and Hong Kong. She is involved in many external and internal funded research projects and publishes widely in the area of assessment, learner autonomy, curriculum, and teacher education. Currently, she is leading a substantial research project entitled "Assessment for Learning in Hong Kong" (Quality Education Fund). Dr Berry develops and coordinates courses, including the MEd Assessment and Evaluation Specialization programme. She provides consultancy services and offers various kinds of professional upgrading training for teachers in and outside Hong Kong. Her research interests include assessment FOR/AS learning, classroom and school-based assessment, curriculum development and implementation, as well as autonomous learning and learning strategies.

Co-editor

Bob Adamson is a Professor at Hong Kong Institute of Education, where he is Head of the Department of International Education and Lifelong Learning. Prior to this, he was Head of the Department of Curriculum and Instruction and the Director of Graduate Programmes. He has worked in schools, colleges and universities in France, mainland China, Hong Kong, Australia and the United Kingdom, before assuming his current position at the Hong Kong Institute of Education in September 2006. Prof Adamson is a former Honorary Director of the Comparative Education Research Centre at the University of Hong Kong, and Past President of the Comparative Education Society of Hong Kong. He has carried out consultancies for the People's Education Press, China; Ohana Foundation, California; and UNICEF. Prof Adamson has published extensively in the field of curriculum studies, with a particular focus on English language teaching and comparative education.

Other Contributors

Paul Black worked as a physicist for 20 years before moving to a chair in science education. He has made many contributions, to curriculum development in the Nuffield Curriculum Projects at primary and secondary levels, and to research into learning and assessment. He was chair of the U.K. government's Task Group on Assessment and Testing in 1988 which formulated advice on the new national assessment system. He has served as Vice-President of the International Union of Pure and Applied Physics, on the ESRC Research Grant's Board, on three advisory groups of the USA National Research Council, as visiting professor at Stanford University, and as a member of the Assessment Reform Group. He is Professor Emeritus of Education at King's College London, and his work on formative assessment with Dylan Wiliam and others has had widespread impact.

Alice Chow is an Associate Professor in the Department of English. She has served as a secondary school teacher and a school inspector, and is involved in pre-service and in-service teacher education. Her research interests are ELT curriculum & method, and school-based professional development. For external appointment, she has served as member of the CDC textbook review committee, and HKEA CE subject committee and provided school-based consultancy services for local primary and secondary schools.

Richard Daugherty is an Honorary Professor in the School of Social Sciences, Cardiff University, UK. Earlier in his career he was a high school teacher of geography and lecturer in geography education. Publications in that field include *Geography into the Twenty-First Century* (Wiley 1996), co-edited with Eleanor Rawling. Richard was President of the Geographical Association in 1989–1990. The main focus of his research in recent years has been on education policy, especially policies on the school curriculum and on student assessment. He has had several advisory roles to government in Wales including chairing the Curriculum Council for Wales (1991–1993), chairing the Daugherty Assessment Review Group (2003–2004) and carrying out a policy audit (2007). Richard has been a member of the Assessment Reform Group since 1992 and has contributed to a series of ARG projects on theory, practice and policy in assessment.

Kathryn Ecclestone is Professor of Post-Compulsory Education at Oxford Brookes University. She has worked in post-compulsory education for the past 20 years, first as a practitioner in youth employment schemes and further education and as a researcher specialising in the principles, politics and practices of assessment and its links to learning, motivation and autonomy. She has a particular interest in socio-cultural approaches to understanding the interplay between policy, practice and attitudes to learning and assessment. Between 2002 and 2004, she was associate director for further and adult education in the ESRC-funded Teaching and Learning Research Programme. She has published a number of books and articles on assessment in post-compulsory education. She is currently directing a project on Improving Formative Assessment in vocational education and adult literacy and numeracy programmes, funded by the Nuffield Foundation, National Research

Centre for Adult Literacy and Numeracy and the Quality Improvement Agency for Lifelong Learning, and finishing an ESRC-funded seminar series for the Teaching and Learning Research Programme on Transitions through the Lifecourse. Kathryn works as a consultant to the National Board of Education in Finland on reforms to assessment and evaluation in Finnish vocational education and is a member of the Access to Higher Education Assessment working group for the Quality Assurance Agency. She is on the editorial boards of Studies in the Education of Adults and is book review editor for the Journal of Further and Higher Education.

Jim Flaitz is a Professor in the College of Education at the University of Louisiana at Lafayette, in the Educational Foundations and Leadership department, where he has taught educational assessment, program evaluation, research design, and statistical analysis of data for the past 25 years. He completed his doctoral studies at the University of Alabama with emphases in educational research and educational psychology. His research interests include classroom assessment and student motivation. He has written, published, and presented extensively on the topic of formative assessment.

John Gardner is a professor of Education in the School of Education at Queen's University, Belfast. He has been engaged in educational research and teacher education at Queen's for 27 years, having begun his career as a teacher in a Belfast grammar school. He has been a head of the Graduate School of Education (1993–2002) and dean of the former faculty of Legal, Social and Educational Sciences (2002–2005). His current teaching areas cover assessment, evaluative research methods and information technology in education. Since 1990, he has been principal investigator or co-investigator in over 30 large and small-scale projects involving over £2.2 million. He has over 100 scholarly publications including five books and 60+ peer-reviewed articles. He is Vice-President (2008–2009) and President (2009–2011) of the British Educational Research Association, a fellow of the British Computer Society, a fellow of the Chartered Institute of Educational Assessors and a council member of the Academy of the Social Sciences. Since 1994, he has been a member of the Assessment Reform Group and is currently a member of the ESRC Teaching and Learning Research Programme Steering Committee. He is a founding member of the Universities' Council for the Education of Teachers – Northern Ireland (UCET-NI), a former member of the General Teaching Council for Northern Ireland and a member of the Research Assessment Exercise (2008) panel for Education.

Eleanore Hargreaves is a lecturer in Assessment for Learning at the Institute of Education, University of London. She teaches and researches Assessment for Learning with a specialism in classroom feedback. She also has a specialism in assessment and in learning plus research and teaching experience in the developing world. She has been working in educational research since 1980, principally researching areas related to educational assessment, as well as primary school learning strategies. Her prime interest is in the use of assessment to enhance learning and her current research focuses on the formative use of self assessment, peer assessment and feedback. Her recent emphasis is on collaborative assessment in classrooms where collaborative learning is needed (in 1998 she was a consultant for the South African Ministry of Education, setting up a system to evaluate the new curriculum and assess its outcomes) She also has skills in test development for the primary phase and in advising on assessment issues and strategies at all levels.

Wynne Harlen, OBE, taught in schools and colleges for 6 years before moving into research in science education, as evaluator of the Science 5/13 project (1967–1973), director of Progress in Learning Science (1973–1977) and deputy director of the Assessment of Performance Unit, science project (1977–1984). She was then Sidney Jones Professor of Science Education and Head of the Education Department at the University of Liverpool for 5 years before becoming director of the Scottish Council for Research in Education. Since 1999 she has been Visiting Professor at the University of Bristol, director of the Nuffield funded project Assessment Systems for the Future (ASF), and a consultant to various UK and international science projects. A founder member of the British Educational Research Association, she was its president in 1993/1994. She was a member of the Secretary of State's original working group on the national curriculum in science and president of the BA's Education section 2001–2002. She was awarded the OBE for services to education in 1991 and received a special award for distinguished service to science education by the Association for Science Education in 2001 and is its president-elect for 2009. Her publications include 25 research reports, over 140 journal articles, contributions to 37 books and 28 books of which she is author or co-author, including Assessment of Learning, arising from the ASF project.

Louise Hayward is a senior lecturer in the School of Education at Glasgow University. She has extensive experience in assessment policy evaluation and provides advice on assessment and inclusive education to Learning and Teaching Scotland and the Scottish Qualifications Authority on a regular basis. She is a member of the Advisory and Management groups for the *Assessment is for Learning* programme and chairs its Research and Development sub-group. Her recent work includes inputs on the Scottish context for inclusive education to the European Masters in Inclusive Education (EUMIE, Linz, Austria)) and a major report on formative assessment to the Scottish Government Education Department. She has been a member of the Assessment Reform Group since 2005.

Mary James is Professor and Associate Director of Research at the University of Cambridge Faculty of Education. From 2005 until the end of 2008 she held a Chair of Education at the Institute of Education, University of London, where she was Deputy Director of the UK-wide Teaching and Learning Research Programme with responsibility for school-based projects. She was director of one of the largest of these projects: Learning How to Learn – in classrooms, schools and networks. She has been a member of the UK Assessment Reform Group since 1992, and is the overseas member of the Curriculum Development Council, of the Hong Kong Government's Education Bureau. She has published extensively in the fields of curriculum, assessment, pedagogy, professional development, school improvement and education policy.

Val Klenowski is a Professor of Education at the Queensland University of Technology in Brisbane, Australia. She currently co-ordinates the Professional Doctoral Program and is engaged in research in assessment. The Australian Research Council Linkage projects for which she is Chief Investigator include research in the use of moderation for achieving consistency in teacher judgment, culture-fair assessment and the use of digital portfolios. She has worked in Hong Kong at the Hong Kong Institute of Education and in the UK at the Institute of Education, University of London. Val has research interests in curriculum, evaluation and assessment. She has become known internationally for her work on the use of portfolios for learning and assessment at all levels from school through to higher education. She has worked as a consultant to Education Queensland and is currently engaged in policy related research with the Queensland Studies Authority. She has also completed consultancy work in Singapore, Malta, Norway, Latvia and Argentina.

Pamela Leung is an Associate Professor in the Department of Chinese. She has had many years of experience in the area of Chinese Language teaching, both in the classroom and as a teacher educator. She has taught at primary, secondary and tertiary levels in Hong Kong and overseas. Her areas of specialization include Chinese Linguistics and related teaching, learning and assessment strategies. Her primary research interest is in teaching effectiveness and classroom practices. Currently, she is involved in research on using Putonghua (Modern Standard Chinese) as the medium of instruction in Hong Kong. The study aims to explore how teachers facilitate students' learning to learn through a non-native language.

Yu-Jen Lu is a PhD candidate in the Graduate Institute of Science Education at the National Taiwan Normal University. He has served for many years as a mathematics teacher leader for the Yilan County Teacher Training Center in Taiwan. Currently, he is the Dean for Academic Affairs of an elementary school in Yilan. He is interested in the development of assessment report system and in issues related to mathematics teacher leadership and mathematics teacher education.

Paul Newton is Head of Assessment Research at Ofqual, the Office of the Qualifications and Examinations Regulator, where his work focuses on issues related to the design and evaluation of large-scale educational assessment systems (including GCSEs, A levels, national curriculum tests, diplomas, etc.). Paul originally trained as a developmental psychologist and has held education research posts within academic, local authority and charitable organisations; but he has spent most of his professional life conducting research for assessment agencies. Paul is a member of the Assessment Reform Group and serves on the Editorial Board of *Assessment in Education: Principles, Policy and Practice*. He has published papers on a range of assessment topics, including: comparability theory; the defensibility of England's national curriculum assessment systems; systems for appealing against results; assessment purposes; and the public understanding of measurement inaccuracy.

David Scott is Professor of Curriculum, Pedagogy and Assessment and Faculty Director of Teaching and Learning at the Institute of Education, University of London. Previously, he was Acting Dean of Teaching and Learning, Director of the International Institute for Education Leadership and Professor of Educational Leadership and Learning, University of Lincoln. Recent research projects include: *Facilitating Transitions to Masters-level Learning through Improving Formative Assessment and Feedback*, Higher Education Academy; *Evaluating Teacher Development*, CAPES, Brazil; *Assessment for Learning* (with the Hong Kong Institute of Education); *Teacher Training and Development*, Save-The-Children Fund, India, European Commission; *Curriculum Structures 14-18 in a Mexican State* (with C. Posner, C. Martin, E. Guzmann), Ministry of Education; *National Curriculum Standards and Structures in Mexico* (with C. Posner, C. Martin, E. Guzmann), Mexican Ministry of Education; *National Curriculum Standards and Structures in Mexico – Pre-Project* (with C. Posner, C. Martin, E. Guzmann), Mexican Ministry of Education; *India Capacity Building to the Elementary Education Programme* (with G. Kingdon, G. Stobart, et al.); *Interdisciplinary and Inter-professional Practice and Training in a Hospital Trauma Team* (with A. Brown); *Roles and Responsibilities of School Business Managers* (with F. O'Sullivan and E. Wood); *How Teams Make a Difference: The Impact of Team Working* (with T. Bush, M. Morrison and D. Middlewood); and *Professional Doctorates and Professional Development in Education* (with I. Lunt, A. Brown and L. Thorne). He has been Editor of *The Curriculum Journal* 1995–2001; Visiting Professor - Lincolnshire and Humberside University 2000–2001; Institute of Education, University of London 2000–2005; and University of Cyprus 2000–2005; and is Series Editor for *International Perspectives on the Curriculum*, Greenwood Press.

Gordon Stobart is Emeritus professor of Education at the Institute of Education, University of London. After teaching English in secondary schools he retrained and worked as an educational psychologist. This led to doctoral studies in applied psychology in the USA as a Fulbright Scholar. After working as Head of Research at London Examinations he became Principal Research Officer for the National Council for Vocational Qualifications and then for the Qualifications and Curriculum Authority. He is a founder member of the Assessment Reform Group (ARG), which campaigns for better use of formative assessment in teaching and learning. He is also a former editor of the international journal Assessment in Education: Principles, Policy and Practice. He has written extensively on assessment and his latest book *Testing Times: the uses and abuses of assessment* was published in March 2008.

Hak Ping Tam is an Associate Professor in the National Taiwan Normal University, where he is the chairperson of the Graduate Institute of Science Education. He graduated from the University of California at Berkeley with a Bachelor degree in mathematics. After obtaining some teaching experience as a secondary school mathematics teacher in Hong Kong, he decided to pursue further training in this area.

He obtained both his Master's and PhD degrees from the Ohio State University, focusing on research methodology, evaluation and applied statistics. Upon graduation, he taught for 4 years as an assistant professor in the Department of Measurement, Statistics and Evaluation at the University of Maryland, College Park. His research interests include mathematics education, statistics education, research methodology, and integrated mathematics and science curriculum. He is now working on projects related to assessment for learning, assessment report system, large-scale assessment and automated Chinese essay scoring system.

Kelvin Tan is an Assistant Professor in the Policy and Leadership Studies Department of the National Institute of Education, Singapore. He is a lawyer by training, but went on to pursue a calling in teacher education. Dr Kelvin Tan is widely consulted by schools in Singapore on alternative and formative assessment issues. He is involved in externally and internally funded research projects on assessment in Singapore, and publishes in the area of assessment for learning, critical perspectives of assessment and phenomenography. His research interests include discursive constructions of assessment for learning, staff development of formative assessment literacy, and teachers' conceptions of student self-assessment.

Part I
Assessment Reform Experiences

Chapter 1
Assessment Reform Past, Present and Future

Rita Berry and Bob Adamson

1.1 The Nature of Assessment

Assessment is one of the most emotive words in the education lexicon. It has a variety of connotations for different people – anxiety, pressure, competition, success, failure, judgment, feedback, fairness, standards, accountability, bureaucracy and drudgery, to mention but a few – depending on the nature of their participation in the assessment process. For schoolchildren, an impending examination, test or euphemistic quiz can be a cause for alarm and despondency; for teachers, there is the administrative burden of setting and grading assessments, with the concomitant concern that they will be judged on their students' results; for admissions officers in tertiary institutions and employers, assessments are required to provide important information for the purposes of selection; for government ministers, assessment results enable them to evaluate the effectiveness of the education system and how it compares with that of other states through the rankings in comparative studies.

These connotations are, of course, only part of the story. Assessment is not necessarily high-stakes, stressful, bureaucratic and linked to accountability, selection and evaluation. It can take many forms and serve many purposes. Assessment can, for example, be formative and summative, formal and informal, external and internal, authentic and inauthentic, oral and written, criterion-referenced, norm-referenced and ipsative, focusing on differentiation and discrimination, and carried out by experts, peers and oneself; it can be used for grading, selecting, diagnosing, determining mastery, guiding and predicting. At different periods of time, different aspects of assessment have been emphasized, according to the prevailing beliefs and theories in education.

Assessment is the subject of intense debate around the world. The diverse requirements of various stakeholders regarding the information produced by assessment processes have led to strains and tensions in education systems. For example,

R. Berry (✉)
Department of Curriculum and Instruction, Hong Kong Institute of Education, Tai Po, Hong Kong
e-mail: rsyberry@ied.edu.hk

R. Berry, B. Adamson (eds.), *Assessment Reform in Education*,
Education in the Asia-Pacific Region: Issues, Concerns and Prospects 14,
DOI 10.1007/978-94-007-0729-0_1,

policy-makers who are keen to deliver a demonstrably-effective, "international standard" education system that meets the social, economic and political needs of society find themselves at odds with the teaching profession when the capacity of the latter to attend to the individual learning needs of students is felt to be constrained by the assessment modalities that are preferred by the former. Although stakeholders share many common goals for education – the creation of a system that brings about high-quality learning – the devil, as ever, is in the detail of what is meant by high-quality learning and what such a system looks like in the situated reality of the classroom. These issues, among others, are explored in this book. It provides the context and themes of current debates, identifies the sources of tensions and challenges, and offers some resolutions to some of the dilemmas.

Assessment could be conceptualized as a form of research, in that it involves the collection of data using valid and reliable instruments, the analysis of the data that has been collected, and the application of findings based on the analysis for specific purposes. There are different types of research, such as evaluative, investigative, interpretive and critical, which determine the specific research questions, data collection methods and analytical processes to be used in the study. The most common type of research associated with assessment is *evaluative*, in that it is concerned with collecting evidence in order to make an informed decision. Other types of research would use or view assessment in other ways. An *investigative* study could look for cause and effect or other interrelationships among variables. This might suggest a scientific approach to student assessment, involving the identification and isolation of relevant variables, and the collection of data that could be analyzed in ways that could establish the probability of one factor being related to another – often using statistical techniques. Such a study would be particularly interesting to researchers who are building or testing theories of learning, for example. An *interpretive* study would attempt to characterize and explain a social phenomenon, such as schooling in a specific context. For this type of study, assessment of student learning might be an object of research studied ethnographically through etic and/or emic perspectives. The researcher would tend to be less concerned with the actual results of the assessment than in the social factors that shape the nature of the assessment and what these factors reveal about the cultural practices and values that underpin them. Thus an interpretive study of a music examination, for instance, might analyze the design of the examination, the range of instruments accommodated by the examination, how the examinee is assessed, the roles and responsibilities of the various parties, and the implications of the outcome – and then endeavor to explain why certain kinds of music and instruments are included or excluded, how the relevant benchmarks are constructed, and what the status of a music student is in that particular society. A *critical* research perspective would examine issues in terms of power relationships, social equity and justice. Assessments of student learning might be investigated for what they reveal about privileging and disadvantaging different sectors of society. For example, a college admission system that requires potential students to demonstrate a high degree of competence in a particular language might be critiqued as favoring students who have ready access to an environment that supports the learning of that language, while disadvantaging those that do not. Such a critical study might form the basis of advocacy for changes to the admission system in order to promote greater equity of opportunity.

This treatment of assessment in this book incorporates a range of research approaches. It is interpretative in that it seeks to identify and explain the nature of assessment policies and practices in various contexts. It is evaluative in that it discerns the strengths and weaknesses of particular philosophies of assessment. It is critical in that it concludes that specific philosophies, policies and practices can be socially inequitable and divisive.

The next section provides an introduction to a number of concepts and issues concerning the purposes, nature and presentation of assessment. It then presents a brief historical overview of assessment in education and identifies shifts in focus and some of the major influences and ideas that have shaped each distinct period. The chapter concludes by outlining the organization and contents of this book.

1.2 Functions of Assessment

The term *assessment* describes a range of actions undertaken to collect and use information about a person's knowledge, attitudes or skills. There are many different ways of categorizing the functions of assessment. The functions are mainly two folds: (1) for making judgments of the performance of individuals or the effectiveness of the system and (2) for improving learning (Berry, 2008a). Assessment is usually carried out in order to evaluate a student's suitability to enter a particular school or profession, or to perform particular tasks (such as piloting an airplane). Alternatively, the assessment of students' achievement could form the basis for the allocation of resources to a school district by the government, or for parents to select a school for their children. On a macro-scale, the Trends in International Mathematics and Science Study (TIMSS), the International Association for the Evaluation of Educational Achievement (IEA), the Programme for International Student Assessment (PISA) and similar comparative studies of student performance pressure national governments to evaluate the effectiveness of their own education system.

How the analysis of the assessment results is presented depends on the intended audience. A recent phenomenon has been the establishment of "league tables" as used for ranking teams or players in sports, as an easily digestible and clearly visible comparative presentation of student performance based on the schools that they attend or the education system in which they are located. And for the results to be easily digestible, the inherent complexities of evaluating student and (according to the logic of the proponents of such tables) school or systemic performance have been eliminated in the analysis, resulting in the simplified presentation of data. Very often, the data that are processed come in the form of numerical scores collected in tests that have been standardized in the interests of reliability (that the scores have been obtained as objectively as possible and thus are trustworthy) and validity (in that the assessment instruments are accurate in assessing what they are designed to assess). However, if the purpose of the assessment is to provide students, parents, teachers and other stakeholders with substantial information as to how the students might develop in their learning, such simplified presentation of data would be insufficient. The evidence for such decisions could be collected from qualitative as well as quantitative means of assessment, and analyzed and presented in ways that set out clearly the pedagogical interventions and strategies that would support the design and development of learning. The issues of reliability and validity are equally important in these forms of assessment as they are in the design of standardized tests.

Assessment, therefore, can be viewed from different angles – political, social, pedagogical, and so on – and it performs a range of functions, including grading, selection, diagnosis, mastery, guidance and prediction (Morris & Adamson, 2010). Grading involves the ranking of students in terms of achievement; selection separates successful students from the rest of the pool; diagnostic assessments help to identify a student's strengths and weaknesses in learning and permit the design of a suitable remedial program; assessment of mastery judges whether the student demonstrates certain competences to a pre-determined level for the purposes of certification or licensing; guidance provides a student with information to assist in making a decision, such as which course of study to take or which career path to follow; predictive assessments are designed to judge how well a student will perform in a particular area of skills or knowledge in the future. Often, a single assessment will perform several functions – an examination in a particular profession, for instance, might be used for grading, selecting and certifying students.

This range of functions has given rise to different modalities of assessment. If the goal is to design an assessment for selective purposes, the designers could well opt for a standardized mode, whereby students are exposed, as far as possible, to a common experience in the interests of fairness. There could be a unified syllabus and process of assessment, with all students handling the same tasks at the same time in replicated conditions, and a marking scheme that can be consistently applied across the board. The assessment would normally take place towards the end of the study of the set syllabus, and would therefore be mainly *summative* (i.e., focusing of summarizing the students' learning of the syllabus) in nature, rather than *formative*, which would be the case if the purpose of the assessment were diagnostic. The selective function would require grading, which implies that the students' performance in the assessment would be *norm-referenced* (i.e., in terms of their ranking in the "league table") if there is a set number of students to be selected, or *criterion-referenced* (i.e., judged against performance criteria) if selection is made on the basis of mastery.

If, however, the purpose of assessment were purely diagnostic, the modality could be very different from a selective process. The assessment would not need to be standardized to the same degree and the arrangements could be less formal and less stressful. Indeed, there might not be a specific intervention – indicators of the student's learning collected in the routine course of study could form the basis of assessment without the need for tests or other tools. The information that is analyzed could include the student's learning strategies as well as learning outcomes, so that guidance can be given in what and how improvements could be made. Such guidance is often *ipsative* – the student's learning is monitored in relation to what is known about his or her prior learning, rather than to external norms or criteria. The assessors are not necessarily authority figures, such as teachers: peer- and self-assessment, if implemented with care, could also provide useful feedback, or – given that the intention is to embed the guidance in future learning tasks – "feedforward".

Assessment has proved problematic and controversial because of its multivalent functions. The disparate goals of external accountability, competitive selection and diagnosis of strengths and weaknesses in learning are difficult to reconcile in a single assessment process. As a result, the nature of assessment that is prevalent in a particular system at a particular time reflects particular priorities, with some functions strongly emphasized and others neglected. Assessment is therefore contested political terrain, encompassing a broad range of viewpoints, practices and values and characterized by power struggles, tensions and compromises.

1.3 Historical Overview

The earliest records of formal assessment dates back to the Western Zhou Dynasty in China (1027–1771 BC), when regular examinations were held to select officials for various ranks of the Imperial civil service. Such posts provided the means for social mobility and were highly prestigious (Berry, 2011; Black, 1998); competition was intense and the examination process was intellectually and physically rigorous. The system also allowed the state to maintain control over far-flung regions by recruiting the local scholar-elites to its service. Wealthy families would employ tutors to prepare male children, often as young as 3 years old, for the examination, immersing them in the requisite canons of classical literature and in the art of refined calligraphy. According to Confucian ideals, successful candidates were required to demonstrate knowledge, wisdom and virtue – qualities that were viewed as essential for the harmonious administration of state affairs at all levels. However, over the centuries, the examination became increasingly formulaic. Towards the end of the Qing Dynasty, in the nineteenth century, the examination centred on the ability of the candidate to compose an "eight-legged" essay. Greater value was ascribed to the candidate's mastery of the rigid rhetorical and poetical structure and calligraphic skills than to the actual thesis of the essay (Hsü, 2000): the focus on form rather than content was a major factor in the abolition of the Imperial civil service examination at the turn of the twentieth century.

The emphasis on classical literature and written rhetoric (in the form of essays) was also a feature of assessment in prestigious schools such as Harrow in the United Kingdom in the early nineteenth century. These examinations were used for selecting students for admission to schools and for promotion to higher grades. As was the case with the Imperial civil service examinations in China, one motivation for these school examinations was the attempt to create a competitive, meritocratic system rather than one based on privilege and patronage (Roach, 1971). The use of examinations as a tool for engineering social equity has, historically, had mixed results particularly when it clashed with other forces such as class systems (Sutherland, 1996).

The twentieth century saw the rise of testing. The notion that human learning could be measured objectively arose from scientific experimentation by researchers in psychologists such as Sir Francis Galton (a half-cousin of Charles Darwin), who specialized in genetic and eugenics; and Alfred Binet, whose eponymous scale was designed to measure intelligence; and behaviourists such as B.F. Skinner and Ivan Pavlov. The purpose of assessment was overwhelmingly summative, the content addressed was primarily discrete cognitive tasks and the mode was largely assessment of student performance in traditional paper-and-paper tests through large scale testing activities (Broadfoot, 2009, p. x). The role of assessment as a diagnostic tool to discern a student's strengths and weaknesses in terms of intelligence, personality, aptitude and behavior became prominent, assisted by the creation of cognitive, affective and psychomotor taxonomies.

The possibilities for large-scale investigations afforded by scientific tests that had been deemed valid and reliable led to a number of developments in the area of assessment. First, from the 1930s, boards of education in the USA began adopting standardized examinations (some of which comprised multiple choice answers and were marked by machines) and, on an international scale, UNESCO and other educational agencies initiated comparative studies of educational achievements among nations, such as the IEA, PISA and TIMSS, from the early 1960s. Second, the notion of standards and benchmarks, which had been a construct of nineteenth century education, became a powerful driver of curricular and assessment reform in the latter decades of the twentieth century – often fuelled by the results of the international comparisons – with the establishment of national frameworks of learning targets and "league tables" of student performance.

These moves also created a backlash. Educators expressed reservations at the amount of formal testing that was required, at the focus on discrete elements of observable learning, and at the emphasis on prediction and control rather than on meaning and understanding (Biggs & Watkins, 2001; Dwyer, 1998; Torrance & Pryor, 1998; Black, 1998; Stiggins, 2004; Wiliam, 2006). There were two main themes to the backlash. The first called for assessments to be more authentic in nature, on the grounds that testing tended to ignore holistic aspects of learning and was often unrelated to real-life situations. According to advocates (e.g., Gipps, McCallum, & Hargreaves, 2000; McTighe & Wiggins, 2004), authentic assessment, in the form of practical, realistic tasks, represents a means to investigate whether students have a comprehensive understanding of the subject matter and of how it is related to their current and future needs in society. The second theme called for assessment to form part of the learning process. Assessment for learning, argued theorists such as Gibbs, Simpson, and MacDonald (2003) and Clarke (2001), could enable learners to self-analyzing, self-referencing, self-evaluating, and self-correcting.

These shifts in perspective can be linked to the emergence of social constructivism as a dominant theory of learning. Social constructivism holds that knowledge is constructed by the learner and developed through experience (Bush, 2006).

Learning is regarded as an active process and is a personal interpretation of the world. Conceptual growth results from the negotiation of meaning, the sharing of multiple perspectives and the changing of internal representations through interactions with the social and the physical environment. Instead of viewing learning outcomes as predictable and instruction as following a pre-determined syllabus, social constructivism maintains that learning outcomes are not always predictable, and instruction should foster, not control, learning (Berry, 2006). Authentic assessment and assessment for learning should be integrated with the learning tasks and not form separate activities; they should also be facilitative in nature and varied so as to acknowledge different perspectives on learning. This entails identifying where students are in their learning progression, diagnosing any difficulties students may be having in their learning, and providing direction to the teacher and the student in the steps to be taken to enhance learning. This focus on the use of assessment to support learning, rather than to document achievement, has come to be referred to as "Assessment for Learning" (AfL) (Berry, 2008a). Teachers are encouraged to devolve the responsibility for AfL practices to their students, making them more self-directed in their own learning through self- and peer-assessment. By doing so, students learn how to monitor their own learning, develop the ability to judge and evaluate their own work and the work of their peers, and think about what to do next (Berry, 2008b). The ability of students to assess their own work contributes to students taking control of their learning, improving learning in the course being studied. All these provide a foundation for lifelong learning (Sadler, 1998). Overall, advocates claim that authentic assessment and AfL, if implemented with care, have the potential to empower and transform students.

1.4 Assessment Policy-Making and Policy Implementation

Policy-making in education is seldom a simple, rational process because policies are often influenced by contradictory or disparate goals that are valued by different stakeholders at the local, regional and international level. Policy-makers have to negotiate and achieve a compromise in an attempt to satisfy the different interest groups, although some interests are more strongly represented in the final outcome than others. As a result, policies often reflect a range of values systems and educational orientations.

Once a policy has been approved, there is no guarantee that it will be faithfully implemented in every classroom in the education system. A process of synthesis can often be discerned, as the policy impacts upon different contexts. Curriculum developers, for instance, interpret a policy according to the prevalent conceptions of the relevant subject community. Examination and assessment authorities design their instruments according to their views, resources and capacities. Educational publishers develop materials with an eye on marketability. Schools adapt a policy according to their ethos, priorities and available facilities and resources. Teachers play a crucial role as gatekeepers in the process by designing and teaching their courses in a manner that reflects their pedagogical beliefs, their understanding of the students' needs, interests and abilities, and the resources at their disposal. Students learn in very individualistic ways. This means that the policy intentions can get transformed by the time they are implemented in the classroom, which has important implications for realistic policy-making (Morris & Adamson, 2010).

Such messiness provides the motivation for the second part of this book. While advocates for assessment for learning, for instance, might argue a cogent and compelling case, these arguments are only valid if the philosophy can be realized effectively in situ. Problems and challenges are inevitable and systemic mechanisms need to be in place to handle them and to provide the means for resolving them.

Chapter authors were invited to explore either the contemporary assessment policies (in Part I) or issues arising from the implementation of assessment for learning practices (in Part II) in a particular context. The aim is to provide an interpretation of why current assessment policies take the form that they do and the role and status of assessment for learning in the policy-making debates, and to identify the problems and challenges that have occurred and the resolutions that might be proposed. There are two caveats about the proposed resolutions. First, the emergent issues are often dilemmas, in that any resolution merely creates a new set of tensions that have the potential to create a backlash. Second, the transfer of one resolution to another context needs to be undertaken with great caution – a degree of adaptation and synthesis may be required.

1.5 Organization of the Book

As this book demonstrates, the AfL movement has produced a variety of policy responses, ranging from the promotion of AfL in schools in Singapore; attempts to strike a balance between classroom and large-scale assessment in a synergistic manner, as in the UK; and efforts by teachers to find a small niche for AfL within the constraints of a powerful standards-based frame, as in many states in the USA. To be implemented effectively, AfL has to be embedded within the complex cultures of classrooms, schools and education systems. As this book also shows, implementation throws up numerous political and pedagogical challenges and dilemmas, often necessitating pragmatic resolutions. For this reason, the book is divided into two parts. The first part focuses on policy; the second on implementation issues.

Mary James' chapter analyses developments with respect to AfL in the UK, which was one of the major centres of research and advocacy for assessment policy reform. James portrays the distinct ways in which AfL has been adopted and implemented in each of the four countries of the UK, and the extent of policy borrowing among them. AfL ideas and practices were developed and disseminated by members of the educational research community, with the UK Assessment Reform Group playing a leading role. However, these pedagogical ideas and practices were then appropriated by government agencies and adapted to meet the political exigencies of educational reform. The interplay between educational and broader political goals produces tensions and dilemmas, and James concludes that effective educational change requires good communication between researchers and policy makers to ensure mutually satisfying outcomes. Jim Flaitz's chapter explores the paradox of No Child Left Behind – how a policy that emphasizes improving the learning of all children has actually squeezed out the opportunities to focus on individualized assessment for learning. The reason lies in the establishment of standards and their application as a means for enhancing the accountability of schools and determining their resourcing. Assessment to demonstrate that the students are meeting the required standards has become essential in determining the financial survival of a school, leaving many teachers fearful of the consequences of experimenting with alternative approaches. Flaitz does discern, however, some green shoots of AfL as teachers in some states seek to redress what they perceive to be an imbalance and rigidity in current assessment practices.

In Chapter 4, Rita Berry looks at the interaction between Chinese culture, with its long tradition of formal, high-stakes assessment, and the ideas underpinning AfL, which are viewed as developing attributes that are desirable for the modern economy. Berry reviews assessment reform initiatives in mainland China, Hong Kong and Taiwan, and identifies the cultural commonalities and the differences bestowed by geopolitics and the specific paths towards economic modernization chosen in each location. She finds that AfL is constrained at the implementation level by mindsets that are strongly influenced by the traditional view of examinations. In setting the policies and providing guidelines, the governments in mainland China, Hong Kong and Taiwan have started the journey down the road to enhancing the quality of teaching and learning through the use of AfL. Turning to Australia, Val Klenowski examines a reverse scenario – the impact of the introduction of standards and national testing on education in Queensland, a state with a strong tradition of teacher empowerment through practices such as externally moderated school-based assessment. Klenowski discusses the emergent tensions and challenges, and cautions against allowing the move towards standards-based testing to undermine this tradition, arguing that teacher-based and authentic assessments, if properly implemented, can also serve the purposes of improving learning, equity and accountability.

Kelvin Tan offers another scenario in Singapore – one in which government policy rhetoric and educational practices both support AfL – and investigates the sustainability of the policy and practices in reality. Tan finds that the reform has encountered unexpected problems, such as the fragmentation of learning, the suppression of students' capacity to become self-regulated learners and a tendency to displace learning with assessment. He suggests that the Singaporean system should boldly strive to bring about radical changes by establishing a robust "threshold" of sustainable assessment that is integrated in and focuses on learning, and that also views the problematic nature of education reform as an opportunity for developing new solutions.

Rita Berry concludes the first part by presenting a broad overview of assessment reforms around the world, with a focus in the experiences and changing landscapes of selected education systems. Berry points out that similar drivers for reform, such as the international "league tables" have produced different policy responses in different places. She also finds that implementation remains a stumbling block for reforms that emphasize AfL. The outcomes of these assessment reforms appear to have been undermined by the dominance of high stakes summative discourse, issues of accountability and the readiness of the teachers for the change necessitated by the assessment reforms. There were pockets of success but a number of issues have to be addressed before the visions of the assessment reforms can be fully realized in the education frontlines.

The complexities of the implementation level are the major focus of Part II. John Gardner, Wynne Harlen, Louise Hayward and Gordon Stobart open this part of the book with a study of the role of teachers in the UK in instituting a complementary mode of AfL within the overall context of external testing and pressure to teach to the test. They find that some teachers are lacking in "assessment literacy", and will need sensitive and carefully planned support and professional development in order to gain their commitment to AfL practices and to ensure that these practices are effective. Eleanore Hargreaves then argues, based on a study of teachers' perceptions of feedback, that even when teachers are "assessment literate" and do provide high-quality feedback, students often do not benefit from it and their subsequent work fails to demonstrate any consideration for the feedback that they receive. The reason for this breakdown in the feedback loop, Hargreaves contends, lies in the social dimensions of the learning enterprise, and how individual students react to positive or negative feedback.

Alice Chow and Pamela Leung describe an assessment project undertaken by a secondary school to improve student learning of languages through strategies such as peer- and self-assessment. The project showed that, with proper induction and support, students were able to turn peer- and self-assessment into effective components of the AfL feedback loop. However, Chow and Leung note that the provision of this induction and support fell to teachers who were often over-stretched in terms of time, and required a considerable degree of "assessment literacy" on the part of the teachers.

David Scott's chapter presents a critical analysis of the beliefs and values that support conventional testing, and the impact that such testing has on student learning. His analysis produces the argument that high-stakes testing leads to the knowledge sets, skills and dispositional states which enable a student to do well in these tests becoming the dominant form of knowledge in the curriculum, and, over time, the student's capacities being increasingly transformed into that dominant form. Drawing on Foucault's critique of examinations, Scott argues that the transformative power of testing allows society to construct individuals in a particular way, embed them in networks of power, and sustain powerful mechanisms of surveillance.

Richard Daugherty, Paul Black, Kathryn Ecclestone and Mary James report five case studies that illuminate the relationship of assessment to curriculum in a school subject (mathematics education in England); a European Commission project to develop indicators relating to learning to learn; workplace learning in the UK; higher education in the UK; and vocational education in England. Although the relationship between curriculum and assessment is often conceptualized in terms of *alignment* or *congruence*, Daugherty et al. show that it is actually more multi-dimensional and multi-level. They tease out four common themes from the case studies: the importance of *construct validity* and *enabling student progression* in programmes of learning and related assessments; the *impact of assessment procedures* on the alignment between intended and actual outcomes from learning; and the exigencies of *system-level accountability as a driver of alignment.*

Hak Ping Tam and Yu-Jen Lu then address an approach to incorporating an AfL dimension into large-scale assessments, which are usually associated with policy-making and accountability. Using examples from Yilan County in Taiwan, they show how the design of software enabled teachers and students to be informed of areas of strength and weakness, while, at the same time, providing administrators with the statistical information that they required for comparisons of student performance across districts and schools. This project provides an example of how a single assessment exercise can integrate different functions.

The final chapter draws together a number of themes arising from the book. It discusses how an apparently simple notion, *assessment for learning*, acquires greater complexity as it moves from idea to realization in specific cultural settings. It suggests that assessment policies and practices need to integrate and accommodate different conceptions and functions of assessment in ways that are compatible with the capacity of those responsible for implementation. It argues that the process of integration and accommodation requires principled pragmatism and sustained professional development on the part of all stakeholders if it is to result in assessment practices that are truly effective, valid and reliable.

References

Berry, R. (2006). Activating learners using the learner autonomy approach: An action research on the relevance of teaching to classroom practice. *Curriculum Perspectives*, *26*(3), 34–43.

Berry, R. (2008a). *Assessment for learning*. Hong Kong: Hong Kong University Press.

Berry, R. (2008b). From theory to practice: Curriculum for autonomous learning. In M. F. Hui & D. Grossman (Eds.), *Improving teacher education through action research*. New York: Routledge.

Berry, R. (2011). Assessment trends in Hong Kong: Seeking to establish formative assessment in an examination culture. *Assessment in Education: Principles, Policy & Practice, 18*(2).

Biggs, J., & Watkins, D. A. (2001). *The paradox of the Chinese learner and beyond*. Hong Kong: Comparative Education Research Centre.

Black, P. J. (1998). *Testing: Friend or foe? Theory and practice of assessment and testing*. London: The Falmer Press.

Broadfoot, P. (2009). Foreword. In C. Wyatt-Smith & J. J. Cumming (Eds.), *Educational assessment in the 21st century: Connecting theory and practice* (pp. v–xii). New York: Springer.

Bush, G. (2006). Learning about learning: From theories to trends. *Teacher Librarian*, *34*(2), 14–18.

Clarke, S. (2001). *Unlocking formative assessment*. Abingdon: Hodder & Stoughton.

Dwyer, C. A. (1998). Assessment and classroom learning: Theory and practice. *Assessment in Education: Principles, policy & practice*, *5*(1), 131–137.

Gibbs, G., Simpson, C., & Macdonald, R. (2003). Improving student learning through changing assessment – a conceptual and practical framework. Paper presented at the European Association for Research into Learning and Instruction Conference, Padova, Italy, Aug 2003.
Gipps, C., McCallum, G., & Hargreaves, E. (2000). *What makes a good primary school teacher? Expert classroom strategies*. London: RoutledgeFalmer.
Hsü, I. C. Y. (2000). *The rise of modern China*. New York: Oxford University Press.
McTighe, J., & Wiggins, G. (2004). *The understanding by design handbook*. Alexandra, VA: Association for Supervision and Curriculum Development.
Morris, P., & Adamson, B. (2010). *Curriculum, schooling and society in Hong Kong*. Hong Kong: Hong Kong University Press.
Roach, J. (1971). *Public examinations in England 1850–1900*. Cambridge: Cambridge University Press.
Sadler, D. R. (1998). Formative assessment: Revisiting the territory. *Assessment in Education*, *5*(1), 77–84.
Stiggins, R. J. (2004). *Classroom assessment for student learning*. Portland, OR: Assessment Training Institute.
Sutherland, G. (1996). Assessment: Some historical perspectives. In H. Goldstein & T. Lewis (Eds.), *Assessment: Problems, developments and statistical issues* (pp. 9–20). Chichester, England: Wiley.
Torrance, H., & Pryor, J. (1998). *Investigating formative assessment*. Buckingham: OUP.
Wiliam, D. (2006). Assessment: Learning communities can use it to engineer a bridge connecting teaching and learning. *Journal of Staff Development*, *27*(1), 16–20.

Chapter 2
Assessment for Learning: Research and Policy in the (Dis)United Kingdom

Mary James

2.1 Assessment Policy in the Context of Education Reform

It is now more than two decades since the UK Government brought in the 1988 Education Reform Act. Its far-reaching powers were designed to create a social market in schooling in England and Wales, which, its Conservative architects believed, would raise standards across the state system. In essence the Act had three linked components. First, it made a commitment to open access to enable parents to choose schools for their children. Secondly, it proposed arrangements for local financial management whereby funds would follow pupils and thus allow successful schools to attract more pupils whilst unsuccessful schools would contract and even close. Thirdly, a new common national curriculum and assessment system would provide parents with a basis for choice because what pupils were expected to learn at various key stages, and how successful schools were in teaching them, would (supposedly) be more transparent. In 1992 the creation of a new framework for inspection through the establishment of the Office for Standards in Education (Ofsted) enhanced this accountability function further.

Although the Act applied only to England and Wales, some aspects were incorporated into policy in Northern Ireland. Scotland, which has always had a separate and distinct education system, watched developments with interest but distanced itself from them. In May 1997, when the Labour Party won the first of three consecutive General Elections, a policy of "devolution" was inaugurated. This entailed the progressive transfer of powers for areas such as health and education from the government's traditional base in Westminster, London, to the new Parliament in Scotland, and to the Assemblies in Northern Ireland and Wales. The argument was that this promotes local control and democracy, although some critics believed it to be wasteful and divisive. This policy of devolution continues under the Conservative

M. James (✉)
Faculty of Education, University of Cambridge, Cambridge, UK
e-mail: mej1002@cam.ac.uk

R. Berry, B. Adamson (eds.), *Assessment Reform in Education*, Education in the Asia-Pacific Region: Issues, Concerns and Prospects 14,
DOI 10.1007/978-94-007-0729-0_2,

and Liberal Democrat "Coalition" Government that emerged after the General Election in May 2010.

The development of assessment policy and, particularly, the aspect that is now known as Assessment for Learning (AfL) needs to be understood against this background because a key feature of the following discussion is the ways in which policy has been variously interpreted, developed and implemented, over time, in the four countries of the UK.

2.2 Initial Influences on Policy with Regard to Assessment for Learning

In England and Wales policy discussion about the purposes of assessment was stimulated when the task of designing a framework for national assessment and testing was given to an expert group set up in 1988 and chaired by Paul Black, an academic researcher. The brief of the Task Group on Assessment and Testing (TGAT) was to devise a system to be both "informative" and diagnostic. By the time the group came to report, these two aspects had had become four distinct purposes: formative, diagnostic, summative and evaluative. The system that TGAT proposed was built on four principles; it would be criterion-referenced, formative, moderated and designed to promote progression. The involvement of teachers would be central and group moderation would help them develop common judgments that would be used for reporting purposes but also, crucially, to enable them to plan next steps in teaching. Unfortunately, these proposals received a hostile reception from some prominent politicians and academics. Margaret Thatcher, the then Prime Minister, perceived it to be a subversion by a left-wing "educational establishment", and some academics, including members of the British Educational Research Association (BERA), saw it as a Trojan horse of the political right. So, starting with the idea of group moderation by teachers, the proposals were rapidly dismantled and few recognizable features remain. The system that was eventually put in place focused on increased testing for summative and, especially, evaluative purposes – i.e., to provide performance tables of aggregated results to judge the effectiveness of teachers, schools, local authorities and the system as a whole, in relation to increasingly challenging numerical performance targets. In a rueful reflection, published almost 10 years after TGAT, Paul Black wrote: "With hindsight, it was naïve to imagine that the government, with its commitment to a market where choice would be guided by tests, would support a complex approach." (Black, 1997, p. 41).

With the political imperative to put in place an accountability system based on tests, where even school inspections would take school performance measured in this way as their starting point, the ideas embedded in TGAT about the possibilities of creating a system to meet formative and summative purposes in combination, with the formative purpose uppermost, were almost lost. The community of academic researchers was consumed by the need to react to, and critique, rapidly developing policy based on frequent whole cohort testing, and it largely failed, at that time, to engage effectively with policy-makers or to clarify the ideas and practices that might offer alternative educational solutions to genuine public concerns about standards of teaching and learning in schools and how to improve them.

A turning point came when Paul Black and Dylan Wiliam, of King's College London, published a pamphlet, *Inside the black box,* derived from an extensive review of research on assessment and classroom learning (Black & Wiliam, 1998). This was commissioned by the Assessment Reform Group (ARG), a group of assessment researchers from all four countries of the UK. The ARG was initially one of several policy task groups set up by BERA in 1989, on the initiative of the then President, John Elliott, who, in response to changes being brought in by the 1988 Act, argued for, "a radically different conception of the primary aim of educational research; namely, to promote worthwhile change by influencing the practical judgements of teachers and policy-makers" (Elliott, 1990, p. 11).

The work of the ARG is described by Richard Daugherty (2007, p. 145) as having two phases. The first, from 1989 to 1995, was characterized as active engagement with policy issues drawing on research evidence and the experience of education professionals to critique policies that were already being implemented. But the second phase, from 1996 to 2010, when the ARG formally "retired", has been more strategic by attempting to influence the policy agenda itself. The commissioning of the review of research by Black and Wiliam, supported by funds from the Nuffield Foundation, was the first step in this more strategic phase.

The central thesis of the *Inside the black box* review was that there is a body of firm evidence that formative assessment is an essential feature of effective pedagogy and its development can raise standards. Moreover, Black and Wiliam put a figure on the size of measured gains and pointed to effect sizes in the range of 0.4–0.7, amongst the largest for any educational intervention. It was probably these figures, and extrapolations that indicated what they might mean in terms of scores on national tests and examinations, and in international surveys of achievement, that encouraged policy-makers to take notice, especially at a time when early gains on the national tests were beginning to level off. However, there was still confusion about what the term "formative assessment" actually meant and, in line with ARG's second phase strategic goal to express issues in a clearer and simpler language, the Group decided to adopt a distinction between assessment *for* learning and assessment *of* learning as a more accessible (less technical) version of the formative/summative distinction. Although the Group continued to debate the wisdom of this – because of similar scope for misinterpretation and confusion – the evidence indicates that the simpler language has, at least, encouraged widespread use. When in 1999 the ARG followed *Inside the black box* with another pamphlet, *Assessment for Learning: Beyond the black box,* and then, in 2002, with a graphically designed poster, *Assessment for Learning: 10 principles* (ARG, 2002a), the new term, and its definition on the poster, was rapidly taken up by policy-makers and practitioners in England and Wales, and elsewhere, including countries beyond the UK. The key event was probably the decision by the Group to find the means to distribute the "principles" to all schools in England, Wales and Northern Ireland.

The next section of this chapter explores the different ways in which the concept of assessment for learning has been interpreted and incorporated into policy in the four countries of the UK. At a time when educational research was criticized for having very little impact on UK policy formation and development (Hargreaves, 1996; Hillage, Pearson, Anderson, & Tamkin, 1998), it is remarkable that developments in assessment for learning provide clear evidence of interactions between research and policy, even if these relationships have not always been straightforward or unproblematic.

2.3 Current Manifestation of AfL Policy in the Four Countries of the UK

At the time of writing, what is most marked is divergence between England and the three "Celtic Fringe" countries: in AfL policy, in assessment policy more generally, and in other aspects of broader education policy. The explanations for this are complex – historical, geographical, economic, political, ideological, cultural and pragmatic – so the ambition of this section is simply to provide a brief description and modest interpretation of some recent AfL initiatives in the four countries of the UK. However, special mention needs to be made of the relative size of these countries. With a population of over 62 million people, England is at least ten times larger, in these terms, than any of the other three countries. This has a profound impact on the ways in which different sections of the education community communicate and interact. There is no doubt that this is more difficult in England, which in the following account, will be dealt with last.

2.3.1 Scotland

Scotland has always taken pride in an education system that is different from that in England. The structures of schooling, the curriculum, the examination system, inspection and the recruitment of teachers have all been developed and managed independently of its neighbour over the border. Scotland was quick to respond to the ideas and evidence on formative assessment/assessment for learning although, characteristically, it started to develop its own distinctive policy. Thus, in 2002, Scotland began setting up a national programme – Assessment is for Learning (AifL) – in which formative assessment is considered as part of a whole assessment system, including pupils' records, personal planning, system monitoring and school evaluation, as well as formative and summative assessment at the classroom level. The intention has been to develop a coherent system for all schools in Scotland that brings together assessment *for* learning, assessment *as* learning and assessment *of* learning. The stated philosophy is to give "considerable freedom to schools and teachers to develop practice within their own context at a pace and in a manner that is suited their needs" (Scottish Government, 2005, p. 3).

Three features of the development of the formative assessment strand are notable: (1) the provision of funding to support teachers' involvement in developing the projects within the programme, (2) support for the participation of university academics (from Scotland and England, especially Dylan Wiliam and Paul Black) which was a source of assurance that the ideas were supported by research evidence, and (3) the fact that the AifL programme was designed using research on transformational change, in particular the work of Senge and Scharmer (2001). The idea was to encourage teachers to engage with the underpinning research and the experience of teachers from England who had worked on the Nuffield Foundation funded King's, Medway, Oxfordshire Formative Assessment Project (KMOFAP) (Black, Harrison, Lee, Marshall, & Wiliam, 2003) and to try out, adapt and develop strategies suited to their own context. Recognizing the failure of previous initiatives in Scotland to embed ideas permanently in the system, those working in AifL in Scotland saw building a sustainable learning community for AifL as a major priority. Thus AifL sought to build learning communities across the education system. In each of the 32 education authorities in Scotland, communities of teachers, headteachers and local authority coordinators worked with national policy-makers, HMIE and researchers from across Scotland. The Research Report (Hayward, Spencer, & Simpson, 2006) on the Scottish AifL initiative notes how important teachers found the opportunities to share their practice through observation and discussion. However, while there was a general impression of successful implementation by those involved in the project, there was a reluctance by some teachers to engage with theories of learning to understand why the strategies "worked" to enhance learning. There was little movement from a pragmatic to a principled rationale. Moreover, there was little evidence that teachers had passed over responsibility for formative processes, especially deciding learning goals, to the pupils themselves. Ownership was still very much with the teachers.

However, by 2008 there was evidence, at least in some local authorities that this was changing. For example, a research report on the formative evaluation of a project designed to explore how teachers were bringing together ideas from AifL with the new curriculum innovation in Scotland, Curriculum for Excellence (see: http://www.LTScotland.org.uk/curriculumforexcellence/ Accessed 22 January 2011). In addition, a second report commissioned by the Scottish Qualifications Authority (SQA) found evidence of teachers developing assessment for learning approaches in the context of high stakes assessment (Standard grade, Intermediate and Higher: all post 16 examination classes). The Highland Council, which was the focus of this study, had taken a particular approach characterized by a professional development programme that encouraged strong and consistent engagement with principles of assessment, that built networks of support, had clear links between assessment, curriculum and learning and teaching, and had contextualized the initiative in a wider policy framework.

Notable, in the Scottish context, is a lack of reference to concerns to raise standards in terms of measured achievements during compulsory schooling. The reason is simple. There are no statutory, standard national tests in Scotland and no league tables of school performance. National monitoring is carried out by means of a sample survey, rather than whole cohort national testing, so that accountability does not directly drive classroom activity. The first Scottish Survey of Achievement (SSA), a sample monitoring survey of English language and core skills, was carried out by the Scottish Executive in May 2005. Assessment materials from the SSA are used to extend an on-line national bank of assessments that teachers can use, when they judge appropriate, to check their own assessments of pupils' progress. In 2007, AiFL was extended to all schools.

2.3.2 Wales

Following devolution of powers to Wales, and the report of the Daugherty Assessment Review Group (DARG, 2004) which was commissioned to advise on a system for Wales, the Welsh Assembly Government decided to discontinue statutory National Curriculum testing, as carried out in England, and to strengthen teachers' summative assessment as the basis for recording, reporting and accountability. From the school year 2008–2009, schools' responsibilities have been revised in relation to end of key stage teacher assessment arrangements. These now emphasize the importance of internal systems and procedures for standardizing and moderating teacher assessment. For assessments of pupils aged 11 at the end of Key Stage 2, primary schools, and the secondary schools to which they are linked, are required to have effective arrangements in place for cluster group moderation and for transfer of information between primary and secondary schools, in order to increase trust in the reliability of information on attainment. For the assessments of pupils aged 14 at the end of Key Stage 3, secondary schools are expected to supply details of their internal standardization procedures as the first stage in a process of national accreditation of secondary schools (by the Welsh Department for Children, Education, Lifelong Learning and Skills – DCELLS). The DARG Report had recommended the introduction of a limited number of "skills tests" in Year 5 (the year before the end of Key Stage 2 and transfer to secondary school). This proposal has evolved into optional skills assessment materials (not test-based), in thinking, communication and number, piloted by DCELLS in 2008, to support teachers in drawing up a skills profile for Year 5 pupils. Whilst the overall policy thrust stemmed from concerns with over-testing, and the lack of trust in professional judgments that this implied, the new direction has detractors. For example, some teachers, especially those of mathematics and science, have been reluctant to give up the statutory tests, and others fear an increase in workload.

In this broader assessment policy context, the DCELLS carried out a specific development programme for Thinking Skills (TS) and Assessment for Learning, which ran from 2006. This built on the insight that there is much overlap between efforts to develop thinking skills across the curriculum and assessment for learning. Both are interested in the development of metacognition, self-regulation, engagement and autonomy in learners, and ways in which teachers can integrate, or "infuse", TS and AfL strategies into subject teaching. To support the development of the programme, an advisory group was formed. The author of this chapter was a member, invited because of her membership of the Assessment Reform Group, and her role as director of a development and research project on learning how to learn through AfL (James et al., 2007). Carol McGuinness, from Queen's University Belfast, who was directing a project on the development of thinking skills (ACTS II), was another member (Information on both of these projects can be found at http://www.tlrp.org Accessed 22 January 2011). Carol McGuinness also contributed substantially to the work with schools in Wales by giving talks at the teachers' conferences that were part of the programme. Other support was provided by DCELLS staff and local authority advisers, although the key element was work by teachers, in 42 schools in ten Local Authorities, to develop their practice from the ideas (principles and practices) to which they were introduced.

External evaluation indicated that, in only five school terms, the development programme improved classroom practice and increased the frequency of creative lessons. This was associated with increased learner engagement and improved attainment for all learners, irrespective of perceived abilities. Although evidence of enhanced performance was difficult to discern, because the move from tests to teacher assessment prevented direct comparisons on stable measures, particular improvements in speaking, listening and behaviour were noted. A 3 year extension programme, beginning in late 2008, was therefore embarked upon to ensure that changes in pedagogy are more broadly embedded. The extension included the successful elements of the pilot:

- close partnership working with local authorities
- coaching/mentoring partnerships between DCELLS staff, local authority officers, school senior managers and teachers
- cluster group partnerships, especially between primary and secondary schools
- local and national networks to disseminate good practice
- ownership by local authority and school staff, and some flexibility on implementation so that their pathways reflect local needs
- funded reflection and planning time for practitioners
- monitoring and evaluation by local authorities and DCELLS.

A specific intention was to use the professional networks already established with international researchers and collaborators to enhance the programme and promote its findings.

2.3.3 Northern Ireland

Although, historically, curriculum and assessment in Northern Ireland (NI) has been tied closely to England, this is now changing quite markedly. In 1999, the NI Minister for Education called for a review of curriculum and assessment arrangements, and the resulting revised curriculum is currently being introduced along with new assessment arrangements (from August 2007). Another important change was a decision in 2001, influenced in part by a devastating critique of the reliability of the 11+ examination (Gardner & Cowan, 2000; but see Gardner & Cowan, 2005 for a more accessible summary), to abolish this selection test for entry to grammar schools, and allow parents and pupils to choose their post-primary schools. One aspect of the new assessment arrangements – the Pupil Profile – is intended to assist them with this choice.

Taken as a whole, the new assessment arrangements are intended to embrace diagnostic, formative, summative and evaluative purposes (i.e., those stated in the 1988 TGAT Report in England). By phased introduction, starting with the first year in each Key Stage in 2007–2008, statutory summative assessment requires every pupil in every year to be assessed by their teachers in (1) areas of learning; (2) cross-curricular skills (communication, using mathematics and ICT); and (3) thinking skills and capabilities (managing information, thinking/problem-solving/decisions, being creative, working with others, self-management). The reliability of these assessments will be assured through teacher moderation. Diagnostic assessment delivered via the Interactive Computerized Assessment System (InCAS) will be used at least once each Key Stage to measure aspects of reading, mathematics and "developed ability". The results of these assessments must be reported to parents and annual parent-teacher meetings arranged to discuss them. An annual pupil profile report will also be produced by the end of May to inform transfer decisions. Alongside all these changes sits AfL to fulfil the formative purpose.

AfL in Northern Ireland represents the "roll out" of a development project begun with 38 primary teachers in 2004 and extended to another 50 primary and post-primary teachers in 2005. The project was described as "action research" in which teachers were encouraged to experiment with aspects of the methodology of assessment for learning and to "adapt the theory and principles of formative assessment to suit their own teaching context and their individual pupils" (CCEA, 2006). The experience of this project has now been distilled into online materials for the Foundation Stage and Key Stages 1, 2 & 3 (See http://www.nicurriculum.org.uk/foundation_stage/assessment/assessment_for_learning.asp for an example. Accessed 22 January 2011) which highlight "five key actions": sharing learning intentions; sharing and negotiating success criteria; feedback; effective questioning; peer- and self-assessment and self evaluation. The emphasis on sharing learning intentions and success criteria reveals the influence of the development consultant, Shirley Clarke, who was involved in live presentations and whose books were provided (e.g. Clarke, 2001); 80% of teachers chose these ideas as their point of departure.

Perhaps this was a good place to start because, for half the teachers in the pilots, the AfL strategies were entirely novel, yet, after a short time positive changes were found. Pupils were described as more confident, persevering and strategic. Teachers were more focused on pupils' needs; they planned for AfL; they were more reflective and had changed their pedagogy. Nevertheless there were concerns over intentions-practice gaps, equity issues i.e. whether the approaches were suitable for all pupils, and the involvement of parents. Moreover there were substantial implications for support for professional development from senior management of schools. The need to share experience with other teachers and to develop practice over time was thought to be important for sustainability. In other words there appeared to be some resistance to these innovations, which is not surprising since Northern Ireland teachers had been embedded in a summative testing culture for so long.

2.3.4 England

In England, ideas associated with AfL were first taken up by the Qualifications and Curriculum Authority: a quasi-autonomous organization set up with public funds to advise government and to implement aspects of policy on curriculum and assessment. Soon after the publication and distribution by ARG of its *AfL: 10 Principles* poster, QCA requested permission to publish the poster on a book mark and on its website. The Association for Achievement and Improvement through Assessment (AAIA), an association created largely by and for assessment inspectors and advisers in local authorities, also took an early interest and developed materials to support AfL development work with schools (See http://www.aaia.org.uk/afl Accessed 22 January 2011). AfL also became established as an element in the Labour Government's Primary National Strategy (PNS) and the Secondary National Strategy (SNS), which were key components of national policy focused on the development of pedagogy. The National Strategies were managed directly by the Department for Children, Schools and Families (DCSF), the name given in 2008 to the government department concerned with schools, formerly the Department for Education and Skills. These national strategies had the status of guidance – they were not mandatory – but the pressure to comply was considerable, not least through the Ofsted inspection process that expected to see the strategies in operation in schools, or very good reasons why they were not.

By 2009 the Primary National Strategy concentrated on literacy and mathematics, and its 2008 renewed materials had a substantial section on assessment for learning. This section had three sub-sections that shifted the focus progressively outwards from teaching and learning interactions in the classroom, to supportive conditions for learning and then to leadership and management and support. This built on an earlier publication (DfES, 2007a) that revealed a shift towards working more with school leaders in supporting improvement in order to embed AfL practice in classrooms because "the greatest prizes are still to be won".

The Key Stage 3 (lower secondary) section on the DCSF Standards Site contained a suite of Assessment for Learning materials for download, including resources on: AfL in everyday lessons, formative use of summative tests, objective led lessons, oral and written feedback, peer and self-assessment, target setting, securing progression, and questioning and dialogue. A report of an action research project with eight secondary schools (DfES, 2007b) also engaged with the challenges of implementing and embedding AfL practice in schools, acknowledging that the results of previous efforts had been equivocal, in terms of raising standards as judged by national test and examination results. This SNS report focused on the impact of AfL on pupil learning and standards, and on the leadership and management of change. The findings indicated that "fundamental to developing AfL in the classroom is developing the independent learner and, fundamental to developing the leadership and management of whole school change is developing distributed leadership" (see Chapter 2, Section 2.2, author's emphasis). Curiously, however, given this work sponsored by the DCSF, the renewed SNS Frameworks published in May 2008 made scant use of AfL ideas although they incorporated some reference into an initiative called Assessing Pupils' Progress (APP). The emphasis throughout the new frameworks was on teachers regularly assessing pupils against target levels, and tracking progress.

Both the PNS and the earlier SNS materials made reference to definitions of AfL and research-base accounts of good practice from the Assessment Reform Group, Paul Black and colleagues at King's College London, and the Learning How to Learn project (James et al., 2007). However, the text of these materials, and especially the newer Secondary Frameworks, also revealed tensions with researchers' definitions of AfL (Personal communication suggests that some of the authors were aware of these tensions). For example, the more recent PNS materials referred to "day-to-day assessment" and the SNS materials to "everyday" assessment. This had two contrasting implications. The first was to reinforce the idea that AfL is part of continual interaction and reflection in classrooms, and integral to teaching and learning. But the second implication was that by changing the descriptor to "day-to-day" or "everyday", AfL can be formative, or summative, or both. Politically this was probably unavoidable because the Labour Government in England had invested a great deal in the development of pupil tracking and planning tools, to help teachers and headteachers use the results of statutory national tests for monitoring, prediction and target setting (see for example: http://www.raiseonline.org/About.aspx. Accessed 22 January 2011). However, one can also argue that what was being promoted was no longer formative assessment, as part of pedagogy, for the purpose of enhancing real and lasting learning, but frequent mini-summative assessment to secure higher performance on tests to meet prescribed targets.

The distinction between learning and performance is a subtle one and not well understood. Measured performance should indeed be an indicator of underlying learning (or what Dweck, 2000, calls "mastery") but debates about the validity and reliability of assessments underscore the difficulties of making such assumptions. It is quite possible to drill pupils to perform well on tests without enhancing their learning and, given the high stakes consequences for schools that perform badly, there is increasing evidence that this has happened in England (ARG, 2002b). One possible explanation for the mixed messages that appeared in DCSF documents is that the authors tried to finesse competing claims between those who were convinced by research that formative assessment is the key to improved learning and achievement, and those who still believed that the pressure of regular testing raises standards. Or the mixed messages may simply be indicative of some confused thinking that has elided "learning" and "performance". A publication from the

DCSF (2008), which launched the Labour Government's Assessment for Learning Strategy, raised such questions.

This new AfL Strategy was a very significant new initiative backed by £150 m of government money over 3 years for the professional development of teachers in AfL. It was supported by the DCSF, QCA (which had become the QCDA), the National Strategies and the Chartered Institute of Educational Assessors. The document began by quoting the ARG's definition of Assessment for Learning and incorporated the ARG's ten principles, albeit unattributed and with a different graphic design (Ibid, p. 5). Much of the rest of the text developed ideas based on the ARG definition that: "Assessment for learning is the process of seeking and interpreting evidence for use by learners and their teachers to decide where the learners are in their learning, where they need to go and how best to get there" (ARG, 2002a). However it also built on the DCSF's own Assessing Pupils' Progress work and its Making Good Progress Pilot (http://www.teachernet.gov.uk/teachingandlearning/schoolstandards/mgppilot/. Accessed 22 January 2011). The idea behind the "Making Good Progress" pilot was to introduce single level tests (SLTs) for teachers to use to check their own judgments, twice a year. On the surface this might look like the Scottish system of banking assessments for teachers to use when they think pupils are ready, but the expectation in England was that standard tests would still be administered to all pupils and the results aggregated, with, at least in the case of the pilot, financial rewards to schools that could show progress of two levels for pupils over a Key Stage. The consultation on the proposed pilot generated concerns that even more testing, which this implies, is not the way forward and more serious effort should be given to developing AfL. However, in its response, the government argued that, by putting AfL together with pupil tracking, formative and summative assessment could be made to work together more effectively. Thus deciding "where the learners are in their learning, where they need to go and how best to get there" had come to mean assessing pupils frequently according to national curriculum levels and sub-levels to track progress, setting new levels as targets and then working (somehow) to attain them. This was not an interpretation that the ARG had in mind when it wrote the definition of AfL although, if "learning" is interpreted as "performance", then the definition is sufficiently ambiguous to make such a reading understandable. A less generous explanation might that the DCSF chose deliberately to appropriate an idea that had gained considerable professional support from teachers in order to take the next pull of the testing lever to meet its performance targets.

Until October 2008, the Labour Government in England seemed unwilling to relinquish any aspect of its testing system as its primary instrument of change. Despite the disastrous experience with missing national test results and poor marking quality in the summer of 2008, it had no obvious plans to rethink the system that was breaking under the strain. In August, Alice Miles (2008), a *Times* columnist, offered her explanation:

> ... in the face of scepticism about the achievements of their Government, these multi-coloured graphs have become the only measure by which they can trumpet their success. This explains the obsession with testing: it has become not a tool of policy, but policy itself.

Then on 14 October, at the height of the financial crisis (a day to bury controversial news – or to save some money?), the Secretary of State for Education, Ed Balls, announced an end to compulsory national tests for 14 year olds (http://www.dcsf.gov.uk/pns/DisplayPN.cgi?pn_id=2008_0229. Accessed 22 January 2011). The proposals were that Key Stage 3 tests would be replaced by improved classroom assessment by teachers and frequent reporting to parents in years 7, 8 and 9. Teacher assessments would be published at national and local authority level only. School Report Cards, along the lines of those used in New York City, would become the mechanism for reporting a wide range of achievements at school level. Standards at age 14, across the education system, would be monitored by national sampling. Assessment for learning was seen to have a role "to help schools use ongoing assessment to drive up pupils' progress". According to the DCSF's Press Notice this involved: "gaining clear evidence about how to drive up an individual pupil's attainment; an understanding between teachers and pupils on what they need to improve; and an agreement on the steps needed to promote individual progress". Given the discussion above, it is worth noting that there was only one reference to pupils' "learning" in the whole four page document.

The announcement of the end of Key Stage 3 tests was widely welcomed by teachers, parents and politicians, including the Opposition parties, and some argued that Key Stage 2 tests should be abolished too. On this matter the Government insisted: "externally marked Key Stage 2 tests were critically important and would continue". However, at a teachers' union conference in April 2009, the then Secretary of State for Education, Ed Balls, said that these tests for 11 year olds were "not set in stone" and that he would work with teachers and parents to reform them, if necessary, after the report, scheduled for May 2009, of an "expert group" on testing made up of headteachers and educational professionals.

Despite this change in policy in England there was little evidence that the underlying rationale had altered significantly. The "drive" was still to raise standards as measured by national curriculum assessment levels; and assessment for learning continued to be seen as an instrument for this purpose. More subtle ideas, about the role of AfL in pedagogy to enhance the learning of capable, resourceful and autonomous citizens in a changing world, seem almost entirely absent.

Recent history of education in England has been characterized by constant change. This has continued. In May 2010, one of the first acts of the incoming Conservative/ Liberal Democrat Coalition Government was to change the name of the DCSF to the Department for Education (DfE). Shortly afterwards it promised what has been popularly called a "bonfire of the quangos" to reduce the levels of government bureaucracy – and to save money in order to reduce the level of national debt. The QCDA was the first quango to be served notice. Within the Department of Education, the National Strategies were also axed. At the time of writing, the future policy profile of AfL is unclear; probably existing material will be placed in an accessible archive for schools to use if they wish. What is more certain is that some form of national testing will continue at the end of the primary phase or at the beginning of secondary schooling and that these results will be published for accountability purposes. The Coalition Government has asked Lord Bew to conduct an independent review of the effectiveness of the current Key Stage 2 tests, and to report to Ministers in June 2011.

2.4 The Extent of Policy Borrowing

The four countries of the UK are constantly looking at one another's policies to see what they might borrow or adapt, or what they should definitely reject. They each regard their particular context as in some way unique, as indeed they are, so they seek to tailor any "borrowed" policy to their own circumstances. Some countries are more inclined to acknowledge the influence of their neighbours than others. For example Northern Ireland gives Scotland's AifL website as a "useful link".

Exchanges between Scotland, Northern Ireland and Wales, and between researchers and policy-makers there, seem more open than with, and within, England. An illustration of this might be the fact that the ARG felt obliged to hold separate seminars for the dissemination of its projects: always a separate one for England and one or more for the other three countries. Unless meetings are held in or near Westminster it is often difficult to meet key policy-makers in England whereas politicians, civil servants, advisers and researchers meet relatively frequently in the other countries. Of course, England has a much bigger and diverse population, and a much more complex bureaucracy with many layers of decision making, even within the area of education. Differences in opportunities for networking might explain, in part, why policy has diverged between England and the Celtic Fringe. Most significantly for AfL, the government in England, in contrast to Scotland, Wales and Northern Ireland, continues to be committed to an accountability system based on published results of summative tests and assessments. Changes in the political party in power have not changed this overall direction. AfL is therefore pressed into the service of this overarching goal, rather than fulfilling a fundamental purpose of its own. No doubt many policy-makers in England see this hard-headedness as a virtue. After all, there is still no strong evidence yet that when AfL (understood as formative assessment as part of pedagogy) moves to the centre of policy it raises performance standards across the system as a whole. For example, results from the Progress in International Reading Literacy Study (PIRLS) 2006 placed England 19th and Scotland 26th in its distribution table of reading achievement in 40 countries (Mullis, Martin, Kennedy, & Foy, 2007, p. 37). This is unlikely to encourage England's policy makers to adopt Scotland's approach. Although school performance tables, based on tests at Key Stage 3, will no longer be compiled in England, any commitment to national sampling for system monitoring is still a long way from policy in Scotland.

It certainly seems that policy makers in Scotland, Wales and Northern Ireland have been more convinced than those in England by the arguments of researchers that a choice does not have to be made between raising performance and good learning because with AfL you can have both. These countries have been convinced enough to reject all whole cohort national testing and the publication of league tables in favour of summative teacher assessment combined with formative assessment. One reason for coming to this common view may be that, rather than directly borrowing from one another, they have each drawn directly on the same pool of evidence, mainly from Black, Wiliam and the ARG. England, as we have seen, has made reference to these sources, but the three other countries have made more use of the researchers themselves as *partners* in the work of development and policy formation. In terms of the impact of educational research on education policy, this must one of the most remarkable examples in recent times.

2.5 Challenges for Educational Change

The story of how AfL has emerged as a focus for policy and practice in the UK, and how it has been variously interpreted and implemented, is a story of relationships between educational researchers and policy-makers. Although some researchers in education are, quite legitimately, content to work in the contributory disciplines of education to produce new knowledge for its own sake, other "educational researchers" seek to use the insights, theories and tools of research to illuminate issues of policy and practice in the hope and expectation that such knowledge will be utilized in the policy context. This is not straightforward because the two different communities of practice – research and policy formation – are characterized by:

- Different time pressures and workflows
- Different priorities and responsibilities
- Different conceptual frameworks and discourse
- Different accountability and incentive systems
- Different cultures and structural positions in society
- Different career structures and pathways

Any attempt to work productively together creates tensions for both groups. The press for quick policy change – to show results before the next election – puts pressure on researchers to deliver ideas and results in a timescale that they find difficult, if not impossible. But sometimes it works the other way and policy-makers are only just getting to grips with certain ideas before researchers have moved on in their thinking, the subtleties of which may be lost on policy-makers who have the task of trying to engineer complex ideas into relatively simple frameworks for action. This may indeed be the case with AfL.

It is notable, from the accounts given above, that a key element of AfL policies in UK countries has been a strategy to introduce teachers to the five or six clusters of AfL practices that were identified in *Inside the black box* and KMOFAP i.e. sharing learning objectives and criteria of quality, feedback, rich questioning, peer and self-assessment, and formative use of summative tests. The common approach thereafter has been to encourage teachers to test and adapt these ideas in their own circumstances and to evaluate the results with colleagues. However, as researchers have found in subsequent projects, such as in the Learning How to Learn project (James et al., 2007) which investigated the conditions in schools that would enable the embedding and spreading of sustainable AfL practice, and as government agencies have discovered in developing AfL projects for national roll out, a number of problems have arisen which were not well dealt with by the early research, notably:

- How to avoid AfL practices becoming mechanistic, ritualized and ultimately meaningless and boring to pupils.
- How to integrate them meaningfully in the flow of lesson activity, not simply added on.
- How to establish, in teachers' minds, a relationship between the practices and the theoretical ideas that underpin them so that they have the intellectual resources to "know what to do when they don't know what to do".
- How to shift AfL from being a teacher-led activity to it being a learner-led activity.
- How to convince teachers that they have the power and responsibility (agency) to make AfL work in contexts of accountability where they feel constrained by mandatory demands for summative assessments and curriculum coverage that tend to take priority.
- How to manage opportunities for teachers to work together to plan, try out, observe, reflect, discuss and revise their AfL ideas and practices.
- How to encourage school managers to become committed to AfL and to accept responsibility for the professional learning of their staff.

The research relating to these questions was not readily available when policy initiatives in the UK countries were put in place so the policies themselves have become experiments from which lessons have be learned. No doubt they will lead to further adjustments in the future. Inevitably, this constant policy tinkering is irritating to teachers and can make them cynical or passive: a state of affairs inimical to the kind of active engagement that successful AfL demands.

Two issues of particular importance have now become a focus of recent work by researchers in the field. The first concerns the theoretical underpinning of AfL practice and how formative assessment might relate more broadly to learning and pedagogy. Chapters in an edited collection from the ARG published in 2006 (Gardner, 2006) began to examine this relationship. Also, in March 2009, a Third International Conference on Assessment for Learning, involving 30 educational researchers and developers from Australia, Canada, Continental Europe, New Zealand, the USA and the UK wrote a position paper on AfL which acknowledged the difficulties of articulating and communicating this relationship (This can be downloaded from: http://www.annedavies.com/assessment_for_learning_ar_a010.html. Accessed 22 January 2011. It is also reproduced in Klenowski, (2009)). They began by noting the widespread use of the phrases *assessment for learning* and *formative assessment* in educational discourse but expressed concern about some of the ways in which the words are interpreted and made manifest in educational policy. They then attempted to clarify the relationship between assessment and learning by emphasising that the primary aim of assessment for learning is to contribute to learning itself. This follows from the logic that when true learning has occurred, it will manifest itself in performance. The converse does not hold: mere performance on a test does not necessarily mean that learning has occurred. Learners can be taught how to score well on tests without much underlying learning.

AfL is therefore the process of identifying aspects of learning as it is developing, using whatever informal and formal processes best help that identification, primarily so that learning itself can be enhanced. This focuses directly on the learner's developing capabilities, while these are in the process of being developed. AfL seeks out, analyses and reflects on information from students themselves, teachers and the learner's peers as it is expressed in dialogue, learner responses to tasks and questions, and observation. AfL is part of everyday teaching, in everyday classrooms. A great deal of it occurs in real time, but some of it is derived through more formal assessment events or episodes. What is distinctive about AfL is not the form of the information or the circumstances in which it is generated, but the positive effect it has for the learner. Properly embedded into teaching-learning contexts, AfL sets learners up for wide, lifelong learning. These ideas were summed up in a short second-generation definition of assessment for learning generated by the Conference:

> Assessment for Learning is part of everyday practice by students, teachers and peers that seeks, reflects upon and responds to information from dialogue, demonstration and observation in ways that enhance ongoing learning.

The second issue from research, with implications for policy, concerns the continuing attention that needs to be given to support for teachers' own learning if AfL is to be effective in classrooms, embedded in schools, spread across schools, and sustained over time. This was the main focus of the Learning How to Learn Project and has also been a theme for another project from the ARG, which has used desk research, interviews and expert seminars to analyze insights emerging from twelve projects, many of which are mentioned in this chapter. The Analysis and Review of Innovations in Assessment (ARIA) project began disseminating its findings in a pamphlet, *Changing Assessment Practice: process, principles and standards* (Gardner, Harlen, Hayward, & Stobart, 2008). The chapter by Gardner and colleagues in this volume is another output.

All these developments indicate that research and policy development are not sequential activities (one before the other) but are necessarily pursued alongside each other. For this reason, the channels of communication have to be open, and deliberate efforts have to be made to engage in dialogue, in order to understand the pressures on, and the possibilities for, evidence informed policy making for effective change. The UK's Teaching and Learning Research Programme (see http://www.tlrp.org), with which the author of this chapter has been involved as deputy director, has been centrally involved in "creative mediation" between the 700+ researchers and 100+ projects in its portfolio and all the potential "users" who might be interested in and benefit from their findings. Andrew Pollard, the director of TLRP from 2002, characterizes its role as a form of "reflexive activism":

> We are trying to build the social capital of educational research – developing relationships and networks, sharing perspectives and building alliances with present and future stakeholders both within and beyond the research community. We are trying to promote collective, open and reflexive debate and action in respect of the changes which need to be faced. We are working on politically engaged impact and dissemination strategies with a view to making a difference. And finally, we are attempting to position ourselves strategically in respect of long-term issues. (Pollard, 2005, p. 4)

This statement could equally characterize the disposition and orientation of the UK's Assessment Reform Group and its belief that researchers, policy-makers and practitioners have to work together in the middle ground of "creative mediation" if research and policy are to contribute to effective educational change.

Acknowledgments The author of this paper is indebted to Richard Daugherty, Carmel Gallagher and Louise Hayward who suggested improvements with respect to the accounts of policy and practice in Wales, Northern Ireland and Scotland, respectively. However, any faults that remain are the author's alone.

References

Assessment Reform Group. (2002a). Assessment for Learning: 10 principles. Assessment Reform Group. http://www.assessment-reform-group.org. Accessed 22 January 2011.

Assessment Reform Group. (2002b). Testing, motivation and learning. Assessment Reform Group. http://www.assessment-reform-group.org. Accessed 22 January 2011.

Black, P. J. (1997). Whatever happened to TGAT? In C. Cullingford (Ed.), *Assessment versus evaluation* (pp. 24–50). London: Cassell.

Black, P., Harrison, C., Lee, C., Marshall, B., & Wiliam, D. (2003). *Assessment for learning: Putting it into practice*. Maidenhead: Open University Books.

Black, P., & Wiliam, D. (1998). Assessment and classroom learning. *Assessment in Education: Principles, policy & practice*, *5*(1), 7–75.

Clarke, S. (2001). *Unlocking formative assessment*. Abingdon: Hodder and Stoughton.

Council for the Curriculum, Examinations and Assessment (CCEA). (2006). *Assessment for learning report*. Belfast: Council for the Curriculum, Examinations and Assessment.

DARG. (2004). *Learning pathways through statutory assessment: Key stages 2 and 3. Final report*. Cardiff: Welsh Assembly Government.

Daugherty, R. (2007). Mediating academic research: The Assessment Reform Group experience. *Research Papers in Education*, *22*(2), 139–153.

Department for Children, Education, Lifelong Learning and Skills (DCELLS). (2008). *Curriculum and assessment update*, Issue 4, Spring. Cardiff: DCELLS, Welsh Assembly Government.

Department for Children, Schools and Families (DCSF). (2008). *The Assessment for Learning strategy*. London: DCSF re: 00341-2008DOM-EN. www.teachernet.gov.uk/publications. Accessed 22 January 2011.

Department for Education and Skills (DfES). (2007a). *Leading improvement using the Primary Framework: Primary National Strategy Guidance for primary headteachers and school leaders*. London: DfES re: 00484-2007BKT-EN. www.teachernet.gov.uk/publications. Accessed 22 January 2011.

Department for Education and Skills (DfES). (2007b). *Assessment for Learning – 8 schools project report: Secondary National Strategy Guidance for School leaders, teachers, school improvement advisers and national policy makers*. London: DfES ref: 00067-2007BKT-EN. www.teachernet.gov.uk/publications. Accessed 22 January 2011.

Dweck, C. S. (2000). *Self-theories: Their role in motivation, personality and development*. Philadephia: Psychology Press.

Elliott, J. (1990). Educational research in crisis. *British Educational Research Journal, 16*(1), 3–18.

Gardner, J. (Ed.). (2006). *Assessment and learning*. London: Sage.

Gardner, J., & Cowan, P. (2000). *Testing the test: A study of the reliability and validity of the Northern Ireland transfer procedure test in enabling the selection of pupils for grammar school places*. Belfast: School of Education, Queen's University Belfast.

Gardner, J., & Cowan, P. (2005). The fallibility of high stakes '11-plus' testing in Northern Ireland. *Assessment in Education, 12*(2), 145–165.

Gardner, J., Harlen, W., Hayward, L., & Stobart, G. (2008). *Changing Assessment Practice: Process, principles and standards*. ISBN 9780853899297. http://www.aria.qub.ac.uk. Accessed 22 January 2011.

Hargreaves, D. (1996). *Teaching as a research-based profession: Possibilities and prospects*. London: Teacher Training Agency Annual Lecture.

Hayward, L., Spencer, E., & Simpson, M. (2006). *Assessment is for learning: Exploring programme success. The Aifl formative assessment project*. Glasgow: University of Glasgow.

Hillage, J., Pearson, R., Anderson, A., & Tamkin, P. (1998). *Excellence in research on schools*. London: Department for Education and Employment.

James, M., McCormick, R., Black, P., Carmichael, P., Drummond, M. -J., & Fox, A., et al. (2007). *Improving learning how to learn: Classrooms, schools and networks*. London: Routledge.

Klenowski, V. (2009). Assessment for learning revisited: An Asia-Pacific perspective. *Assessment in Education: Principles, Policy & Practice, 16*(3), 263–268.

Miles, A. (2008). Today's SATs result: Government 0 Pupils 0, *Times Online*. 6 August. http://www.timesonline.co.uk/tol/comment/columnists/alice_miles. Accessed 22 January 2011.

Mullis, I., Martin, M., Kennedy, A., & Foy, P. (2007). *PIRLS 2006 international report: IEA's Progress in International Reading Literacy in Primary Schools in 40 countries*. Boston: Boston College. http://timss.bc.edu/pirls2006/intl_rpt.html. Accessed 22 January 2011.

Pollard, A. (2005). *Taking the initiative? TLRP and educational research*. Educational Review Guest Lecture, 12th October 2005, School of Education, University of Birmingham. http://www.tlrp.org. Accessed 22 January 2011.

Scottish Government. (2005). *AifL – Assessment is for Learning information sheet*. http://www.scotland.gov.uk/Publications/2005/09/20105413/54156. Accessed 22 January 2011.

Senge, P., & Scharmer, O. (2001). Community action research: Learning as a community of practitioners, consultants, and researchers. In P. Reason & H. Bradbury (Eds.), *Handbook of action research: Participative inquiry and practice*. Thousand Oaks, CA: Sage.

Chapter 3
Assessment for Learning: US Perspectives

Jim Flaitz

3.1 Introduction

In the USA, educational policy-making is largely a state and local matter, rather than a federal or national area of involvement. With a few major exceptions, federal engagement in education had been limited to providing supplemental funding of compensatory education programs until recently, with the enactment of the No Child Left Behind (NCLB) Act in 2002, an early initiative in the presidency of George W. Bush. The act marked the culmination of a movement that characterized the USA as being in crisis, due in large part to an educational system that was not producing a workforce with the requisite skills for economic competitiveness. Key elements of the educational reform included a call for the establishment of rigorous standards in certain "core" subjects as a means to promote excellence in education and to make schools accountable for the academic performance of their students. With the passing of NCLB, funding for state and local education in the federal budget was consolidated and made contingent upon the states adopting the framework of NCLB.

While a range of initiatives have been introduced around the world to promote assessment as a tool for enhancing student learning, NCLB has been driving practices in the opposite direction. Although systemic changes to education at the national level for the purpose of greater accountability have been a common theme in many contexts internationally, those reforms have nonetheless created a certain amount of space for pedagogically-oriented initiatives such as assessment for learning. This space is more constrained in the USA, although educators have been attracted to complementing test-based practices with alternative, formative assessments. The difference in the available pedagogical space, suggests Popham (2006a, p. 90), stems from the fact that education reform in the USA produced "test frenzy", while the reforms in other education systems were less frenetic. Additionally, what seems most compelling in the case of the USA is the degree of politicization of

J. Flaitz (✉)
Educational Foundations and Leadership Department, College of Education at the University of Louisiana at Lafayette, Lafayette, LA, USA
e-mail: jflaitz@louisiana.edu

R. Berry, B. Adamson (eds.), *Assessment Reform in Education*,
Education in the Asia-Pacific Region: Issues, Concerns and Prospects 14,
DOI 10.1007/978-94-007-0729-0_3,

educational reform, in combination with strong, private sector interests representing the testing industry. Shortly after the passage of NCLB, Popham offered the wry observation at a national educational research meeting that it would perhaps be more appropriate to refer to the legislation as "No Test Publisher Left Behind", in reference to the almost total focus placed in the legislation on the use of high-stakes tests (the near exclusive domain of private test publishers) to gauge attainment of standards by students.

This chapter explores and explains the constraints imposed upon many US schools and teachers by recent reforms such as NCLB that mitigate their opportunities to explore alternative approaches to assessment. It presents a snapshot of contemporary assessment practices, in particular those that are associated with NCLB and then investigates some practices in the spirit of assessment for learning that have managed to survive or emerge as educators at the state and local level struggle to reconcile the powerful influences of high-stakes testing with the more fundamental mandate to promote learning.

3.2 Economic, Political and Ideological Background to Education Reform in the USA

In their study of education and national development, Fägerlind and Saha (1989) propose a triadic framework for analyzing reform that covers economic, political and ideological perspectives. These perspectives – which are often intertwined – can provide a contextual explanation for the ideas that underpin NCLB.

A key precursor to NCLB was a document published in 1983, by the National Commission on Excellence in Education, *A Nation at Risk*. This report raised the specter of the USA losing its economic competitiveness and falling behind other economies because the educational foundations of American society were "being eroded by a rising tide of mediocrity" (National Commission on Excellence in Education, 1983, p. 1). The danger, claimed the report, was signaled by poor performances in international comparisons of student achievement, national surveys and test scores, and other indicators, and was exacerbated by economic changes that required even higher levels of educational excellence:

> Knowledge, learning, information, and skilled intelligence are the new raw materials of international commerce and are today spreading throughout the world as vigorously as miracle drugs, synthetic fertilizers, and blue jeans did earlier. If only to keep and improve on the slim competitive edge we still retain in world markets, we must dedicate ourselves to the reform of our educational system for the benefit of all – old and young alike, affluent and poor, majority and minority. Learning is the indispensable investment required to success in the "information age" we are entering. (National Commission on Excellence in Education, 1983, p. 2)

A second theme that is present in the discourse of *A Nation at Risk* concerns equity across different economic and racial groups:

> We do not believe that a public commitment to excellence and educational reform must be made at the expense of a strong public commitment to the equitable treatment of our diverse

> population. The twin goals of equity and high-quality schooling have profound and practical meaning for our economy and society, and we cannot permit one to yield to the other either in principle or in practice. To do so would deny young people their chance to learn and live according to their aspirations and abilities. It also would lead to a generalized accommodation to mediocrity in our society on the one hand or the creation of an undemocratic elitism on the other. (National Commission on Excellence in Education, 1983, p. 7)

Attention to diversity arose from political forces such as the civil rights movement that led to the desegregation of schools in the 1960s, and the War on Poverty that also dated back to presidency of Lyndon B. Johnson.

The solution to the perceived decline in students' academic performance and to the problems of equity, according to the authors of *A Nation at Risk*, lies in the promotion of excellence, which is to be achieved by setting high standards and focusing on core subjects such as mathematics, English, history/US government, and science, while rejecting at the same time "undemanding and superfluous high school offerings" (*ibid,* p.9). As the problem is framed as being a national issue, it follows that some form of national framework of standards would be required. The argument that *A Nation at Risk* makes reflects a social and economic efficiency orientation to educational aims. According to this orientation, the role of schools is to prepare future citizens who will be economically productive (Schiro, 2008).

The ideological linkage between economic productivity and education represents a third theme that influenced NCLB, namely, accountability. The notions that schools should be accountable and that a measurable output of the education system is student performance in standardized tests, are derived from a view of education as an economic commodity existing in a marketplace (Nelson, 2007). Calls to make schools more accountable for the public funding they received had been heard increasingly since the inauguration of federal programs such as Title I in the mid-1960s (O'Day, 2002). By calling for the establishment of standards to measure academic performance, *A Nation at Risk* facilitated the introduction of a system that makes schools accountable for the funding that they receive.

The rhetoric of *A Nation at Risk* consists of vilifying the current state of affairs in US schools and then promoting a particular vision of change for which, according to the document, there was strong public support: "Of all the tools at hand, the public's support for education is the most powerful" (National Commission on Excellence in Education, 1983, p. 8), although a cynic might retort that members of the public are highly unlikely to fail to support ideas such as educational excellence. Politicians at the state and federal level seized the opportunity to nail their colors to the mast of educational reform, with the result that NCLB enjoyed broad bipartisan support in both the House of Representatives and the US Senate.

3.3 No Child Left Behind

The NCLB legislation established a new direction in federal policy toward public education. However it did not mandate a national curriculum or set of standards, rather it mandated that states develop and adopt standards; it did not mandate a specific national testing scheme, rather it mandated that states develop or adopt standardized tests in literacy and numeracy of demonstrated validity and reliability. It stipulated that the academic achievement standards should include at least three levels of achievement – advanced, proficient and basic–and that descriptions of the competencies associated with each level should be provided (US Department of Education, 2002). NCLB further required that only objective knowledge should be assessed, although states were allowed flexibility in determining the types and combinations of assessment to be used, on condition that all the standards were covered in depth and breadth, and that results could be reported in terms of the standards. A further requirement was that the assessments would have to be designed so as to be valid and accessible as far as possible for students with disabilities and those whose proficiency in English was limited. Assessment under NCLB has three main characteristics: it is high-stakes, designed to serve the purpose of accountability, and based on standards.

3.3.1 High-Stakes Assessment

The USA is a relatively recent entrant into the world of high-stakes testing for judging student learning and school effectiveness. One area where high-stakes testing has a history has been in the arena of university admissions, where the practice of requiring applicants to sit for either the Scholastic Aptitude Test/Scholastic Assessment Test (SAT) or the American College Testing (ACT) tests of "scholastic aptitude" has been in effect for over 70 years (Isaacs, 2001; Lawrence, Rigol, Van Essen, & Jackson, 2002). These tests are privately developed, administered and scored, and universities use the scores, in conjunction with other relevant applicant information (high school Grade Point Average, extracurricular activities, etc.) in making admissions decisions. In early days, the use of these high-stakes, standardized assessments for university admissions were initiated at the behest of private universities and the most selective of public universities, who were looking for an objective source of evidence of academic potential that could be efficiently applied to a growing pool of applicants from very different academic backgrounds.

Ironically, the introduction of high-stakes testing to university admissions began as an egalitarian effort (to level the playing field among applicants by providing a common measure of educational readiness). As university-going exploded after World War II (due to the return to the workforce of millions of young men), universities found themselves in the dilemma of selectively admitting applicants, and turned to the use of high-stakes tests. In the 1960s and 1970s, as the societal view of higher education shifted to that of an essential prerequisite for economic opportunity, many universities began to use the standardized test scores for placement decisions (determining which students would be required to take remedial coursework in preparation for the regular curriculum, and which students would be eligible for advanced placement, exempting them from introductory level required courses, or routing them to more accelerated versions of those courses). This placement process, which may be unfamiliar in other parts of the world, is a reflection of an abiding view of students as being differentiable based on aptitude, running into a parallel view that access to public education (including university education) is an entitlement and a critical foundation for personal economic success. Consequently, public universities were in many instances admitting students who were less prepared for university-level studies. Because these tests used for university admissions by design focus on *aptitude* (general abilities) rather than on achievement of specific academic outcomes, the direct connection to such matters as "narrowing of the curriculum" or "teaching to the test" is less clear. Because for much of the history of university-admissions standardized testing, college-going was just one of many legitimate post-secondary paths a student might take, the proportion of students taking these tests has never been as high as is the case in other nations where such tests are mandated. Many high schools developed "college preparatory" curricula, but students largely self-selected for these curricula. Until relatively recently, conventional wisdom was that "teaching" to such tests was impossible, because the focus of the tests was on aptitudes that were a life-time in the making (in more recent times, several highly successful test-preparation companies have claimed substantial success in preparing students for these tests).

In the 1980s, individual states began to develop or adopt high school graduation examinations (which, however, did not supplant existing, high-stakes tests designed for use in university admissions) and required students to attain a minimum performance on literacy and mathematics tests in order to obtain a high school diploma (Jacob, 2001; Marchant & Paulson, 2005). These tests were *minimum competency* tests in the sense that the thresholds of performance set for them were based on "minimum" expectations for high school graduates. Prior to that time, there had been only one instance (New York state) of state or local educational agencies using high-stakes tests or examinations to make decisions about student progression, graduation, or selection to university. Instead, most states were using low-stakes testing at selected grade levels to generate comparative data on students and schools, which was putatively used for student advisement and school improvement.

An important cultural artifact that underpins much of the history of standardized testing in the USA has been a widely held belief by many in the public that differences in student school outcomes are primarily due to intelligence, which is viewed as a relatively immutable characteristic (Shepard, 2000). Consequently most standardized testing done in the schools up until the 1980s held neither students (because they could not control their own intelligence) nor schools (because they could not influence student intelligence) accountable for learning outcomes. Those views became less tenable in the face of persistent "gaps" in achievement between racial groups, and less relevant when educational quality began to be indicted as the prime cause of loss of international economic competitiveness. Those views have been largely abandoned in an era of accountability for educational outcomes. However, the past thinking has left its mark on the nature of many of the high-stakes tests still in use prevalently in the USA (multiple-choice items pitched at *aptitudes for learning* as much as at *outcomes of learning*). Since the 1990s, high-stakes testing has increasingly been used as a mechanism for introducing greater levels of accountability, at the state, district, and school levels, for student achievement.

3.3.2 Assessment for Accountability

One important difference in the way high-stakes testing in the USA has developed in comparison to other parts of the world is in the purpose of the tests. In the USA, beginning in the 1990s at the state level, and more recently at the national level with the implementation of NCLB, high-stakes testing has increasingly been used as a mechanism for introducing greater levels of accountability, at the state, district, and school levels, for student achievement. The recognition that the tests being used as a mainstay in the determination of school impact on student learning were neither designed for that purpose, nor validated for that use has been slow to come, and only recently have states moved to develop or adopt state-mandated assessments that are explicitly linked to the standards adopted by the state for student achievement.

As an element in judging school outcomes, test scores are used in two ways to influence school practices, first by making public the record of performance of schools on the tests, by way of a "report card" which compares the performance of schools at similar levels across districts within states, and second by putting into place sanctions and incentives for schools, based on those report cards. Thus schools identified as "needing improvement" may be required to provide supplemental educational support (SES) to students whose performance lags that of their peers. Another sanction applied to schools with repeated failure to achieve annual yearly progress (AYP) is the provision that parents may remove their students from that school and relocate them to a school of their choice. The ultimate sanction for consistent failure to achieve AYP is the restructuring or closing of a school.

NCLB mandated that states develop accountability plans, but left it to the states to design those plans. While school improvement and gains in student achievement are the intended goals of the legislation, there is very little in the language of the act that would spell out how schools and states will achieve those gains and improvements. With the strong focus in the legislation on test score performance, and the mandate that standardized achievement tests be the tool for accountability, it is perhaps not surprising that diverse assessment tools associated with formative functions for learning are not part of the testing landscape. An advocate of alternative assessment approaches, Richard J. Stiggins, argues:

> Politicians routinely ask, How can we use assessment as the basis for doling out rewards and punishments to increase teacher and student effort? They want to know how we can intensify the intimidation associated with annual testing so as to force greater achievement. How we answer these questions will certainly affect schools. But that impact will not always be positive...
>
> School administrators in federal, state, and local education agencies contribute to our increasingly damaging assessment crisis when they merely bow to politicians' beliefs and focus unwaveringly on the question of how to make our test scores go up...
>
> We are a nation obsessed with the belief that the path to school improvement is paved with better, more frequent, and more intense standardized testing. The problem is that such tests, ostensibly delivered to "leave no student behind," are in fact causing major segments of our student population to be left behind because the tests cause many to give up in hopelessness – just the opposite effect from that which politicians intended. (Stiggins, 2002, pp. 758–579)

To date, the goal of most schools is simply to achieve AYP, as represented by the standardized achievement test results. Because this enterprise is in its infancy, relatively speaking, expressions of concern over "narrowing" of the curriculum, over-emphasis on test preparation, or failure of the high-stakes tests to take account of other, important, but more difficult to assess, learner outcomes have been largely confined to academics and professional education groups. Despite a wealth of evidence from past high-stakes testing efforts at the state level that revealed a fundamental disconnect between the *testing for accountability* approach and meaningful improvements in school outcomes (e.g., Carnoy, 2005; Darling-Hammond, 2004; Toch, 2006), and despite the emergence of similar evidence relevant to the NCLB impact (Nichols, Glass, & Berliner, 2005), the political sway of accountability combined with the relative simplicity and cost-effectiveness of standardized testing largely blunted those concerns while maintaining the ascendancy of standardized tests. Of course the paradox, as pointed out by Stiggins above and reinforced by Black and Wiliam (2005), is that the emphasis on accountability as the tool for raising standards of learning, and the use of standardized tests to measure learning outcomes, is the greatest obstacle to making gains in student achievement.

> The final irony is that it is precisely the demand for accountability which has produced unprecedented pressure to improve education systems that is likely to be the biggest impediment to achieving that improvement. (Black & Wiliam, 2005, p. 260)

3.3.3 Standards-Based Assessment

Even before NCLB, with its emphasis on high-stakes testing, school improvement plans, and state accountability systems, many states had already embarked on significant reform initiatives in response to the Improving America's Schools Act of 1994, which was earlier federal legislation aimed at promoting the adoption of world-class content standards by the states. A part of the reform was the development of performance standards (specifications of what students should know and be able to do in each content area at each grade level) and standards-based assessments to measure student attainment of the standards (e.g., Marzano & Kendall, 1996).

Direction for these reforms was taken in many states from the work of the National Research Council, which offered this description of a successful standards-based assessment system:

> Research suggests that a successful system of standards-based assessment is coherent in three fundamental ways. Curriculum, instruction, and assessment all align with the standards, targeting the same goals for learning, and working together to support students' developing understanding (**horizontal coherence**). All levels of the system (classroom, school, district, state) possess a shared vision of the goals of education, of purposes and uses of assessment, and of the criteria for competent performance (**vertical coherence**). Finally, the system needs to take into account how students' learning develops over time. Learning progressions, descriptions of successively more sophisticated ways of thinking about an idea and laying out in words and examples what it means to move toward more expert understanding establish **developmental coherence** (National Research Council, 2005, emphasis in original).

In most states that were early, voluntary, adopters of the standards-based initiative, these assessments were intended to be low-stakes tests for both students and schools, providing information with which instructional decision-making could be guided. However, with the implementation of NCLB, achieving world-class standards, and using mandated, high-stakes examinations to hold schools accountable for achieving those standards became the context within which almost all testing took place. Although states continue to have a degree of autonomy in establishing their own content standards, the National Technical Advisory Council (NTAC) advises the Secretary of Education and the Assistant Secretary for Elementary and Secondary Education on matters relating to the approval of the design and implementation of standards by individual states. Nonetheless, significant variations in standards occur across states. A study of the standards in three states – California, Georgia, and Pennsylvania – showed that there were differences, inter alia, in the content of the academic standards, the difficulty level of their performance standards, and the methods for calculating AYP and AYP trajectories, and that these differences stemmed from contextual factors that pre-dated NCLB, such as the state's prior use of similar standards-based systems (Hamilton et al., 2007). The scope for variations has the advantage of allowing states to take local contextual factors into account but it complicates the national standardization goals of NCBL.

3.4 Assessment for Learning Under NCLB

It is clear that, although NCLB is not mandatory in the states, its provisions for rewards and punishments, including the threat of withdrawing federal funds from non-compliant states, has brought about a systemic framework that, at least potentially, works against the principles of assessment practices that are concerned with formative functions. In a system of high-stakes testing where schools rather than students are the focus of the testing, and are the ones being held accountable for the results of the tests, the need for school-based, formative assessment as a component of the testing program has not been identified as a priority. Indeed, when the impetus behind the testing program is a suspicion that schools have somehow failed to fulfill their mandate to provide quality educational experiences to their students, and must be held accountable through the results of these tests, it should not be surprising that schools and teachers would not be seen as appropriate partners in the enterprise.

Alternative assessments, such as teacher observation of students, portfolios of student work produced during regular classroom instruction, and student performance in standardized tasks, are recognized by the NTAC for students with particular cognitive learning difficulties, provided that such assessments are aligned with state standards. Otherwise, there has been little scope within NCLB frameworks for alternative assessments. In an analysis of state assessment programs conducted in 2001 (Goertz, Duffy, & Le Floch, 2001), local assessments were found to be relatively rare among the states, and for most states that had any local assessment component, the component was most often a standardized achievement test adopted at the district, rather than the state level. However, one direct response to NCLB has been the emergence of school-based assessment to take on that very role, primarily as a mechanism for identifying those students at greatest risk of "failing" to make AYP on the end-of-the-year standardized tests (Black & Wiliam, 2005; Olson, 2005; Popham, 2006a, 2006b). Also referred to as *benchmark assessments* or *interim assessment systems*, in many instances these "formative assessments" are simply repackaged versions of the end-of-the-year high-stakes tests intended to be administered at various times earlier in the year to detect students who may be lagging (Popham, 2006b). Increasingly these tests are being developed and marketed by third parties, and have come to represent a growth industry, as schools, desperate to achieve their AYP goals, search for whatever means may be available to them to raise student test scores.

However, as Popham (2006a, 2006b) points out, in many instances the diagnostic utility of these tests is very limited, and their use in genuinely formative fashion is rare. Quoted in an article by Olson (2005), Robert Slavin observed, "If you're looking, as you should be, at the full range of development that you want kids to engage in, you're going to have to look at their work products, their compositions, their math problem-solving, their science and social-studies performance." While the practice of interim assessments appears to be growing among the schools (particularly schools struggling to achieve AYP), and does in a general way represent school-based assessment, it fails in several important respects to accomplish many of the aims associated with the concept in other parts of the world (broadening the base of curriculum being assessed, promoting assessment for learning, contextualizing assessment of performance skills in authentic settings, embedding assessments within the learning experience). What it does seem to represent is at best, an alignment of assessments occurring in the school setting with those being administered as the accountability measures, designed to support student achievement of learning outcomes represented on the high-stakes tests.

While most states opted for the use of traditional testing instruments (standardized achievement tests, multiple choice item formats), some states chose to employ less-traditional assessment systems, including the use of portfolios and performance assessments embedded within the learning activities in the schools. Cromey and Hanson (2000) reported on schools in Michigan, one state that had begun the process of reforming its schools several years earlier. In their study, two groups of schools were selected, one group that had well-developed school-based student assessment systems and a second group, matched on important school and student characteristics, that had less well-developed assessment systems. The purpose of the study was to identify those features of the schools with well-developed systems that distinguished them from the schools with less well-developed systems. Several significant differences were noted. The schools with well-developed systems:

- aligned their local curriculum, standards, and assessments to the state content standards
- analyzed assessment results to monitor student progress.
- used state assessment results to check the validity of local assessment systems

- used assessment results to evaluate the efficacy of local curriculum and instructional practices
- limited the number of student assessments used to those that are purposeful and can be aligned to local curriculum and state standards
- allocated time for teachers to collaborate, reflect and make data-based decisions-individually or in teams- based upon student assessment data and their instructional implications.

In some states high-stakes tests for high-school graduation have been supplanted by end-of-course (EOC) examinations. The best-known EOC examinations are the Advanced Placement, New York Regents, and International Baccalaureate examinations. Fifteen states include, or will soon include, EOC examinations as part of their high school assessment systems. Unlike traditional high school graduation examinations that might be administered at any grade level from grade 10 to grade 12, and might focus on learning outcomes associated with grades 8 through 12, and unlike standardized achievement tests that might focus at a specific grade level, but would typically assess across a range of subjects with relatively few items per subject, the EOC examination is a purpose-designed examination that, as its name suggests, is administered at the end of the course, making it grade and subject specific. However, like the exit examinations, they are administered by a third party rather than the teacher and, as such, allow comparability among schools and courses. Advocates of such tests argue that they offer a better basis for judging student achievement in the various subjects included in the high school curriculum, and unlike the other test formats, can provide a more valid source of evidence of student achievement in the particular subjects taken. While EOC examinations represent an approach taken in some states to address some of the problems found to be associated with traditional high-stakes testing, they nevertheless fall short as "school-based assessments" in most important respects. Although they can serve to "broaden" the curriculum by testing in many subjects, and can represent tasks that involve more complex learner outcomes than are commonly found on traditional standardized achievement tests, they are not carried out by teachers, in schools, and the tasks which are set for students are not embedded in their learning, and consequently cannot serve as the basis for supporting learning and providing constructive feedback on that learning.

One state that has developed a form of school-based student assessment modeled on those principles is Vermont. Quoting from the Vermont "Core Principles" document,

> The Vermont School Quality Standards call for a balance of both classroom based and school based assessment. At the classroom level, formative assessment reflects individual student "learning in progress". Beyond the classroom, the school based system needs to generate feedback that enables teachers and other members of the educational community to determine consistency in meeting shared expectations for student learning across all classes and grade levels. A comprehensive assessment system encompasses both classroom and school-based assessments. (Vermont Department of Education & Standards & Assessment, 2006, p. 1)

Another important feature of the Vermont School Quality Standards is the role of collaboration. To again quote from the core principles document,

> Most importantly, teachers, administrators, and other members of the school community need to engage collaboratively in the decision making process, with ongoing dialogue about the relationship between learning goals and assessment. Finding the time and opportunity for collaboration is a significant challenge for a school. When such dialogue becomes part of the school's culture, significant rewards come in the form of continuity, professional development and improved student learning. (Vermont Department of Education & Standards & Assessment, 2006, p. 1)

Perhaps the most visible example of a state committed to local, school-based assessment is Nebraska (Nebraska Department of Education, 1999), with its STARS (School-based, Teacher-led, Assessment & Reporting System). Nebraska was the only state to successfully resist the NCLB mandate to base accountability decisions on nationally recognized standardized tests of achievement, largely due to its aggressive moves to demonstrate that its existing system of school-based assessments were capable of producing valid and reliable evidence of student achievement (Roschewski, Isernhagen, & Dappen, 2006). Nebraska's 517 school districts design their own assessment systems which include a portfolio of teachers' classroom assessments, district tests that measure how well children are meeting locally developed learning standards, a state writing test and at least one nationally standardized test. The last component was not originally part of the STARS program, but was instead part of the compromise Nebraska reached with the US Department of Education which allowed it to retain its assessment and accountability system. Nebraska teachers at the district level worked to align their curriculum and assessment practices to the state content standards. Standards-based classrooms are achieved as each teacher clearly articulates the learning targets, aligns instruction to the learning targets within each of the content standards, and assesses whether or not students are meeting the targets outlined by the content standards.

To ensure quality in the locally developed and administered assessments, each year a District Assessment portfolio, which includes a sample of actual assessments used in the classrooms at each grade level, is assembled and submitted to the Nebraska Department of Education. Department of Education personnel, working with consultants from the Buros Center for Testing, examine the assessment materials and evaluate them against 6 quality assessment criteria. In a recent evaluation of the STARS assessments, Brookhart (1999), noted that generally the alignment of teacher developed assessments to state content standards was good, although the reliability of teachers' judgments of student outcomes using those assessments was uneven, with teachers able to reach consensus in mathematics more consistently than in reading (the two areas assessed).

3.5 Recent Developments

For at least the past 30 years, changes in educational policy in the USA, particularly at the national level, have been driven by ideological views of the proper role of the national government, as well as the proper role of public education. Many of the mandates associated with NCLB reflected a conservative ideology that tended to view public education and its employees as fundamentally flawed and responsible for many of the failings in American society. With a significant change in national leadership (in both legislative houses as well as the executive) in the most recent rounds of national elections, some of that ideology is beginning to shift. While support for the major tenets of NCLB seems to remain relatively solid, there is evidence of at least some rethinking of the rigidity of some aspects of the assessment component of the legislation. One such shift has been the move by the Department of Education to allow more states to propose alternative models for achieving the aims of the legislation. Although the reliance on high-stakes testing aligned to state educational standards remains a constant, such alternatives as end-of-course examinations are being allowed.

Another major development has been the proposal of a "value-added" model for judging student achievement and school/teacher impact on student learning (Shurtleff & Loredo, 2008). The value-added model essentially uses a sophisticated statistical modeling approach to predict the test-score performance of each child, allowing for the impact of individual differences as well as past test performance. By "controlling" for those factors, the argument is that it becomes possible to detect the impact of instruction on the performance of the students on the test. Of course, all this arises from the underlying purpose of finding a way to hold individual teachers accountable for their impact on the learners in their classes, and so, unfortunately, it has proved controversial among educators.

Finally, in 2009, the US Department of Education introduced a new initiative referred to as "Race to the Top", which provided a multi-billion dollar competitive grant to the states to promote educational innovations and reform (US Department of Education, 2009). While the purposes of the grant are to encourage educational excellence and the improvement of underachieving schools, one controversial provision has been the requirement that states tie teacher pay and retention to the performance of their students on the state's high-stakes tests. "Race to the Top" and "value-added assessment" actually work hand-in-hand, as the one represents the means whereby the other is proposed to be achieved.

3.6 Conclusions

Even before NCLB, with its emphasis on high-stakes testing, school improvement plans, and state accountability systems, many states had already embarked on significant reform initiatives aimed at promoting the adoption of world-class content standards by the states. Even in those states like Vermont and Nebraska, where significant commitment to an assessment system that performs diverse functions has been in evidence, the use of the assessment results is problematic (because they are being used to judge the quality of the school and teachers, in addition to appraising the competence of the students) even if the rationale (assessment that supports learning) and the assessment approach (portfolios, performance assessments) may represent shared qualities. Unfortunately, these examples are the exception, with more evidence of states and school districts rushing to adopt "formative assessment" systems that represent little more than "early warning systems" for student difficulties in achieving AYP (Sharkey & Murnane, 2006).

Although most educational experts and assessment experts endorse the sorts of approaches taken in Nebraska and Vermont (e.g., Darling-Hammond, 2004; McMunn, McCloskey, & Butler, 2004; Shepard, 2000; Sirotnik, 2002; Wilson & Sloan, 2000), the reality is that as pressure grows on schools to make their annual yearly progress on the standardized achievement tests, the "oxygen" needed to simultaneously support the more educationally sound school-based assessment systems is likely to disappear (e.g., Mitchell, 1997).

What is perhaps most interesting to note is the comparative enthusiasm and support shown by professional education organizations and teachers in the USA for school-based, formative assessment systems. Perhaps this is in part because many US schools and teachers have had more than a decade of experience with standards-based assessment, but very limited experience with national examinations (and the attendant pressures to shape the curriculum to those examinations). More likely, the attitudes of US teachers are being shaped by the accountability focus of the high-stakes tests, which places them in the unenviable position of being held responsible for the achievement of high levels of proficiency by all learners, irrespective of contextual factors, levels of resources, or any other considerations.

It has become something of a truism in the assessment community that "assessment drives curriculum", and the higher the stakes associated with the assessment, the more strongly the assessment will determine the priorities of schools, teachers, and students in matters of curriculum choices, instructional practices, classroom assessment approaches, and learning strategies. So long as the stakes associated with performance on public examinations are as high as they are, it will be difficult to create a climate conducive to meaningful school-based assessment. Classroom teachers are in some cases retreating from assessment for learning practices (often at the direction of school leaders) out of a fear that they will not be preparing students for the types of assessment and learning outcomes reflected on the high-stakes tests. School-based assessment, as it is conceived in some settings elsewhere, as a means of enhancing the validity of the traditional public examinations while supporting assessment for learning approaches in the classroom, is not part of the high-stakes assessment equation in the vast majority of US states.

In those few states, school districts, and individual schools where a commitment to an assessment model in which teachers collect and use evidence of student learning to support their learning, where the assessments are "authentic" and extended, and embedded in meaningful learning activities, where students actively participate in the learning, and the assessment of that learning, it seems inevitable that those schools will find themselves under greater pressure each year to focus more explicitly on achieving those NCLB mandated targets, reflected in test scores, at the expense of focusing on the learning. Because it has been demonstrated that schools that focus their efforts on increasing test scores on a specific test do typically see test score rise *on that test,* without producing a commensurate increase in the underlying learning, the practices that lead to that increase (drilling on the test/practicing test-taking, modeling classroom assessments on the high-stakes tests, de-emphasizing or eliminating subjects in the curriculum not represented on the test, focusing instruction on the types of learning outcomes, usually lower-level, represented on the tests) will be difficult to resist, particularly for schools that serve student groups that traditionally under-perform on standardized achievement tests.

One implication of the US experience has to do with the use of high-stakes tests for holding schools and teachers directly accountable for student test performance. Tests that began as "monitoring" mechanisms eventually evolved into "accountability" tools. In the USA, much of the impetus behind accountability testing has been political, and those winds have begun to shift with a change in national administrations. It is unlikely though that the role of standardized achievement tests will diminish significantly in the foreseeable future, nor that the role of school-based assessment, as a formal part of accountability will necessarily rise. More promising is the prospect for assessment for learning practices at the classroom level to grow as schools become disillusioned with the "quick-fix" strategies that can only produce short-term and superficial results, especially for those student subgroups that are traditionally least successful in standardized testing situations.

References

Black, P., & Wiliam, D. (2005). Lessons from around the world: How policies, politics and cultures constrain and afford assessment practices. *The Curriculum Journal*, *16*(2), 249–261.

Brookhart, S. M. (1999). Teaching about communicating assessment results and grading. *Educational Measurement: Issues and Practice*, *18*(1), 6–13.

Carnoy, M. (2005). Have state accountability and high-stakes tests influenced student progression rates in high school? *Educational Measurement: Issues and Practice*, *24*(4), 19–31.

Cromey, A., & Hanson, M. (2000). *An exploratory analysis of school-based student assessment systems*. North Central Regional Educational Laboratory (ERIC document).

Darling-Hammond, L. (2004). Standards, accountability, and school reform. *Teachers College Record*, *106*(6), 1047–1085.

Fägerlind, I., & Saha, L. J. (1989). *Education and national development: A comparative perspective* (2nd ed.). Oxford: Pergamon Press.

Goertz, M. E., Duffy, M. C., & Le Floch, K. C. (2001). *Assessment and accountability systems in the fifty states*. Consortium for Policy Research in Education, Number RR-046. Philadelphia: University of Pennsylvania.

Hamilton, L. S., Stecher, B. M., Marsh, J. A., McCombs, J. S., Robyn, A., & Russell, J. L., et al. (2007). *Standards-based accountability under No child left behind: Experiences of teachers and administrators in three states*. Santa Monica, CA: The Rand Corporation.

Isaacs, T. (2001). Entry to university in the United States: The role of SAT and advanced placement in a competitive sector. *Assessment in Education*, *8*(3), 391–406.

Jacob, B. A. (2001). Getting tough? The impact of high school graduation exams. *Educational Evaluation and Policy Analysis*, *23*(2), 99–121.

Lawrence, I., Rigol, G. W., Van Essen, T., & Jackson, C. A. (2002). A historical perspective on the SAT: 1926–2001. New York: College Entrance Examination Board. http://professionals.collegeboard.com/profdownload/pdf/rr20027_11439.pdf. Accessed 7 May 2010.

Marchant, G. J., & Paulson, S. E. (2005). The relationship of high school graduation exams to graduation rates and SAT scores. *Educational Policy Analysis Archives*, *13*(6), 1–15.

Marzano, R. J., & Kendall, J. S. (1996). *A comprehensive guide to designing standards-based districts, schools, and classrooms*. Alexandria, VA: Association for Supervision and Curriculum Development.

McMunn, N., McCloskey, W., & Butler, S. (2004). Building teacher capacity in classroom assessment to improve student learning. *International Journal of Educational Policy, Research, & Practice*, *4*(4), 25–48.

Mitchell, K. (1997). What happens when school reform and accountability testing meet? *Theory into Practice*, *36*(4), 262–268.

National Commission on Excellence in Education. (1983). *A nation at risk: The imperative for educational reform: A report to the Nation and the Secretary of Education, United States Department of Education*. Washington, DC: National Commission on Excellence in Education.

National Research Council. (2005). *Systems for state science assessment*. Washington, DC: National Academies Press.

Nebraska Department of Education. (1999). School-based Teacher-led Assessment & Reporting System: A planning guide for Nebraska schools. http://www.nde.state.ne.us/. Accessed 12 November 2006.

Nelson, C. (2007). Accountability: The commodification of the examined life. *Change: The Magazine of Higher Learning*, *36*(6), 22–27.

Nichols, S. L., Glass, G. V., & Berliner, D. C. (2005). High stakes testing and student achievement: Problems for the No Child Left Behind Act. Educational Policy Research Unit. http://www.asu.edu/educ/epsl/EPRU/documents/EPSL-0509-105-EPRU.pdf. Accessed 20 November 2006.

Olson, L. (2005). Benchmark assessments offer regular achievement. *Education Week*, *25*(13), 13–14.

O'Day, J. A. (2002). Complexity, accountability, and school improvement. *Harvard Educational Review*, *72*(3), 293–329.

Popham., W. J. (2006a). Diagnostic assessments: A measurement mirage? *Educational Leadership*, *64*(2), 90–91.

Popham, W. J. (2006b). Phony formative assessments: Buyer beware!. *Educational Leadership*, *64*(3), 86–87.

Roschewski, P., Isernhagen, J., & Dappen, L. (2006). Nebraska STARS: Achieving results. *Phi Delta Kappan*, *87*(6), 433–437.

Schiro, M. S. (2008). *Curriculum theory: Conflicting visions and enduring concerns*. Los Angeles: Sage Publications.

Sharkey, N. S., & Murnane, R. J. (2006). Tough choices in designing a formative assessment system. *American Journal of Education*, *112*(4), 572–588.

Shepard, L. A. (2000). The role of assessment in a learning culture. *Educational Researcher*, *29*(7), 4–14.

Shurtleff, D. S., & Loredo, J. (2008). Beyond No Child Left Behind: Value-added assessment of student progress. National Center for Policy Analysis. http://www.policyarchive.org/handle/10207/bitstreams/11781.pdf. Accessed May 7, 2010.

Sirotnik, K. (2002). Promoting responsible accountability in schools and education. *Phi Delta Kappan*, *83*(9), pp. 662–674.

Stiggins, R. J. (2002). Assessment crisis: The absence of assessment FOR learning. *Phi Delta Kappan*, *83*(10), 758–765.

Toch, T. (2006). Turmoil in the testing industry. *Educational Leadership*, *64*(3), 53–57.

US Department of Education. (2002). No Child Left Behind Act. http://ed.gov/policy/elsec/leg/esea02/107-110.pdf. Accessed 19 July 2010.

US Department of Education. (2009). Race to the Top Program: Executive summary. US Department of Education. http://www2.ed.gov/programs/racetothetop/executive-summary.pdf. Accessed 5 May 2010.

Vermont Department of Education, Standards & Assessment. (2006). Core principles of high quality local assessment systems. http://education.vermont.gov/new/pdfdoc/pgm_curriculum/local_assessment/core_principles_06.pdf. Accessed 16 November 2006.

Wilson, M., & Sloane, K. (2000). From principles to practice: An embedded assessment system. *Applied Measurement in Education*, *13*(2), 181–208.

Chapter 4
Educational Assessment in Mainland China, Hong Kong and Taiwan

Rita Berry

4.1 Introduction

China is traditionally examination-oriented. For centuries, summative tests have been frequently used at schools as the sole assessment method to make judgments on student performance and high stakes public examinations are used for making decisions on educational upward movement and social mobility. "*The Book of Rites*" and "*The Book of Learning*", both Chinese ancient volumes, recorded that in the Warring States period (475 BC–221 BC), students were required to sit for examinations at the end of school years one, three, five, seven, and nine. These examinations had different assessment focuses, with year one concentrating on assessing students' reading abilities, year three on learning attitudes and social abilities, year five on aspects that demonstrated a broad range of learning and attitudes towards the teachers, year seven on abilities in presenting sound arguments during discussions and in recognizing the achievements of others and in year nine on reasoning, self-esteem and the ability to take further what had been inspired by their teachers. At the end of the 9 years of learning, students were expected to demonstrate in the examinations a good grasp of various kinds of skills and moral qualities in addition to the knowledge they had learnt from their teachers. Judging by the focuses of the examinations, education in these early days seemed to associated with whole person development. However, until very recent times, assessment was not used for supporting learning.

4.2 The Changing Climate of Educational Assessment in Mainland China

At the national level, although there have been many changes in the government policies over the last 3,000 years, examinations have served as the main instrument for making decisions on educational opportunities and government official

R. Berry (✉)
Department of Curriculum and Instruction, Hong Kong Institute of Education, Tai Po, Hong Kong
e-mail: rsyberry@ied.edu.hk

R. Berry, B. Adamson (eds.), *Assessment Reform in Education*,
Education in the Asia-Pacific Region: Issues, Concerns and Prospects 14,
DOI 10.1007/978-94-007-0729-0_4,

selection. Many dynasties in China followed a three-stage imperial examination system, including (in sequence of advancement) the local examination, the regional examination, and finally the highest level examination organized by the central government (with some variations in individual dynasties). As the system became more established over time, examinations focused more and more on assessing candidates' scholastic achievements, such as testing their ability in producing a high quality "eight-legged essay" (Eight-legged essays have a rigid discourse structure comprise eight parallel parts). This impacted on the teaching and learning at school level. As with the summative tests in schools, these examinations judged candidates' performance by the product, not on the process of learning. An example of the imperial assessment system is presented by Fig. 4.1 below.

It was not until the nineteenth century that the Qing Dynasty, started to make a major change to the assessment system. The increased interactions between the East and the West triggered a series of reforms including the "Westernization Movements" and the "Modernization Initiatives". These reforms gave new directions in educational assessment policies. The imperial examinations were officially abolished in 1906 and replaced by a three-tier national examination system for assessing students at the end of the three major stages of schooling – primary, middle and senior secondary. Acting on the guidelines of the government ("*Presented School Regulations*" 1904), schools administered five kinds of tests, including non-regular tests, during term time, mid-term examinations, end-of-year examinations,

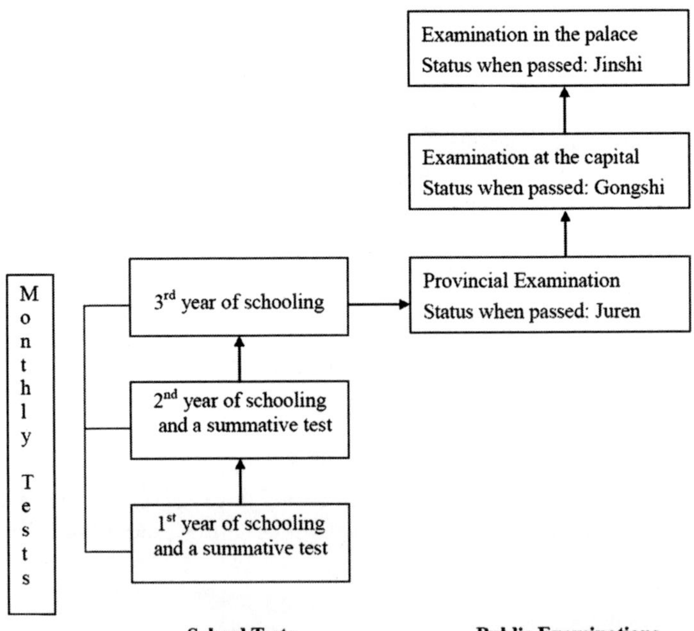

Fig. 4.1 An example of the imperial assessment system

graduate examinations and entry examinations for further education. Standards were set for each stage of learning with 60–80 representing excellent, 40–60 above average, 20–40 average and below 20 fail. At this stage, educational assessment was a synonym of educational testing and carried clear connotations of comparing, grouping and selecting (Wu, 1996). Despite the major make-over of the assessment system, the function of assessment showed little change. Examinations were still used as a tool for driving learning and for making summative judgments of learning. A common practice at school was for the teacher to give students some questions resembling those in the examinations. Using the designated reading list, students prepared answers to the questions and then brought the answers for a discussion with their peers. After that, individually, students wrote down their answers in the question papers. Students swapped papers and marked them against the model answers (Hou, 1996). Although the learning activities were more interactive and more self-directed than previously, central to teaching remained the goal of gearing students to pass the examinations, resulting in the "narrowing" of learning. At this point of time, in China, educational assessment was terminologically and ideologically synonymous with examinations, and examinations were basically used for measuring success.

Assessment for Learning (AfL) made a fleeting appearance in China after the Second World War, when political and economic situations worldwide underwent a metamorphic change. Western countries, led by the USA and the UK, and socialist nations led by then Soviet Union, entered the Cold War period. As a member of the socialist bloc, mainland China modeled its education system and assessment policies on those of the Soviet Union (Feng, 2006). Grading replaced percentiles for judgments of performances (Distinction 5, Good 4, Pass 3, Fail 2, Poor 1) in schools. There were six domains to refer to when grading the students: (1) knowledge and skills; (2) level of understanding; (3) sustainability of knowledge; (4) application of knowledge; (5) written and verbal presentation skills; and (6) errors. Many assessment methods were used, including continuous observation of student work in the classroom, questioning, written assignments, quizzes, and tests (Dong, 1998). To what extent the information collected from the students was used to support learning is unknown. Judging by the focuses and methods of assessment, an educated guess would be that there were some forms of formative assessment in the classroom assessment practices in this period of time. However, following the increased tension between China and the Soviet Union, and the turmoil in education arising from the Cultural Revolution in the 1960s, these new found assessment practices came to a total halt. The country subsequently resumed its old assessment practices.

China adopted the Open Door Policy in 1978 and in 1984, the Chinese government made a historic decision to shift the country from a planned economy to a market economy. This shift triggered a series of wide-ranging educational reforms (Yang, 1999). In 1993, the government disseminated a policy document entitled "*The outlines of China's educational reforms and developments*" (Ministry of Education, the Republic of China 1993), which emphasized that one target of the reforms was to raise the quality of the labour force through the provision of enhanced education. New policies in the guidelines included an overhaul of assessment policies and practices. There were two distinct strands to assessment reforms: one impacting on senior secondary education and the other on basic education. The senior secondary reforms placed stronger emphasis on the quality of teaching and examination modalities whilst the basic education reform focused more on classroom assessment. The guidance document, published by the government in 1990, detailing the new assessment policies for the senior secondary – "*Provisional regulations for senior secondary schools educational assessment*" (Ministry of Education, the Republic of China 1990), was converted to a more advanced policy document entitled "Evaluation policies on subject teaching in regular secondary schools" (Ministry of Education, the Republic of China 2002) in 2002. This official document is still in effect.

The assessment reform in basic education was closer to the heart of assessment for learning. In July 2001, the Education Department in China issued "The Outlines for Basic Educational Reform (Pilot)" (the "Outlines"). The measures in this document were piloted in 38 experimental districts in 27 provinces, marking the beginning of China's curriculum reform for basic education. When compared to the "Teaching Guidelines", which formed the previous policy and which had been criticised for placing too strong an emphasis on the product of learning, the new Outlines underlined the significance of learning processes. Chang (2002) summarises the aspirations of the Chinese government for basic education curriculum reform as follows:

1. The focus of teaching is on providing students with "whole-person education". The new curriculum stresses the development of students, giving equal emphasis to the learning process and the product.
2. It emphasises the application of knowledge. This entails knowing how to apply the knowledge in real life situations. It promotes exploration, application, participation, communication and cooperation.
3. The Task-based Approach is promoted in the new curriculum. Students will learn through completing tasks.
4. The aim of assessment is to stimulate learning. The new curriculum encourages self-, peer-, and parental assessment in addition to teachers'.
5. The new curriculum requires teachers to make use of the resources available to them for teaching. They are also encouraged to make suggestions to help enrich the new curriculum.

There were strong signals from the government that the country's assessment system should change from being over-reliant on the selection function of assessment and that assessment should be used for enhancing teaching and supporting learning. It was suggested that a new assessment system should be established to address three different aspects: (i) student whole person development; (ii) teacher continuous professional growth; and (iii) curriculum advancement. Based on these suggestions, the Education Department issued and disseminated a notification document to all schools entitled "*On the implementation of assessment reforms of primary and secondary schools*" requiring schools to use AfL as a major focus in their schools' educational planning. Teachers were advised to use various methods of assessment and open-ended assessment items to understand students' learning needs and potential so that support could be provided to help their further development. The content of examinations needed to be related to real life situations to enhance students' ability in knowledge transfer and application of knowledge.

To meet the requirements stipulated in the policies from the central government, the education departments of some provinces and local districts responded in a variety of ways. Several provinces volunteered to be involved in the government's pilot scheme on assessment reforms. For example, in the north, the provincial government in Heilongjiang (2007) focused on three aspects in their new classroom assessment directives: (i) classroom assessments should be student-centred and the methods used should be multi-faceted; (ii) students should be assessed on different perspectives including fundamental knowledge and skills, learning skills and methods, attitudes and values; and (iii) judgments of students' attitudes and performances should be made by observing students work and behaviours during class time and by analysing students' assignments. The teacher should connect assessment activities with teaching objectives and everyday classroom activities. Down south, education authorities in the city of Taicang, Jiangsu Province (2007) proposed "Six seriousnesses in teaching" to help strengthen teaching qualities. In essence, teachers were required to adopt a serious manner in designing student assignments, selecting the types of assignments for students, marking student assignments, giving feedback, acknowledging achievements and improving student learning. Further south, Guangzhou, a major city in Guangdong province, was one of the first places to experiment with assessment for the new senior secondary examinations. The city developed a chart in 2004 to assess students summatively and formatively. When making judgments of the performance of the students, the results of both types of assessment would be used (The Research of the Education Department, Guangzhou & Guangdong Province, 2007). Another province-wide project being conducted in Guangdong was entitled "On research of assessment tools for and of Basic English learning", a key project of basic education in the 15th Guangdong Education Development Plan. The assessment tools developed ranged from those used formatively in the classroom to those for making summative judgements, such as an English oral test (see Gu & Berry, 2008).

Scholars generally agreed that the country has recently placed more attention to AfL and to integrating assessment into everyday teaching and learning (Wang, 2007). However, Wang (2008) finds the country exhibits two major inadequacies in classroom assessment. First, teachers are generally unprepared for AfL. Their understanding of AfL was limited and therefore they were not able to see the value of AfL for teaching and learning. Second, teachers did not know how to integrate assessment into teaching and learning. In the classroom, assessment was mainly used for confirming taught knowledge. There were very few assessment activities designed for supporting learning and the quality of the assessment activities was generally low. A questionnaire survey conducted in Hubei Province by Jing, Hang, and Zhang (2007) to investigate teachers' classroom assessment practices in the primary found that, although teachers were very enthusiastic about the new AfL advocated by the government, the teachers generally demonstrated insufficient knowledge of assessment for learning and how it could be implemented in the classroom. Parents and students were still very deeply steeped in the examination culture. They did not seem to be very interested in the new assessment initiatives stipulated in the education reforms. To gain a deep understanding of the current classroom assessment situation in the mainland, Berry and Gao (2009) conducted a case study in Guangzhou. The study invited the participation of three teachers from a local primary school who taught Chinese, English, and Mathematics respectively. Research was carried out through class observations, dialogue with the teachers and the study of lesson plans and assignments. Analysis of data showed that, although there were signs of improvement in using assessment for learning purposes, AfL still lacked fundamental developments. Teachers did not have a clear understanding of the concepts of assessment for learning and their assessment practices in the classroom did not meet the standards required by the assessment reform.

In sum, with the publication of *The Outlines* (Ministry of Education, the Republic of China 2001), it became evident that assessment reform is one of the main foci of the mainland's new wave of educational reform. However, research into the implementation of the policies discovered a notable disparity in the activities at the school level and the guidelines distributed to different levels of the educational ministry. The disparity may possibly be linked to the mainland's examination-based mentality and a general insufficient understanding of AfL on the part of the teachers in particular.

4.3 The AfL Movements in Hong Kong

The assessment system operating in Hong Kong has long been criticized as being very examination-oriented. Examinations in Hong Kong are very high stakes, being the key to social mobility through access to higher education and enhanced employment opportunities. Choi (1999) comments that examinations remain at the "heart of the community", both feeding and feeding off the "Chinese culture that academic credentials are superior to other qualifications" (p.405). Many schools prepare students to get through the system by drilling them with past test papers and testing them relentlessly. Teaching content focuses on meeting the requirements of the examinations.

In the last two decades, the call in education worldwide for a change of assessment culture, from treating assessment as the means of making final judgments of performance to using assessment to support learning, has been echoed by some advocates in Hong Kong. Biggs (1996) points out that in Hong Kong, for years, educators had based their assessment practices on assumptions inappropriately adopted from psychology and from the testing establishment. He then drew people's attention to the other function of assessment – to educate and pointed out that there is a need to change the assessment climate in Hong Kong. The Hong Kong SAR government has responded positively to the AfL movement as reflected by the two major reform initiatives over the past two decades. The Target-Oriented Curriculum

(TOC) in the 1990s was a large scale attempt to link assessment with learning. TOC was a form of outcome-based education in which students progressed towards specified learning targets through carrying out tasks (Morris, 2002). The assessment method of TOC was to collect information about the students' learning outcomes during the learning process. This form of assessment required teachers to record students' learning outcomes in a highly detailed fashion, which teachers found very difficult to handle and too time-consuming to carry out. The formative assessment initiatives of the TOC were unfortunately not well received despite their good intentions (Berry, 2008). Though perceived as unsuccessful, the AfL concepts embedded in the TOC were regarded as theoretically sound. In 2000, the government initiated another round of major assessment reform with AfL highlighted in the reform agenda. The Curriculum Development Council (CDC, 2002) states that:

> All schools should review their current assessment practices and put more emphasis on assessment for learning. The latter is a process in which teachers seek to identify and diagnose student learning problems, and provide quality feedback for students on how to improve their work. Different modes of assessment are to be used whenever appropriate for a more comprehensive understanding of student learning in various aspects. (Chapter 5, p. 1)

In its most recent published assessment guidelines (Curriculum Development Council, 2009), Hong Kong government argues that:

> Assessment is an integral part of the curriculum, pedagogy and assessment cycle. It involves collecting evidence about student learning, interpreting information and making judgements about students' performance with a view to providing feedback to students, teachers, schools, parents, other stakeholders and to the education system. (Booklet 4, p. 1)

The new round of assessment reform included two initiatives – the Basic Competency Assessment (BCA) for primary education and junior secondary and School-based Assessment (SBA) for secondary education. Both of them are used as instruments for pushing ahead with AfL.

BCA is a low-stake assessment tool that aims at enhancing teaching and learning in the areas of English language, Chinese language and Mathematics. There are two main components of BCA, namely, Student Assessment and Territory-wide System Assessment. Student Assessment is a resource bank provided through the internet for the purpose of assisting teachers in developing and selecting the appropriate task for their students. Territory-wide System Assessment is conducted by the government across Hong Kong (Berry, 2011).

SBA is regarded as a general term for the assessment conducted in schools which contributes to the certification system in Hong Kong and also aims at becoming an integral part of teaching and learning. By 2007, Hong Kong Certificate of Education Examination subjects (equivalent to O Level) and 14 Hong Kong Advanced Level Examination subjects (equivalent to A Level) will have SBA components. In time, SBA will become a major component in all 24 subjects within the new Hong Kong Diploma of Secondary Education (which the first cohort will take in 2012), the combined examination students will take at the end of the 6 year schooling for the new 3+3+4 education structure (6 years secondary and 4 years tertiary education).

The message of the SBA initiatives is that assessment should be seen as an integral part of the learning and teaching cycle. There should be a de-emphasizing of the summative tests, in favour of formative assessment, which is supported by the diversification of assessment strategies and tasks, providing quality feedback and involvement of different parties including students.

Hong Kong society has shown different responses to the AfL movements. In his study related to the Target-Oriented Curriculum, Carless (2005) found that the teachers encountered resistance from parents, as well as lack of support from colleagues and school policies. Kennedy, Chan, Fok, and Yu (2008) points out that in Hong Kong, even though there has been considerable support for the principles of AfL, the high stakes nature of assessment gives it a role and function that can trivialise these plans. Berry (2010) further argued that, although AfL has been accepted for some time, Hong Kong still has yet to effectively implement the plans and policies as set. Many schools in Hong Kong are traditional in their assessment practices and are not using assessment in the service of teaching and learning.

4.4 The "Multivariate Approach" Assessment Reforms in Taiwan

As with mainland China and Hong Kong, Taiwan has a deep-rooted examination culture. Taiwan experienced five main forms of government, with, in chronological sequence, occupation by Holland and Spain (1624–1662), the Ming Dynasty (1662–1683), the Qing Dynasty (1683–1895), the Japanese occupation (1895–1945) and the Republic of China (1945–present). During the occupations by Holland (38 years) and Spain (16 years in only northern Taiwan), education was purposefully linked with religious preaching and was used as a major political means for consolidating the colonial rule. Though criticized as inimitable to Taiwanese traditions and culture of the time, this period witnessed its first educational establishments on the island (Zhuang, Xie, Huang, & Xu, 1994). However, it was not until the Ming Dynasty that Taiwan instituted its examination system. Basically, Taiwan followed mainland China's imperial examination systems in the Ming and Qing Dynasties. Education was mainly focused on preparing students for the imperial examinations, which had the sole purpose of selecting government officials. During the Japanese occupation, education and its related examination system came to an almost total halt. In the early days of this colonial period, education for Taiwanese children was almost non-existent. Whether it was a political or resource allocation decision, the Japanese government maintained a tight control on schooling for the local people. With increased criticisms and pressure from the public, the Japanese government slowly opened up some education opportunities for the natives over time (Xu, 1993).

After the defeat of the Japanese in the Second World War and in the aftermath of the civil war in China, the education system was quickly re-established by the new government that was formed on the island – the Republic of China. Following the modern trend, Taiwan used a three-tier system of primary, secondary and tertiary education. Traditional paper-and-pencil tests were used for the country's high stakes public examinations and the test items were developed to test hard retainable knowledge. At school, teaching was content-based and encouraged memorization of facts. This was heavily criticized by scholars in Taiwan as problematic and harmful to learning. The "410 (10 April 1994) big protest march", initiated by a professor at the University of Taiwan, was successful in raising the government's awareness of the prevailing problems in the education system and its examination system. The government then proposed a wide range of reforms in education with which "Multivariation" was a key element of the assessment reform. The concepts of AfL, though not explicitly spelt out, was embedded in the reform agenda. The core of the reform was to de-emphasize the single use of traditional paper-and-pencil tests and to encourage diversification of assessment– for example, the use of multidimensional strategies (e.g., project assessments) and parties (various assessors) and different pathways for education.

At the vanguard of a series of reforms related to assessment was the university entrance examination. In 1996, different pathways to tertiary education were created to replace the high stakes public examination. Candidates would be considered either by their special talents and/or their performance in the aptitude tests in (i) the general subject-based aptitude tests, which took place at the end of the final year of secondary schooling; and (ii) the specific subject examinations, which took place in July in the same academic year (Wu, 2004). It was believed that by removing the one-off public examination for university admission, the stakes could be reduced, and that it would be fair to acknowledge students' achievements of various kinds rather than judging them purely by their academic results.

The assessment reform in Kaoshung, a major city in south Taiwan, beginning in 1996, focused on test item design for higher secondary public examinations. The reform adopted the principle that the design of test items should be able to challenge students' different learning perspectives, such as critical thinking skills and their abilities in knowledge application, but not encouraging regurgitation of factual knowledge. It was believed that the change could create a backwash effect on teaching and learning (Li, 1999). In Taipei, there was an educational call for student-centredness to be central in the reform. Authoritarian styles of teaching were discouraged. Teachers would take up the roles of counselors and consultants to student learning. Students would be given opportunities to set their own learning goals and plans as well as to select the learning content, but would be responsible for the consequences of their choice. Assessment would be multi-faceted including both quantitative and qualitative means. Teachers were to observe and record student learning during the learning process and to facilitate independent learning through students' self-assessment (Deng, 1998).

A large-scale nation-wide curriculum reform entitled "The 9 year curriculum" in primary and secondary education was introduced in 2001. The new curriculum replaced subjects with ten basic competences and seven learning domains. While tests were purposefully developed to assess students' abilities in these new learning focuses (e.g., basic competence tests), the reform strongly emphasized the use of various kinds of strategies including learning portfolios to assess students. Assessment could be performance-based or authentic. To be in-line with the new assessment policies, the reform in Tainan province required a change in classroom assessment. In its official document disseminated to schools in 2008, (Tainan Education Department, 2008) the education department highlighted the use of multidimensional assessment for teaching and learning. Teachers were to use different kinds of strategies to assess students (e.g., performance-based assessment, oral tests and authentic assessment) and to integrate them into their everyday teaching.

The "multivariate approach" assessment reform initiatives have triggered different responses. Many scholars heavily criticized the multiple pathways to tertiary education, commenting that it was in fact unfair for the students from the lower income families. The new initiatives demanded students to demonstrate achievements in different areas such as dancing and playing musical instruments. Because of limited resources, the students from the lower income families were in a disadvantageous position to meet the demands. Statistical evidence showed that only three candidates from the lower income families had been accepted to read at the University of Taiwan in 2008. In addition, the multiple pathways, meant to reduce pressure, actually intensified the pressure because of the increased number of hurdles to university education (Qiu, 2009). The People's Daily Overseas (2010) reported that half of the people involved in a recent opinion poll survey expressed their wish to restore the high-stakes senior school public examination.

There were a number of widespread misconceptions about the multivariate approach to assessment. For example, some teachers thought that the approach would mean a total ban on paper-and-pencil tests. Others perceived that it equated the use of learning portfolios or performance assessment or authentic assessment. From observations in his four rounds of school visits to twenty-five provinces, Li (2006) found that teachers generally lacked knowledge and skills for developing good quality paper-and-pencil tests. Teachers adopted different kinds of assessment strategies (e.g., learning portfolios, learning journals and oral presentations) just for the sake of using them. Their knowledge of assessment strategies was actually very limited. They did not understand the strengths and weaknesses of individual kinds of assessment strategies and therefore were not able to use them effectively. Generally speaking, teachers were not able to link assessment activities with teaching and learning objectives.

4.5 Conclusion and Implications

For thousands of years, Chinese people have been very used to examinations and have culturally accepted high-stakes examinations as a means to determine their future prospects. The assessment practices at schools are often teacher-led with a strong emphasis on getting students to demonstrate factual knowledge. Scholars generally found these kinds of assessment practices problematic and argued that they narrowed teaching, encouraged rote-memorisation and restrained students from achieving their full potential. Around the turn of the twenty-first century, there was an international call for a paradigmatic shift of assessment, asking policy-makers to recognize that, besides selection and accountability, AfL is a very important function of assessment (Black, Harrison, Lee, Marshall, & Wiliam, 2003; Carless, 2005; Gu & Berry, 2008; Li, 2006; James et al., 2007; Stiggins, 2008; Stobart, 2008). Assessment should be used to diagnose where students have been successful and not so successful. The information should subsequently be used for providing direction for improving teaching and enhancing learning (Berry, 2005). Mainland China, Hong Kong and Taiwan took the new conceptions of assessment on board and responded in their own particular ways. All three places initiated large-scale national-wide assessment reforms to address the deeply entrenched examination culture. They formulated policies with the intention of reducing excessive use of tests and examinations and encouraging the use of AfL. They set guidelines for the reference of local governments and education units and supported local education units in trying out the new assessment conceptions in a number of pilot implementation projects. Despite these foundations, researches into teachers' assessment practice in the classroom found that teachers in the three areas were generally unprepared for the new assessment conceptions. On the whole, teachers were not capable of translating AfL theories into classroom practices. Teachers who were enthusiastic about AfL were particularly frustrated because, although there were policies and guidelines available for them to refer to, there were no concrete ways available to help them use assessment for teaching and learning purposes.

Teachers do need more detailed and substantial ideas to help them implement AfL in their classroom teaching. There is increasing agreement that to be effective in raising student achievement, teacher professional development needs to attend to both *content* and *process* elements (Reeves, McCall, & MacGilchrist, 2001; Wilson & Berne, 1999; see Chapter 8 by Gardner et al.). On the *content* side there should be input that helps equip teachers with AfL knowledge and skills. The input will entail empowering teachers with the AfL concepts and showing them in concrete terms how AfL can be implemented in real contexts. The *process* side will mean having mechanisms or plans to facilitate teachers self development so the newly acquired knowledge and skills could be sustained. Black and Wiliam (1998) and the Assessment Reform Group (1999) point out that there is firm evidence to show that AfL can raise standards. However, standards can be raised only if teachers are willing and are able to tackle AfL. The growing body of research suggests that improving teacher quality and their capacity to use assessment as central to learning may be the most effective way to attain this goal (Wiliam, 2008; see Chapter 8 by Gardner et al.). In setting the policies and providing guidelines, the governments in mainland China, Hong Kong and Taiwan have started the journey down the road to enhancing the quality of teaching and learning through the use of AfL. There are however, many challenges ahead of them in embedding AfL into the culture of the classroom.

References

Assessment Reform Group. (1999). Assessment for Learning: Beyond the Black Box. http://www.assessment-reform-group.org.uk/publications.html. Accessed 17 April 2008.

Berry, R. (2005). Entwining feedback, self and peer assessment. *Academic Exchange Quarterly, 9*(3), 225–229.

Berry, R. (2008). *Assessment for learning*. Hong Kong: Hong Kong University Press.

Berry, R. (2010). Teachers' orientations towards selecting assessment strategies. *New Horizons in Education, 58*(1), 96–107.

Berry, R. (2011). Assessment Trends in Hong Kong: Seeking to establish formative assessment in an examination culture. *Assessment in Education: Principles, Policy & Practice, 18*(2).

Berry, R., & Gao, L. (2009). *Teachers' classroom assessment practice in China*. Paper presented at the International Conference on Primary Education. Hong Kong Institute of Education, Hong Kong.

Biggs, J. (1996). *Testing: To educate or to select?* Hong Kong: Hong Kong Educational Publishing Co.

Black, P., Harrison, C., Lee, C., Marshall, B., & Wiliam, D. (2003). *Assessment for learning: Putting it into practice*. Maidenhead, Berkshire, England: Open University Press.

Black, P., & Wiliam, D. (1998). Inside the black box: Raising standards through classroom assessment. *Phi Delta Kappan, 80*(2), 139–147.

Carless, D. (2005). Prospects for the implementation of assessment for learning. *Assessment in Education, 12*(1), 39–54.

Chang, X. (2002). *A comparison between the outlines and the teaching guidelines*. Sichuan: Sichuan Province Chengdu Oriental Bilingual School. (in Chinese).

Choi, C. C. (1999). Public examinations in Hong Kong. *Assessment in Education, 6*(3), 405–417.

Curriculum Development Council (CDC). (2002). *Basic education curriculum guide: Building on strengths (Primary 1 – Secondary 3)*. Hong Kong: Author.

Curriculum Development Council (CDC). (2009). *Senior secondary curriculum guide (Secondary 4 – 6)*. Hong Kong: Author.

Deng, Y. (1998). *Open education and education reform*. Kaohsiung: Kaohsiung Fuwen Publisher. (in Chinese).

Dong, Y. (1998). *An analysis of teaching in China*. Beijing: People's Education Press. (in Chinese).

Education Department, City of Taicang, Jiangsu Province. (2007). Opinions on the implementation of "Six Seriousnesses in teaching" to strengthen teaching and learning in City of Taicang. Retrieved 20 March 2009 from http://www.tcldxx.cn/sms/news/readnews.jsp?id=1992. Accessed 20 March 2009. (in Chinese)

Feng, D. (2006). China's recent curriculum reform: Progress and problems. *Planning and Changing, 37*(1&2), 131–144.

Gu, Y., & Berry, R. (2008). Assessment reform in China: A pilot study of implementing English oral summative exam for basic education. In Y. C. Lo & M. Yung (Eds.), *School curriculum reform and teacher professional development: Experience sharing in Mainland China, Hong Kong and Macau* (pp. 41–64). Hong Kong and Macau: The Association for Childhood Education International Hong Kong and Macau. (in Chinese).

Heilongjian People's Office. (2007). Provincial UppeSecondary School Curriculum Reform Working Proposal, Memorandum from Heilongjian People's Office to Provincial education department and other departments. http://law.baidu.com/pages/chinalawinfo/1692/70/23919c47abe399c22450046c40a94ece_0.html. Accessed 20 March 2009. (in Chinese)

Hou, W. (1996). *Introduction to educational evaluation*. Shijiazhuang: Hebei Education Press. (in Chinese).

James, M., McCormick, R., Black, P., Carmichael, P., Drummond, M., & Fox, A., et al. (2007). *Improving learning how to learn: Classrooms, schools, and networks*. London: Routledge.

Jing, Li., Hang, S., & Zhang, C. (2007). Investigation and analysis of implementation of assessment in primary English teaching. *Teaching and Management, 2007*(18). (in Chinese).

Kennedy, K. J., Chan, J. K. S., Fok, P. K., & Yu, W. M. (2008). Forms of assessment and their potential for enhancing learning: Conceptual and cultural issues. *Educational Research for Policy and Practice*, *7*(3), 197–207.
Li, K. (1999). *Multiple teaching evaluation*. Taipei: Psychological Publishing Co., Ltd. (in Chinese).
Li, K. (2006). *Teaching evaluation*. Taipei: Psychological Publishing Co., Ltd. (in Chinese).
Ministry of Education, the People's Republic of China. (1990). *Provisional regulations for senior secondary schools educational assessment*. China: Ministry of Education. (in Chinese).
Ministry of Education, the People's Republic of China. (1993). *The outlines of China's educational reforms and developments*. China: Ministry of Education. (in Chinese).
Ministry of Education, the People's Republic of China. (2001). *The outlines for basic educational reform (Pilot)" (or generally called "The Outlines")*. China: Ministry of Education. (in Chinese).
Ministry of Education, the People's Republic of China. (2002). *Evaluation policies on subject teaching in regular secondary schools*. China: Ministry of Education. (in Chinese).
Morris, P. (2002). Promoting curriculum reforms in the context of a political transition: An analysis of Hong Kong's experience. *Journal of Education Policy*, *17*(1), 13–28.
People's Daily Overseas. (2010). How Taiwan students facing the university entrance exam, from one exam to multiple-entrance program. http://211.89.225.4:82/gate/big5/www.nihaotw.com/xw/xwfl/tw/201005/t20100507_563467.htm. Accessed 13 May 2010. (in Chinese)
Qiu, S. (2009). The research of the multiple-entrance program. *Ming Chuan Education Electronic Journal*, *1*, 83–93. (in Chinese).
Reeves, J., McCall, J., & MacGilchrist, B. (2001). Change leadership: Planning, conceptualisation and planning. In J. MacBeath & P. Mortimore (Eds.), *Improving school effectiveness* (pp. 122–137). Buckingham: Open University Press.
Stiggins, R. (2008). *Student-involved assessment for learning* (2nd ed.). Upper Saddle River, NJ: Pearson/Merrill Prentice Hall.
Stobart, G. (2008). *Testing times: The use and abuses of assessment*. London, New York: Routledge.
Tainan Education Department. (2008). http://www.tnc.edu.tw/edumsg/showmsg.php?msg_id=28779&from_unit=tnc. Accessed 13 May 2010 (in Chinese)
The Research of the Education Department, Guangzhou, Guangdong Province. (2007). Report of the pilot study of Guangzhou High school new curriculum (Septmember 2004 to July 2007). In M. Chan (Ed.), *Experiment and exploration*. Guangzhou: South China University of Technology Press. (in Chinese).
Wang, H. (2008). Reflection on classroom assessment. *Journal of Agricultural University of Hebei (Agriculture and Forestry Education Edition)*, *10*(2), 142–145. (in Chinese).
Wang, L. (2007). An investigation of the assessment theory and practice of university English teachers. *Crazy English (Teacher)*, *2007*(8), 48. (in Chinese).
Wiliam, D. (2008). Changing classroom practice. *Educational Leadership*, *65*(4), 36–42.
Wilson, S. M., & Berne, J. (1999). Teacher learning and the acquisition of professional knowledge: An examination of research on contemporary professional development. In A. Iran-Nejad & P. D. Pearson (Eds.), *Review of research in education* (pp. 173–209). Washington, DC: American Educational Research Association.
Wu, G. (1996). A cause analysis of the development of education evaluation in Western countries. *Elementary & Secondary Schooling Abroad*, *2000*(3), 19–21. (in Chinese).
Wu, W. (2004). An analysis of Taiwan educational reforms. The 1st HongKong Principal's Conference 2004. http://www.ied.edu.hk/cric/new/principalconference/papers/keynote-taiwan.pdf. Accessed 13 May 2010. (in Chinese)
Xu, N. (1993). *History of Taiwan Education*. ShTaBook. (in Chinese)
Yang, G. (1999). *Evolution of the governing patterns in modern China*. Beijing, China: BNU Press.
Zhuang, M., Xie, Z., Huang, H., & Xu, M. (1994). *Brief history of Taiwan education* (pp. 44–46). Fujian, China: Fujian Education Press. (in Chinese).

Chapter 5
Assessment Reform and Educational Change in Australia

Val Klenowski

5.1 Introduction

The recent experience of assessment reform in Australia with an explicit focus on the emergent assessment policies at the levels of the nation and the state are analyzed in this chapter. The implications for teachers' classroom practice are made explicit. To begin a review of recent developments in assessment in Australia will be presented and issues relating to the use of standards for both accountability and the improvement of learning will be discussed.

These are changing times in Australia with the development of a national curriculum, national student assessment and reporting of school education outcomes. In 2007, the six states and two territories of Australia developed individual approaches to the use of standards in the implementation of curriculum, assessment and reporting. In February 2008, the interim National Curriculum Board was established to set the *core content* and *achievement standards* in Mathematics, Science, History and English from Pre-school to Year 12. Most recently, in May 2009, the Australian Curriculum, Assessment and Reporting Authority (ACARA) assumed responsibility for the work of the National Curriculum Board (April 2008–May 2009). ACARA now has responsibility for a national curriculum from Kindergarten to Year 12 in specified learning areas, a national assessment program aligned to the national curriculum that measures students' progress and a national data collection and reporting program. The latter is intended to support analysis, evaluation, research and resource allocation and accountability and reporting on schools and broader national achievement.

V. Klenowski (✉)
Queensland University of Technology, Brisbane, QLD, Australia
e-mail: val.klenowski@qut.edu.au

R. Berry, B. Adamson (eds.), *Assessment Reform in Education*,
Education in the Asia-Pacific Region: Issues, Concerns and Prospects 14,
DOI 10.1007/978-94-007-0729-0_5,

5.2 Drivers for Educational Change in Australia

Global drivers for curriculum and assessment reform in Australia are apparent from policy makers' responses to international measures of educational attainment such as the results from the Programme for International Student Assessment (PISA), developed by the Organisation for Economic Co-operation and Development (OECD) or the Trends in International Mathematics and Science Study (TIMSS) of the International Association for the Evaluation of Educational Achievement (IEA). Important questions of whether we are comparing like with like have not always been considered. Nevertheless, governments have used the results from international comparisons to justify the introduction of ongoing curriculum change. In Australia the use of international comparative data, for example TIMSS data, has identified significant State and Territory differences in Australia. So it was no surprise when the new Labor Government in 2008 introduced plans for a National Curriculum in Mathematics, Science, History and English in primary and secondary schools by 2011 to be extended to include languages, geography and the arts.

International comparisons have highlighted equity issues for Australia as Indigenous children have scored significantly lower than non-Indigenous children (Klenowski, 2009a, 2009b). Australian schools are not adequately addressing inequalities and when compared with other developed countries, Australia is underperforming: "high in quality but low in equity" (McGaw, 2004). The analysis of the 2003 PISA data suggested that Australia was "over-represented in the lowest categories of maths proficiency and under-represented in the highest" (Australian Council for Educational Research (ACER), 2004, p. xiii). The achievement of students overall was high; however there were wide differences between the high and low achieving students.

This trend appeared to persist in PISA 2006 that assessed science as the main domain with reading literacy and mathematics as minor domains. The analysis of these results indicated that Indigenous students were under-represented among the highest scoring students and over-represented among low scoring students. For example, "[i]n scientific literacy 40% of Indigenous students performed below the OECD 'baseline' and were judged to be at serious risk of not being able to participate adequately in the twenty-first century workforce or to contribute as productive future citizens." In mathematical literacy the percentage was 39% and in reading literacy 38% (ACER, 2007). These latest results of PISA 2006 showed a continued widening of the gap in academic achievement between Australia's Indigenous students and non-Indigenous students with minimal improvement since 2000.

Headlines such as "PISA shows Indigenous students continue to struggle" (ACER, 2007) reflect areas of real inequity in Australia's education system. Reports (Ibid; Thomson, 2008) indicate that Australia's lowest-performing students are most likely to come from Indigenous communities, geographically remote areas and poor socioeconomic backgrounds. In terms of averages, about 40% of Indigenous students, 23% of students from the lowest category of socioeconomic status, and 27% of students from remote schools, are not meeting a proficiency level in science that the OECD deems necessary for full participation in today's workforce and society.

These recent PISA results indicate that in Australia issues of inequity need to be addressed to ensure access to quality education for all students (Thomson, 2008).

5.3 National Levers for Educational Change in Australia

Apart from such global factors as international comparative analyses of achievement data there have also been national drivers for curriculum and assessment reforms in Australia. These developments are derived in part from an earlier investigation of the introduction of an Australian Certificate of Education (ACE) aimed at achieving greater consistency in senior secondary arrangements for curriculum, assessment and certification, more comparable student results across Australia, and more consistent standards of student achievement (Masters, Forster, Matters, & Tognolini, 2006). A further study (Matters & Masters, 2007) investigated what was common content, what was essential curriculum content and whether achievement standards were comparable in the final year of schooling, in English (including Literature), Mathematics, Chemistry, Physics and Australian History.

Significant consistency in what was assessed was identified; however, it was also found that different jurisdictions use different methods of assessment such as external examinations or teacher-devised assessment instruments. This finding raised the important issue of whether achievement standards can be compared across jurisdictions, or whether the existence of different assessment methods hinders comparison. The study recommended that a curriculum "core" be identified for each nominated senior school subject to specify explicitly what students would be expected to learn no matter where in Australia they live. To achieve a nationally consistent description of how well students are expected to learn the core in each subject it was recommended that a set of achievement standards be developed.

Other origins for these curriculum and assessment reforms that have been identified include the ministerial agreement on national goals at the Hobart Declaration of 1989, the Adelaide Declaration of 1999 and the National Declaration on Educational Goals for Young Australians of 2008. There is a sense that the nation as a whole can do better than its parts and that the nation's capacity would be greater if all jurisdictions worked together to achieve more efficiency and reduce duplication (McGaw, 2009).

5.4 Background

In Australia benchmark testing began in 1999 when the first annual literacy tests (reading and writing) for Year 3 and Year 5 students were conducted. The nationally agreed literacy and numeracy benchmarks for Years 3, 5 and 7 represent minimum standards of performance. In 2008 the National Assessment Program – Literacy and Numeracy (NAPLAN) was introduced, students in Years 3, 5, 7 and 9 sit the same national tests in reading, writing, spelling, grammar and punctuation and numeracy. In addition, National Assessment Program assessments are also taking place and involve triennial sample assessments in science at Year 6, in civics and citizenship at Years 6 and 10 and in ICT literacy at Years 6 and 10 (Harrington, 2008).

5.5 Current Context

By May 2009 the National Curriculum Board had, through a process of consultation, managed the development of four framing papers in the subject areas of English, Mathematics, Science and History. This work was handed over to the new, independent, statutory authority ACARA, which now has responsibility for the management and the implementation of the national curriculum (to be referred to as the Australian Curriculum), national student assessment and reporting of school education outcomes. There is also an intention to establish a standards-referenced framework to "invigorate a national effort to improve student learning in the selected subjects" (National Curriculum Board, 2008, p. 3). Table 5.1 outlines the curriculum development timelines.

For the other disciplines of geography and languages the curriculum framing will occur from June 2009 until May 2010, curriculum development from May 2010 until December 2010, consultation from February 2011 until May 2011 and publication from July 2011 until August 2011. The Arts will be developed a year behind this timeline.

Table 5.1 Australian curriculum development timelines

Stage	Activity	Timelines K–10	Timelines senior years (11/12)
Curriculum framing	Confirmation of directions for writing curriculum for the learning areas of English, mathematics, the sciences and history	April, 2009	April, 2009
Curriculum development	Two step process for development of curriculum documents Step one – broad outline; scope and sequence Step two – completion of "detail" of curriculum	April–Dec, 2009	June–Jan, 2010
Consultation	National consultation on curriculum documents and trialing	Jan–April, 2010	Mar–June, 2010
Publication	Publication of national curriculum documents in print and digital format	June–July, 2010	July–Sept, 2010

Source: National Curriculum Board (2009).

The Australian Curriculum is to have a futures orientation and will identify the essential skills, knowledge and capabilities that all young Australians are entitled to learn. A futures orientation includes an understanding that our society is becoming more complex and that increasingly Australians will need the knowledge and the skills to interact in a global environment. This requires knowing how to learn, adapt, create and communicate effectively, and interpret and use information more fluently and critically. A continuum of learning in literacy and numeracy skills will form the foundation for the national curriculum. It will be a web-based document. That is, web technologies will be used to embed links and enable multiple views and access. The three elements of the national curriculum framework will comprise; curriculum content, achievement standards and a reporting framework.

The curriculum content element of the Australian Curriculum will provide teachers with the expectations of what should be taught and what students are expected to learn, that is, knowledge, skills and understanding. Curriculum content will be described for a particular learning area at a particular year level for example, Mathematics, Year 5 (ACARA, 2009).

The achievement standards aim to provide "an expectation of the quality of learning that students should typically demonstrate in relation to the content by a particular point in their schooling (that is, the depth of their understanding, the extent of their knowledge and the sophistication of their skills)" (ACARA, 2009, http://www.acara.edu.au/verve/_resources/The_Shape_of_the_National_Curriculum_paper.pdf#xml=http://search.curriculum.edu.au/)

The aim is to provide achievement standards for each year of schooling across K–10 using a descriptor of the quality of learning that draws together the knowledge, skills and understanding typically expected for that year. The representation of the standards for every year will include a statement of expected learning, a set of generic grade descriptors and a set of work samples that illustrate typical learning (ACARA, 2009).

Course specific standards are to be developed for Years 11–12 with a range of levels of achievement expected of students studying the particular course. The standards aim to assist in reporting to students and parents, to aid consistency of assessment and reporting across Australia and to fulfil the purpose of selection required of assessment for post-school pathways. It is intended that the Year 11–12 standards will be designed to be applicable in jurisdictions with external examinations and with school-based assessment.

Finally the reporting framework aims to provide consistency in nomenclature to describe the quality of achievement associated with each A–E grade for use across K–10. It is intended that the use of the five-point scale will indicate the extent to which a student has met the achievement standard for a particular year of school. To illustrate, students who achieve a grade of C or above will have met the standard for that year/stage. The grade C would indicate a satisfactory level of achievement while an A grade would indicate an outstanding level of achievement. Conversely a grade of D or E would suggest that follow-up is required and further investigation by teachers, students and parents might be needed (ACARA, 2009).

It is also intended that annotated student work samples will be used to demonstrate the different standards. This collection of work samples will build on the work that is currently established in the Australian states and territories. It is anticipated that this collection will provide a common and national reference point for greater consistency in teacher judgement within and between classrooms, schools, states and territories.

Such changes to curriculum and assessment make considerable demands on teachers who need to be informed, prepared and resourced to implement this level of change. It is most important that teachers are aware of the literacy demands of national curriculum and assessment for the implementation of a national curriculum requires the development of teachers' capacity to use the learning power of assessment to improve the outcomes for all students.

5.6 Emergent Issues

Teachers need to be aware of the accountability context within which they work and appreciate how the practices that they engage in are mediated by structures beyond their control, such as national policy about what they are supposed to assess and how that is to be recorded and reported. In such a context an important emergent issue is for teachers to maintain a strong sense of responsibility by developing their professionalism through building their assessment literacy and practices.

The use of achievement standards to assess student learning, as planned for in the Australian Curriculum, is a new phenomenon for teachers in Australia. Standards-driven reform in the Australian context involves the use of achievement standards as the basis for judgments of student learning (depth of understanding, extent of knowledge and the level of sophistication of skills) with the intended aims of informing the teaching and learning process and of reporting and tracking student progress.

Assessment literacy is a fundamental issue for teachers and is defined, not from a traditional view of skills, knowledges and cognitions that reside within an individual, but rather a view of literacy as a visible social practice with language, text and discourse (Gee, 2003). To raise the assessment literacy of teachers there is a need to understand, and practice, the fundamental principles of assessment design. That is "fitness for purpose" and the mode of assessment should impact positively on teaching and learning (Gipps, 1994).

The use of achievement standards for assessment and reporting will further require the development of teachers' assessment literacy and assessment practices. This will be illustrated by referring to the particular case of the Australian state of Queensland where extensive research has been conducted to study the standards-driven reform in the middle years of schooling (Klenowski & Wyatt-Smith, 2008; Wyatt-Smith & Klenowski, 2008; Klenowski & Adie, 2009; Wyatt-Smith, Klenowski, & Gunn, 2010).

5.7 The Case of Queensland

Queensland has a long history of externally moderated standards-referenced assessment that supports teachers' judgments in assessing the quality of student work. It was in 1972 that Queensland schools introduced a system of school-based assessment as a response to public dissatisfaction with the Senior Public Examination papers, set by the university. In 1966 and 1967, 68% of students failed to attain a pass in their Physics senior examination. The public lost confidence in the examination system and called for a review. The Radford Report of 1970 was the result. Externally-set senior examinations were abandoned and an alternative system developed that valued more systematic collection of student achievement data by the teacher. Teachers' professional judgment was recognised and privileged in the senior years of schooling. The support for developing teachers' assessment capability in the middle and primary years of schooling for achieving consistency of teacher judgment is only a recent development.

The Queensland Curriculum, Assessment and Reporting (QCAR) Framework was developed from 2005, implementation began in 2008 and a review of the extended trial was conducted prior to full implementation in 2009. The framework comprises the Essential Learnings (ELs) that identify what students should know, understand and be able to do; standards that articulate the quality of student achievements described on a five point scale from A to E; the assessment bank that provides a collection of online assessments and resources that relate to the ELs and standards; and the Queensland Comparable Assessment Tasks (QCATs) that are authentic, performance-based assessment tasks and guidelines for reporting and that outline how schools might provide information about students' learning (Queensland Studies Authority (QSA), 2009). The QCATs are designed to assess a selection of ELs in English, Mathematics and Science in Years 4, 6 and 9.

Queensland has conceptualised the framework from the view that assessment should be an integral part of teaching and learning. While the QCAR framework promotes the practice of embedding assessment into classroom practice, the report on the 2008 extended trial of the QCATs found that teachers needed greater familiarity with the standards and the suggested approach to making judgments (QSA, 2009). The implication is that with the move to a national curriculum and the related use of achievement standards there will be a need for all teachers in Australia to familiarise themselves with the standards and develop their understanding of how to use them when making judgments about student work. For although at the national level the intention is to help teachers interpret the standards by providing annotated samples of work indicative of the standard, the research indicates that the judgement process involved for the teacher is more complex than this (Klenowski & Wyatt-Smith, 2008; Wyatt-Smith & Klenowski, 2008).

In Queensland the use of the QCATs is intended to allow students to demonstrate their best work and "[a]s much as possible... avoid the flavour of point-in-time tests" (Queensland Department of Education and the Arts, 2005, p. 9). The information collected from the QCATs is considered to be low-stakes data and it is not intended that it be used for measuring school or teacher effectiveness (Queensland Department of Education and the Arts, 2005). Rather the intention is to build teachers' assessment capacity and assessment literacy by demonstrating the nature of quality assured assessment tasks that are designed to be authentic and performance-based. Teachers are also provided with resources, such as the assessment bank, guides to assist teachers in making judgments about the quality of the students' responses, model answers and a range of annotated samples of student responses reflective of each standard. This level of resourcing is intended to support the development of shared understanding about the interpretation and application of standards (QSA, 2009).

Teachers have indicated the value of meeting as a community of learners at moderation meetings to share their understanding and use of the standards (Klenowski & Adie, 2009). It is through the processes of discussion, critique and analysis of student responses that teachers have the opportunity to validate or adjust their interpretations of the standards in relation to the judgments they have made. Providing teachers with a common discourse in terms of the criteria (assessable elements) and the standards (task specific descriptors) facilitates teachers' understanding of how well students have completed the QCAT.

To help teachers understand the value of the assessment data and how it can be used to modify teaching and learning the QSA provides a report to schools on the implementation of the QCATs, based on the analysis of all the data collected. QSA collects a random sample from Queensland schools of teacher judgments representative of standards A to E for analysis. The resultant report provides teachers with insights into the way students typically responded. The teacher uses this information for teaching and learning purposes. The intent is that the report will contribute to a better understanding by teachers of student strengths, development of consistency of teacher judgement and comparability of reported results of student achievement and progress. Moderation processes have been found to support consistency of teacher judgments and a large number of Queensland Years 1–9 teachers have gained practical experience of this practice (QSA, 2009).

5.8 Challenges for Teachers at the National Level

Where there is a growing international trend for using standards not just for accountability but also for the purpose of improving learning, it is important to understand their different purposes (goals) and functions (roles). In Australia, standards are currently being used in different contexts to fulfil different functions.

To illustrate, in the context of the NAPLAN, the standards fulfil a particular role.

> For each year level a national minimum standard is located on the scale. For Year 3 Band 2 is the national minimum standard, for Year 5 Band 4 is the national minimum standard, for Year 7 Band 5 is the national minimum standard and for Year 9 Band 6 is the national minimum standard. The skills that students are typically required to demonstrate for the minimum standard at each year level are described on the back page of the student report.

These standards represent increasingly challenging skills and require higher scores on the national scale (NAPLAN, 2009, http://www.schools.nsw.edu.au/learning/7-12assessments/naplan/nms/index.html).

In 2009, league tables emerged to represent these results for the Australian states. In Queensland, the state government is keen to raise standards as represented by the results of NAPLAN testing and in 2009 the premier advised schools to sit practice NAPLAN tests in Years 3, 5, 7 and 9 as she was disappointed by the overall results of the 2008 tests which she indicated were designed to assess if students were meeting "national standards in numeracy, reading, writing, spelling, punctuation and grammar" (Bligh, 2009). Currently in Australia, there are no statements about the expected learning of literacy and numeracy and no standards to inform them about the expectations of quality. There are only summary statements of skills assessed to inform parents about their child's report. Here the term is used in reference to national minimum standards and the Queensland premier's response to the NAPLAN testing program highlights how the meaning of the term *standard* differs in that it is used as a level of attainment or point of reference as measured by a yardstick or as in this case band levels on a scale.

The concern for teachers is that by emphasising that the NAPLAN test is the measure or reference point, the consequent action by teachers will be to narrow their focus to that which is tested or measured. In other words the curriculum too will be narrowed and teachers will emphasize in their teaching that which has been specified in the test. What becomes evident is that in this context of accountability when the stakes are high not only will there be an impact on teaching, there will be consequences at the level of the school, the system and the nation. It is possible that high-stakes accountability testing can have benefits such as raising expectations, providing a clearer focus for teaching and learning, motivating achievement, challenging patterns of school performance and providing useful information to stakeholders for governing and allocating resources. There are also some costs such as the detrimental impact of setting targets that distort the system by encouraging teachers to teach to the test, with excessive time allocated to drill and practice, booster tests and the like. Inexorable pressures emerge to pervert the system such as the manipulation of the drop out or retention rates of students for the purposes of achieving targets, result or grade inflation and entry selection to maintain one's position on the league table (Stobart, 2008). The No Child Left Behind legislation in the USA is an example where the push to raise standards has led to enormous pressure on teachers and distortions in the teaching of a holistic curriculum with the reduction in authentic and challenging learning experiences for students (Marsh, 2009; see Chapter 3 by Flaitz).

The Queensland premier's response to the NAPLAN results demonstrates how governments are becoming increasingly anxious about education standards particularly as reflected in such national or international comparisons of student achievement. This is because of the expected critical contribution of raising standards in education to economic growth and competitiveness. There is also increasing individual (particularly parental) anxieties because of the growing importance of formal qualifications in determining success in terms of life chances.

In Queensland, standards for improvement of student learning provide a generic description of the expected quality of student work and offer a common language for teachers to use in discussing student work (QSA, 2007). The aim is to improve learning by indicating the quality of achievement that is expected and in so doing provide the basis for judgments about the quality of students' work. Research indicates that standards are useful for the purpose of informing teachers' work and in contributing to quality teaching and learning experiences (Klenowski, 2006, 2007; Sadler, 2005; Wyatt-Smith & Castleton, 2004). In the context of the QCATs, the achievement standards function by monitoring the growth in student learning and by providing information about the quality of student achievement for improvement purposes. The intended purpose of these standards is to assist teachers in identifying areas for improvement in teaching, curriculum design or development. The provision of these standards make explicit for teachers what to teach and the level of performance expected for a particular age group and in this way they contribute to the demand for public accountability at the local professional level of the teacher (Harlen, 1994; Wilson, 2004).

As suggested earlier these standards are also intended to promote teachers' professional learning, focused on good assessment practices and judgement of the quality of student achievement against system level benchmarks or referents. In addition it is expected that teachers using the standards will present more meaningful reports and engagement with assessment as a learning process.

5.9 Future Challenges

These are changing times for Australian teachers in terms of the changing curriculum and assessment demands. There are lessons that can be learnt from the research conducted in other countries, like those of the United Kingdom, where there have been years of experience of national curriculum and testing systems.

In a time of economic uncertainty, it is important for governments to be accountable and to develop policy that will maintain high standards for all. The use of national tests and examinations as the basis for school, local government, state and national accountability is on the increase in Australia, and such trends globally have given rise to standards-driven reforms. The policy rationale for such change, which includes testing, is that it will improve standards of teaching and learning regardless of the student's religion, race, gender, socio-economic or socio-cultural background. However, the cost-benefits of using testing in this way are not always economical or successful. There are alternative approaches for schools and teachers to demonstrate accountability that places less emphasis on test results. Important questions need to be considered and mistakes that other national systems have encountered need to be avoided in Australia.

While both large-scale standardised tests and authentic, teacher assessment can contribute to improved learning and accountability the question of balance remains. There are important ethical questions to consider in assessment change efforts. The social impact of changes to education systems is not something to be taken lightly when the impact on students results in them being turned off learning or labelled as failures. Unhealthy competition between schools, teaching to the test, increased stress levels for children, parents and teachers, and huge costs are just some of the reactions to testing that is high-stakes.

There is also evidence that internationally the gap between children with and without access to high-quality education is growing. In assessment terms this raises the important equity issue which is not simply a technical consideration of the test or assessment itself. Whether testing systems take into consideration socio-cultural representations of achievement, the limitations of current assessment practices and the consequences of how the assessment evidence is used are further significant considerations in this time of assessment change in Australia.

References

Australian Council for Education Research (ACER). (2004). In S. Thomson, J. Cresswell, & L. De Bortoli (Eds.), *Facing the future: A focus on mathematical literacy among Australian 15 year-old students in PISA 2003*. Camberwell: ACER.

Australian Council for Educational Research (ACER). (2007). *PISA shows Indigenous students continue to struggle*. Media release, 4 December 2007. Camberwell, Australia: ACER.

Australian Curriculum, Assessment and Reporting Authority (ACARA). (2009) *The Shape of the National Curriculum Paper: A Proposal for Discussion*. http://www.acara.edu.au/verve/_resources/The_Shape_of_the_National_Curriculum_paper.pdf#xml=http://search.curriculum.edu.au/. 12 June 2009.

Bligh, A. (2009). *Letter to parent*. Brisbane: Queensland Government.

Gee, J. P. (2003). Opportunity to learn: A language-based perspective on assessment. *Assessment in Education: Principles, Policy and Practice, 10*(1), 27–46.

Gipps, C. (1994). *Beyond testing: Towards a theory of educational assessment*. London: Falmer Press.

Harlen, W. (1994). *Concepts of quality in student assessment*. Paper presented at the American Educational Research Association conference, New Orleans.

Harrington, M. (2008). 19 November 2008, no. 60, 2008–09, ISSN 1328–8091. Australian Curriculum, Assessment and Reporting Authority Bill 2008

Klenowski, V. (2006). *Evaluation report of the pilot of the 2005 Queensland Assessment Task (QAT)*. Brisbane: Queensland Studies Authority, http://www.qsa.qld.edu.au/research/reports.html. Accessed 15 June 2009.

Klenowski, V. (2007). *Evaluation of the effectiveness of the consensus-based standards validation process*. http://education.qld.gov.au/corporate/newbasics/html/lce_eval.html. Accessed 15 June 2009.

Klenowski, V. (2009a). Australian Indigenous students: Addressing equity issues in assessment. *Teaching Education, 20*(1), 77–93.

Klenowski, V. (2009b). Public education matters: Reclaiming public education for the common good in a global era. *Australian Educational Researcher, 36*(1), 1–26.

Klenowski, V., & Adie, L. E. (2009). Moderation as judgement practice: Reconciling system level accountability and local level practice. *Curriculum Perspectives, 29*(1), 10–28.

Klenowski, V., & Wyatt-Smith, C. (2008) *Standards-Driven Reform Years 1–10: Moderation an Optional Extra?* Paper presented at the Australian Association for Research in Education conference, 30 November – 4 December, 2008, Brisbane, Queensland.

Marsh, C. (2009). *Key concepts for understanding curriculum*. London: Routledge.

Masters, G. N., Forster, M., Matters, G. N., & Tognolini, J. (2006). *Australian certificate of education: A way forward*. Melbourne: Australian Council for Educational Research.

Matters, G. N., & Masters, G. N. (2007). *Year 12 curriculum content and achievement standards*. Brisbane: Australian Council for Educational Research.

McGaw, B. (2004). Australian mathematics learning in an international context. In I. Putt, R. Farragher, & M. McLean (Eds.), *Mathematics education for the third millennium: Towards 2010* (p. 29). Proceedings of the 27th annual conference of the Mathematics Education Research Group of Australasia. Melbourne: MERGA.

McGaw, B. (2009). Building a national curriculum, Keynote address, Queensland Studies Authority, Issue 1, 9 April. http://www.qsa.qld.edu.au/publications/8203.html. Accessed 20 September 2009.

National Assessment Program – Literacy and Numeracy (NAPLAN). (2009). *National Minimum Standards*. http://www.schools.nsw.edu.au/learning/7-12assessments/naplan/nms/index.html. Accessed 2 June 2009.

National Curriculum Board. (2008). *The Shape of the National Curriculum: A Proposal for Discussion*. www.ncb.org.au/our_work/preparing_for_2009.html. Accessed 5 November 2008.

National Curriculum Board. (2009). *The Shape of the Australian Curriculum*. http://www.acara.edu.au/verve/_resources/The_Shape_of_the_Australian_Curriculum_-_precis.pdf. Accessed 20 June 2009.

Queensland Department of Education and the Arts. (2005). *Queensland curriculum assessment and reporting framework*. Brisbane, Australia: Department of Education and the Arts.

Queensland Studies Authority (QSA). (2007). *Information statement April 2007: Standards draft 2*. Brisbane, Australia: Queensland Studies Authority.

Queensland Studies Authority (QSA). (2009). *Capability statement*. Brisbane, Australia: Queensland Studies Authority.

Sadler, D. R. (2005). Interpretations of criteria-based assessment and grading in higher education. *Assessment and Evaluation in Higher Education, 30*(2), 175–194.

Stobart, G. (2008). *Testing times: The uses and abuses of assessment*. London: Routledge.

Thomson, S. (2008). Lessons to learn from high achievers, *The Age*. http://www.theage.com.au/news/education-news/lessons-to-learn-from-high-achievers/2008/02/01/1201801039731.html. Accessed 30 October 2008.

Wilson, M. (Ed.). (2004). *Towards coherence between classroom assessment and accountability*. Chicago: University of Chicago Press.

Wyatt-Smith, C., & Castleton, G. (2004). Factors affecting writing achievement: Mapping teacher beliefs. *English in Education, 38*(1), 37–61.

Wyatt-Smith, C., & Klenowski, V. (2008). *Examining how moderation is enacted within an assessment policy reform initiative: You just have to learn how to see*. In: 34th International Association for Educational Assessment (IAEA) Annual Conference, 7 – 12 September 2008, England, Cambridge.

Wyatt-Smith, C., Klenowski, V., & Gunn, S. (2010). The centrality of teachers' judgement practice in assessment: A study of standards in moderation. *Assessment in Education: Principles, policy & practice., 17*(1), 59–75.

Chapter 6
Assessment for Learning Reform in Singapore – Quality, Sustainable or Threshold?

Kelvin Tan

The education system in Singapore has been transformed since its independence from colonial British rule in 1965. Reforms have occurred in three distinct phases: the *survival* phase from 1959 to 1978; the *efficiency* phase from 1979 to 1996; and the *ability-driven* phase from 1997 to the present. This chapter concentrates on assessment reform in Singapore in the third phase, and examines its impact on the nature and quality of students' learning, with particular reference to assessment for learning initiatives in schools. It argues that assessment reform in Singapore tends to emphasize and perpetuate structural efficiency at the expense of the quality of learning. It suggests that the notion of a threshold level of reform (Trafford & Leshem, 2009) could be a useful way of framing assessment reform in order to achieve a sustainable level of transformation. The chapter concludes that it is not enough for assessment reform to merely achieve a higher level of effective assessment and learning and argues that the education system requires assessment reform to be radical and ambitious enough to attain a new threshold for assessment and learning in Singapore schools.

6.1 Introduction

The education system in Singapore has been transformed beyond recognition since its humble beginnings in 1965. Then, following its independence from colonial British rule, the under-resourced system was not capable of meeting either the citizenship or the economic challenge (Gopinathan, 1999). A slew of reforms has brought about much needed change and progress, leading the respected *Times Educational Supplement* (1997, p. 1) to label Singapore as the "most academically successful nation in the world".

There are three distinct phases in the transformation of the Singapore education system (Tan, 2006a). The *survival* phase from 1959 to 1978 was about producing

K. Tan (✉)
Policy and Leadership Studies Department, National Institute of Education, Singapore
e-mail: Kelvin.tan@nie.edu.sg

R. Berry, B. Adamson (eds.), *Assessment Reform in Education*,
Education in the Asia-Pacific Region: Issues, Concerns and Prospects 14,
DOI 10.1007/978-94-007-0729-0_6,

trained workers in the context of post war industrialization and mass unemployment. The *efficiency* phase from 1979 to 1996 was prompted by the report on the Ministry of Education in 1979 which sought to address the problem of inefficiency in the 1970s. Then, up to 30% of students dropped out of the education system (Ministry of Education & Singapore (MOE), 1979). The most significant phase is the *ability-driven* phase from 1997 to the present, described by one writer as the "big bang" in educational reforms because the entire education system was reviewed (Gopinathan, 2001).

This chapter examines assessment reform in Singapore since 1997, and its impact on the nature and quality of students' learning. In particular, the impact of assessment for learning (AfL) initiatives in schools is examined. It is argued that much of assessment reform in Singapore emphasizes and perpetuates structural efficiency at the expense of the quality of learning. The notion of a threshold level of reform (Trafford & Leshem, 2009) is suggested as a way of framing assessment reform to achieving a sustainable level of transformation. The chapter concludes that it is not enough for assessment reform to merely achieve a higher level of effective assessment and learning. It is argued that the Singapore education system requires assessment reform to be radical and ambitious enough to attain a new threshold for assessment and learning in Singapore schools.

6.2 Recent Educational Developments and Assessment Reform in Singapore

In 1997, the Ministry of Education (MOE) of Singapore announced a new vision for education intended to produce school leavers capable of thriving in the new Millennium. This vision represents a watershed in Singapore's education system and was termed "Thinking Schools Learning Nation" (TSLN). It sought to replace an efficiency-driven education system with an ability-driven system. The emphasis was to motivate students to "value learning, empower them to use information for problem solving purposes, enabling them to work in teams to lead, share and follow, to learn in an open ended manner valuing divergence, encouraging a questioning attitude and developing communication skills" (Gopinathan, 1999, p. 299).

Senior Minister Goh Chok Tong, then Prime Minister of Singapore, explained TSLN as a vision for a total learning environment, for students, teachers, parents, workers, companies, community organizations and the government (Goh, 1997). Under the "umbrella" vision of TSLN, various initiatives were launched to address the different needs to begin, sustain and pursue the ambitious vision. Syllabi, examinations and university admission criteria were changed to encourage thinking out of the box and risk-taking. Students' involvement in project work and exposure to higher order thinking questions resulted in greater creativity and independent as well as inter-dependent learning (Ng, 2005).

In 2004, Prime Minister Lee Hsien Loong commented in his inaugural National Day Rally speech that "We have got to teach less to our students so that they will learn more" (Lee, 2004). The term "Teach Less, Learn More" (TLLM) quickly became a catch phrase amongst policy-makers, principals and teachers, and eventually became a major policy initiative in the Singapore education system (Ng, 2008).

Since then, TLLM is frequently mentioned in relation to ideas and practices aimed at enhancing student learning and promoting thinking students. For many teachers, TLLM represents the pedagogical embodiment of producing thinking students that would develop and construct a nation of future learners (Tan, 2007).

Politicians are increasingly aware that what is taught, and how, can be indirectly asserted through the control of high-stakes assessment. Educational assessment has thus become a highly contested area as the focus of complex political, economic and cultural expectations for change (Filer, 2000). Singapore's national high-stakes assessment system is intended to perform a number of important institutional tasks such as to provide an objective and politically acceptable measure of student learning and to allocate students into different curriculum tracks and schools based on their academic performance (Hogan, Towndrow & Koh, 2009).

In Singapore, the centralized bureaucracy of the education system exerts its central authority in and through assessment policy by creating and perpetuating a centrally-planned and common assessment framework. This common assessment framework applies to all schools in Singapore, and is in turn administered by a central examination authority, The Singapore Examinations and Assessment Branch, which is part of the MOE. As students take the same national examinations, there is the perception of a level playing field for all, regardless of their ethnic and socio-economic status. Students' subsequent progression into schools and institutions of higher learning and placement into courses at each educational level is based on their performance in common national examinations. These are meant to reflect the notion of a common, level playing field and the principle of meritocracy.

The Singapore Examinations and Assessment Board of the MOE has purportedly developed new assessment practices to cater to the pedagogical changes of TLLM. For example, Sellen, Chong, and Tay (2006) argue that an assessment shift in the form of a greater emphasis on coursework and new assessment items and methods have been developed in the past few years to cultivate thinking skills and foster a capacity and desire for lifelong learning. Specifically, these changes include the introduction of

- Project Work for pre-university students in 2003 as part of university admission criteria
- Science Practical Assessment as a coursework initiative for secondary and pre-university students
- Source-based items in Social Studies and History for secondary school students
- Data response items in Geography for secondary and pre-university students
- Case study items in Economics for secondary and pre-university students

But do the new ways of designing assessment and utilizing assessment result in schools actually enhance students' learning in a manner consistent with the stated intentions of TSLN and TLLM? This begs the question of the prevailing purposes of assessment in the Singapore education system – whether assessment is merely to serve a gate-keeping function to sort students for school admission (Gregory & Clarke, 2003), or also meant to enhance the quality of students' learning in the process of assessment as well. The utility of national examinations as a sorting mechanism should also be understood against the backdrop of the intensive competition amongst schools and the school ranking system.

Assessment may be said to serve multiple purposes, and one way of determining what constitutes effective assessment (and therefore effective assessment reform) is in terms of its fitness of purpose, i.e., the purpose(s) that assessments seek to fulfill in any given context. Hence, it is instructive to ponder what assessment is actually meant to achieve in relation to learning in Singapore.

Formative and summative assessment are commonly understood as "assessment *for* learning" and "assessment *of* learning" respectively. Hence, assessment used primarily to measure the extent or nature of what students have learned is understood as *summative* assessment. This would include high-stakes national examinations and school tests and assessment for streaming students into different ability levels. In contrast, assessment practices that involve the generation and use of feedback primarily intended to enhance what students may learn is categorized as *formative* assessment. Formative assessment comprises of activities primarily designed and undertaken by teachers, and/or by their students, to provide information to be used as feedback that would then enhance students' learning (Black & Wiliam, 1998).

When Prime Minister Lee Hsien Loong first mooted the "Teach Less, Learn More" initiative in his inaugural National Day address on 22 August 2004, he said: "We've got to teach less to our students so that they will learn more. Grades are important – don't forget to pass your exams – but grades are not the only thing in life and there are other things in life which we want to learn in school." Perhaps this belies an implicit recognition of the adverse effects of high-stakes summative assessment. Assessment practice may be said to shape students' experience of learning, and even schooling, in drastic ways. Whilst assessment is seen as a necessary evil to meet the need to measure and compare students, the side effects of summative testing cannot be ignored.

A recent nation-wide investigation into the intellectual quality of assessment tasks in schools suggests that assessment practices by and large may not be oriented towards students' understanding, let alone utilize assessment to enhance understanding. In 2004–2005, a major research project was undertaken to examine the quality of teacher assignments and associated student work in Singapore schools (Koh & Luke, 2009). Altogether, 6,526 samples of teachers' assessment tasks and associated student work from Primary 5 and Secondary 3 lessons in English, Social Studies, Mathematics, Science, Chinese Language, Malay Language, and Tamil Language in 59 Singapore schools (30 primary schools and 29 secondary schools) over 2 years (2004–2005) were collected and analyzed. At the same time, classroom observations were made in order to situate the instructional and formative practices of teachers with the assessment tasks. The types of assessment tasks included daily class work, homework assignments, major assignments/projects, and teacher-made tests.

The findings of this study were that assessment tasks focused heavily on assessing students' memorization of factual and procedural knowledge. The assessment tasks were found by the investigators to be of low authentic intellectual quality in all subject areas except for Primary 5 Social Studies, the only non-examinable subject in Singapore elementary schools in the study. The consequent student work demonstrated a high level of reproduction of factual and procedural knowledge. Likewise, a similar study in Hong Kong involving 300 teachers from 14 primary and secondary schools by Brown, Kennedy, Fok, Chan, and Yu (2009) found its sample of Hong Kong teachers to strongly associate using assessment to improve teaching and learning by making students accountable through examination preparation practices. From the study, Brown et al. (2009) suggested broader Chinese cultural norms concerning examinations to be a significant part of school culture that would impede the assessment reform agenda in Hong Kong and other Confucian societies such as Singapore (see Chapter 4 by Berry).

Such concerns over the prevailing negative effects of examination practices on students' learning prompted the MOE in Singapore to re-examine the relationship between assessment and learning in primary schools. In April 2009, the Primary Education Review and Implementation (PERI) Committee called for examinations for Primary 1 and 2 to be replaced by school-based holistic assessment practices to support learning. It was argued that in these early years (typically 7–8 years of age), too much emphasis on semestral examinations would impede students' confidence and desire to learn, and prevent students (and teachers) from understanding and using assessment to support and improve learning (Klenowski, 2009).

Such a decreased emphasis on semestral examinations provides opportunities for teachers to in turn emphasize AfL. However, recent studies would suggest that even formative assessment practices without overt high-stakes summative assessment pressures would be challenging in their own right. Webb and Jones (2009) reported a study in Jersey, United Kingdom, wherein activity theory was utilized to examine the formative assessment processes of six primary school teachers and their classes. Formative assessment was identified by the participating teachers as "a philosophy of learning focused on learners taking responsibility for their learning by developing understanding of what and how they were learning through a two way feedback process" (p. 176). The study revealed difficulties in dealing with "the contradiction between the culture in the existing classroom community and the new mediating artefacts, particularly peer feedback and dialogue" (p. 175). In particular, the teachers in the study voiced the need for ample time to establish an appropriate culture in the classroom community and emphasized the importance of attaining such conditions *before* formative assessment practice can be developed. It is not certain whether such conditions can be said to exist in Singapore schools for formative assessment practices to flourish.

6.3 What Does Formative Assessment Do for Learning in Singapore?

The TLLM initiative encapsulates new pedagogical aspirations in teaching and assessment in bringing about new levels of thinking and desired learning for students. It enjoys unprecedented levels of financial support and assumes the status of policy. For example the MOE announced in January 2008 generous resources over the next 3 years for schools embarking on TLLM initiatives (MOE, 2008). Ominously known as the "TLLM Ignite! Package", the recent initiative promises to provide up to 100 deserving schools each year with up to $15,000 per school as well as a range of human resource support and expertise.

The TLLM initiative hints at what assessment practice should be achieving from the viewpoint of enhanced pedagogy. On the website of the MOE (MOE, 2007), it is stated that assessment supporting enhanced pedagogy and learning in TLLM should be conducted "more qualitatively, through a wider variety of authentic means, over a period of time to help in their own learning and growth, and less quantitatively through one-off and summative examinations."

I argue that this not happening in Singapore schools. Instead, the intended "qualitative" approach to assessment is perverted by quality assurance pressures that distort and fragment what students actually learn.

There is a dominant quality assurance discourse in Singapore education in the form of excellence models, external validations and inspections of schools all based on performance indicators (Ng, 2003). Whilst assessment may provide a basis for assuring academic standards and reliable procedures may give the impression of good order, the presence of quality assurance processes on assessment does not in itself mean that there is good quality assessment practice. Instead, quality assurance procedures may have a potentially detrimental effect on student learning. Bloxham (2009, p. 214) warns of the following detrimental effects of quality assurance on students' learning:

- It creates an illusion of confidence which may skew assessment design away from that which supports learning towards that which provides certification and "quality assurance".
- Extensive external moderation may delay the return of work and accompanying feedback to students.
- Anonymous marking may render dislocation between tutor and students, and undermine the dialogic quality of feedback.

Ironically, such processes tend to look for quantifiable performance indicators which may or may not reflect the complexities and subtle nuances of quality change (Ng, 2008). This is especially true for TLLM and its consequent assessment discourse. Firstly, it should be pointed out that TLLM originated as a passing remark in a speech. Whilst it has subsequently been repeated and reconstructed as a policy, the term "Teach Less, Learn More" itself is nothing more than a slogan. And slogans face inherent limitations in articulating pedagogical guidelines and assessment reform (Tan, 2008).

A qualitative approach to assessment that TLLM requires emphasizes the holistic dimension of assessment and learning. Qualitative assessment may be described as assessment practices that encourage open-ended responses (as opposed to standardized instruments), permits meaningful student involvement (as opposed to unilateral testing) and takes place over a period of time (as opposed to controlled environments) in order to prompt, judge and enhance holistic understandings (Tan, 2007).

Can we claim that students in Singapore are prompted by assessment practices to achieve holistic understanding of different topics and ideas in relation to each other? A relational, holistic understanding of relevant concepts is indeed a tall order and a high ideal to strive for in assessment practice, and TLLM.

Tests and examinations are typically conducted in controlled environments and this is useful and convenient from the view of managing students and handling marking loads. The purpose of such assessment is not primarily intended to enhance the quality of student learning, but in the case of national examinations in particular to function as "gatekeepers to educational opportunities throughout the Singaporean education system" (Gregory & Clarke, 2003, p. 70). In Singapore, standardized tests and examinations are administered at different stages in the school system, and better students streamed into studies on the arts and sciences whilst weaker students are channelled to vocational-technical training (Tan, 2006b). The cost of emphasizing such clinical conditions for high-stakes assessment of learning is the tendency to isolate students through assessment practice and to give the impression that knowledge can be reduced to periods of intense examination. Because tests and examinations need to reduce the examination of learning to a fixed period of time, this in turn pressures the forms of learning to be demonstrated in isolated instances of different learning outcomes.

This impacts teaching and learning activities, often leading to the compartmentalization of the curriculum into disparate and unrelated segments. The compartmentalization of different topics into different questions avoids the needs for students to make connections of their knowledge. The increasing modularization of syllabi does not help either, creating artificial modularizations of knowledge with accompanying assessment practices isolated within artificial modularized boundaries. The resultant situation is akin to what Sadler (2007) describes as *decomposition*, of segmenting the whole into manageable units such that it is difficult to "the make the bits work together as a coherent learning experience that prepares learners to operate in intelligent and flexible ways" (p. 389). Consequently, students experience the curriculum in a linear fashion, moving from one topic to the next without necessarily making sense of the subject as a whole. More often than not, a reductionist view of learning is constructed and perpetuated.

6.4 What Should Assessment Reform Actually Do for Learning in Singapore?

Having examined the effects of high-stakes assessment and the limitations of formative assessment practices in schools, I now discuss the potential for orientating assessment practices in more constructive ways to enhance students' learning in Singapore. Three recommendations are made:

- Emphasizing clarity of standards for formative purposes of assessment and feedback
- Making formative assessment sustainable to enhance future learning
- Recognizing the importance of self-assessment in formative assessment

6.4.1 The Critical Need for Clear Standards in a Norm Referenced Assessment System

What are standards? In common discourse, standards are whether the results of a programme of study or an examination show a level of satisfaction/achievement. But in terms of functioning as a yardstick for gauging whether learning (or enhancement of learning) has actually taken place, standards need to be more unambiguously defined *before* tests and examinations.

Hawe (2002) describes standards-based assessment or standards-referenced assessment as emphasizing "explicit specification of standards, the use of teachers' qualitative judgments and development of shared understandings regarding the interpretation and operationalization of these standards" (p. 94). Buckles, Schug, and Watts (2001) argue that clear descriptions of standards of performance are important for informing students what they are expected to learn and how they should perform in their assessed work and for informing teachers how they can assess students accordingly.

Assessment for summative purposes can also be used for feedback, but only if certain conditions are present. For example, summative assessment which is purely norm-referenced and is not standards-based has poor clarity for offering feedback for enhancing learning.

Assessment in Singapore schools is commonly understood and labelled as either summative or formative. The annual examinations serve as a reference for describing all preceding forms of school assessment. Typically, assessment is described as continual assessment (CA) or semestral assessment (SA). Both CA and SA are viewed as summative assessment in view of the fact that the marks for both assessments count towards the final computation of a student's academic attainment. The final aggregate result is high stakes for students because it determines whether they can progress to the next academic year and their placement into an ability-differentiated class. Such high-stakes assessments are viewed as summative assessment. Any assessment that does not count towards the computation of marks for progression and placement is considered formative.

However, the backwash effect of high-stakes assessment in Singapore poses challenges to utilizing assessment, especially formative assessment practices, for enhancing learning in Singapore schools and classrooms. High-stakes national examinations do not report students' learning against pre-defined standards. Instead, each student is given a numerical score which represents his or her aggregate score for all examined subjects. This aggregate score is then used to rank students' eligibility for acceptance into his or her school of choice. It is used to discriminate an annual cohort of roughly fifty thousand students to decide on the allocation of school places based on the notion of meritocracy. But the aggregate score in itself does not indicate what, or how well, a student has learnt anything.

Preceding school assessment in Singapore is meant to prepare students for such a high-stakes examination, and the backwash effect of norm-referenced national assessment can be seen in numerous schools' practice of reporting their students' assessment outcomes in terms of *banding*, i.e., which discriminated level of students' academic achievement their results fall under. Such bands do not describe standards of learning, but merely pinpoint where they stand in relation to their peers' academic results. Such practices do not encourage students to understand standards in order to benefit from their teachers' feedback. Formative assessment practice is difficult, if not impossible, in such circumstances.

6.4.2 Formative Assessment Must Be Sustainable to Enhance Future Learning

Whilst the importance of formative AfL is commonly recognized in schools, the place and use of formative assessment for long term learning is not as obvious. Boud (2000) had identified formative assessment practices to be vital to achieving sustainable assessment but observed that discussion of formative assessment in the literature and in practice "has made relatively little contribution to current assessment thinking" and that "new thinking is therefore required to build sustainable assessment" (p. 159).

In this regard, a criticism may be levelled against purported formative assessment practices in Singapore for being myopic. Such formative and feedback practices focus unstintingly on assisting students to achieve better results in the next high-stakes assessment, but do not assist students to strengthen their capacity for learning beyond their formal education. The myopic attention to academic attainment raises questions about the quality of learning, and whether assessment practices may be said to displace learning under the guise of seeking to enhance the same learning. For example, Torrance (2007) warns of the possibility of over-emphasizing the detailed description of assessment criteria to be attained as a basis for "good" formative assessment practice. Instead, he warns that this may lead to unthinking compliance in assessment-driven learning, a phenomenon he describes as *assessment as (a substitute for) learning*.

The idea of sustainable assessment seeks to achieve present learning outcomes without compromising on students' capacity for future learning. Sustainable assessment can be understood as "assessment that meets the needs of the present without compromising the ability of students to meet their own future learning needs" (Boud, 2000, p. 151). Perhaps the most critical requirement for students to meet their own future learning needs is their capacity to judge what their own learning needs are and how they can go about meeting these needs. My view is that students will need to be involved in and empowered through assessment practices in order for suitable assessment to have a chance. Self-assessment ability is therefore a critical ingredient for students' lifelong learning.

6.4.3 The Importance of Self-Assessment in Formative Assessment

Student self-assessment is identified closely with effective formative assessment, i.e., assessment practices that emphasize the enhancement of learning. Both Sadler

(1998) and Black and Wiliam (1998) emphasize the need for formative assessment to involve students in generating and understanding feedback that explains the gap between the state revealed by feedback and the desired state. Sadler (1998) goes further by arguing that "any formative assessment that is not self-assessment involves (merely) communication... (and) that the communication is from the teacher to the learner" (p. 79). But how seriously should we take the notion of students assessing themselves in schools? If student self-assessment is understood as a pre-requisite for formative assessment to take place, then should it be optional or mandatory in schools? This question does not have unanimous consensus in the literature.

For example, some teachers may believe in the value of student self-assessment, but yet allow their students the option of not participating in self-assessment activities at all in order to lessen the disciplinary effects of self-assessment. Leach, Neutze, and Zepke (2001) advocate such an approach, arguing that self-assessment should be optional for learners and the freedom to choose whether or not to assess themselves represents a form of empowerment. I am generally hesitant about the notion of optional self-assessment being empowering for students and would not agree with this approach for two reasons.

Firstly, students who choose not to self-assess are not necessarily empowered since this decision may be a sign of their docile and disciplined condition in the first place. After all, it is not inconceivable that students will decide against self-assessing their work because they lack confidence, in themselves or in the teacher, to do so. Secondly, reducing self-assessment as an option contradicts the general consensus that self-assessment should be a central focus and attribute of formative assessment and education in general. I argue that self-assessment cannot be a critical element and an optional practice at the same time. If students are expected to be able to judge their own learning in order to understand and act on teachers' feedback, then self-assessment cannot be presented as an option for them to dismiss. Conversely, if self-assessment is a practice that can be ignored by students, then it is difficult for teachers to insist on it as part of their formative feedback practice.

6.5 Conclusion: Towards a Threshold of Sustainable Assessment in Singapore

In order for assessment to enhance imminent learning and safeguard students' capacity for future learning, there will need to be a different kind of assessment reform in Singapore. Such reform needs to be focused on establishing the quality and enhancement of students' learning as a priority, and needs to introduce changes that will unlock the true potential of formative assessment in Singapore schools. I argue that assessment reform needs a threshold concept in order to address structural obstacles to learning and unlock the true potential for assessment to enhance immediate and long term learning.

Meyer and Land (2003) coined the term "threshold" as a metaphor to describe a certain level of learning-gain such that passing through this threshold (portal) means that the learner acquires transformed capabilities in conceptualization. Such a threshold thus represents a gateway for the learner to understand the accompanying concepts and theories. Likewise, Davies and Brant (2006, p. 113) describe a threshold concept as presenting "levels of understanding in a subject (or activity) that can be used in assessment for learning".

Four attributes of threshold concepts are suggested by Meyer and Land (2003), and I shall use these attributes to expound what it would mean for assessment reform in Singapore to attain a threshold of sustainable assessment.

Firstly, a threshold level of assessment reform in Singapore needs to be *irreversible* so that new perceptions and understandings of what assessment should do for learning will not be reversed. Huge parental interests and anxiety in students' future careers often hinge on students' academic results in national examinations. Parents, as stakeholders, are not necessarily interested in utilizing assessment to enhance their children's learning. They are likely to be far more concerned whether assessment or AfL practices would jeopardize their children's academic results in any way. Assessment reform in Singapore should be directed towards achieving the present and future learning needs of students in ways that cannot be reversed or undermined by resistant parents.

Secondly, just as assessment should not atomize learning which is hitherto holistic and integrated, assessment reforms should also be coherent and *integrative.* Reformed assessment changes should seek to cohere assessment practices in schools. Just as learning and the curriculum should be holistic and understood in relation to its constituent parts, assessment practices should be designed and practised as an integrative whole to preserve the integrity of students' learning. This would go a long way towards preventing the atomizing of curriculum through assessment modularization.

Thirdly, assessment reform can be valuable as a catalyst for transforming the direction and value of education. To reframe assessment reform in a way that makes learning important, it is critical to recognize that assessment is bounded by, and therefore can act as the *pivot* for, the different forms of learning and understanding that a holistic education can bring about. Education in Singapore is essentially pragmatic, and assessment is seen as the most direct opportunity to secure sought-after school places, and eventually stable lucrative careers. Assessment reform that is directed at emphasizing the epistemological richness of learning different subjects and disciplines would instead redirect assessment outcomes from its regulatory features towards emphasizing its learning features (Boud, 2007).

Finally, assessment reform should be *potentially troublesome* in raising new perceptions that may be quite unfamiliar, or which raise new issues concerns. A well-regarded education system will find it hard to admit to areas for improvement, even if it implicitly does so by an unrelenting pursuit for continuous progress. However, the rhetoric of continual steady progress may sometimes disguise troubling issues which act against the direct interests of some students. Although there have been inevitable mistakes in educational policy over the years (Gopinathan, 1999), such admissions have not been publicly disclosed.

A threshold level of assessment reform would help to bring about a greater level of confidence, perhaps to a sufficient level of reassurance that would permit the MOE, schools leaders and teachers to publicly admit to troublesome issues to address in and through assessment practices. Just as formative assessment seeks to bridge the gap between present and desired levels of learning, a threshold of assessment reform can articulate the gap between the troublesome issues that plague assessment practices in Singapore schools and the desired levels of irreversible, pivotal and integrative learning that the nation and its learners may aspire to.

References

Black, P. J., & Wiliam, D. (1998). Assessment and classroom learning. *Assessment in Education: principles, policy and practice*, *5*(1), 7–75.

Bloxham, S. (2009). Marking and moderation in the UK: False assumptions and wasted resources. *Assessment and Evaluation in Higher Education*, *34*(2), 209–220.

Boud, D. (2000). Sustainable assessment: Rethinking assessment for the learning society. *Studies in Higher Education*, *22*(2), 151.

Boud, D. (2007). Reframing assessment as if learning were important. In D. Boud & N. Falchikov (Eds.), *Rethinking assessment in higher education: Learning for the Longer Term* (pp. 14–25). London: Routledge.

Brown, G., Kennedy, K., Fok, P. K., Chan, J., & Yu, W. M. (2009). Assessment for student improvement: Understanding Hong Kong teachers' conceptions and practices of assessment. *Assessment in Education: Principles, Policy and Practice*, *15*(3), 347–363.

Buckles, S., Schug, M., & Watts, M. (2001). A national survey of state assessment practices in the social studies. *Social Studies*, *92*(4), 141.

Davies, P., & Brant, J. (2006). *Business, economics and enterprise: Teaching school subjects 11–19*. London: Routledge.

Filer, A. (2000). *Assessment: Social practice and social product*. London: Routledge Falmer.

Goh, C. T. (1997). Shaping our future: Thinking schools, learning nation. SingaporeGovernment Press Release. Speech by Prime Minister Goh Chok Tong at the Opening of the 7th International Conference on Thinking, 2 June.

Gopinathan, S. (1999). Preparing for the next rung: Economic restructuring and educational reform in Singapore. *Journal of Education and Work*, *12*(3), 295–308.

Gopinathan, S. (2001). Globalisation, the state and education policy in Singapore. In J. Tan, S. Gpopinathan, & W. K. Ho (Eds.), *Challenges facing the Singapore education system today*. Singapore: Pearson Prentice Hall.

Gregory, K., & Clarke, M. (2003). High-stakes assessment in England and Singapore. *Theory into Practice*, *42*(1), 66–74.

Hawe, E. (2002). Assessment in a pre-service teacher education programme: The rhetoric and the practice of standards-based assessment. *Asia-Pacific Journal of Teacher Education*, *30*(1), 93–106.

Hogan, D., Towndrow, P., & Koh, K. (2009). The logic of confidence and the social economy of assessment reform in Singapore: A new institutionalist perspective. In E. Grigorenko (Ed.), *Assessment of abilities and competencies in the era of globalization*. New York: Springer.

Klenowski, V. (2009). Assessment for Learning revisited: An Asia-Pacific perspective. *Assessment in Education: Principles, Policy & Practice*, *15*(3), 263–268.

Koh, K., & Luke, A. (2009). Authentic and conventional assessment in Singapore schools: An empirical study of teacher assignments and student work. *Assessment in Education: Principles, Policy and Practice*, *16*(3), 291–318.

Leach, L., Neutze, G., & Zepke, N. (2001). Assessment and empowerment: Some critical questions. *Assessment and Evaluation in Higher Education*, *26*(4), 293–305.

Lee, H. L. (2004). Our future of opportunity and promise. Singapore Government Press Release. Address by PrimeMinister Lee Hsien Loong at the 2004 National Day Rally at the University Cultural Centre, National University of Singapore, 22 August.

Meyer, J. H. F., & Land, R. (2003). *Threshold concepts and troublesome knowledge: Linkages to ways of thinking and practising within disciplines* (Occasional Report No. 4). Swindon, UK: TLRP/ESRC.

Ministry of Education, Singapore (MOE). (1979). *Report on the ministry of education 1978*. Singapore: Author.

Ministry of Education, Singapore (MOE). (2007). What is Teach Less Learn More? http://www3.moe.edu.sg/bluesky/tllm.htm. Accessed 29 June 2009.

Ministry of Education, Singapore. (2008). More support for School's "Teach Less, learn More" initiatives: Ministry of Education Press Release.

Ng, P. T. (2003). The Singapore school and the school excellence model. *Educational Research for Policy and Practice, 2*(1), 27–39.

Ng, P. T. (2005). Students' perception of change in the Singapore education system. *Educational Research for Policy and Practice, 3*(1), 77–92.

Ng, P. T. (2008). Educational reform in Singapore: From quantity to quality. *Educational Research for Policy and Practice, 7*, 5–15.

Sadler, D. R. (1998). Formative assessment: Revisiting the territory. *Assessment in Education, 5*(1), 77–84.

Sadler, D. R. (2007). Perils in the meticulous specification of goals and assessment criteria. *Assessment in Education, 14*(3), 387–392.

Sellen, R., Chong, K., & Tay, C. (2006). Assessment shifts in the Singapore Education System. 2006 Annual IAEA Conference, Singapore.

Tan, C. (2006a). Education developments and reforms in Singapore. In C. Tan, B. Wong, J. Chua, & T. Kang (Eds.), *Critical perspectives on education*. Singapore: Pearson Prentice Hall.

Tan, C. (2006b). Creating thinking schools through "Knowledge and Inquiry": The curriculum challenges for Singapore. *The Curriculum Journal, 17*(1), 89–105.

Tan, K. H. K. (2007). In K. H. K. Tan (Ed.), *The case for qualitative approaches to assessment. Alternative assessment in schools: A qualitative approach*. Singapore: Pearson Education South Asia.

Tan, K. H. K. (2008). In J. Tan & P. T. Ng (Eds.), *Rethinking TLLM and its consequential effects on assessment. Thinking schools, learning nation: A decade of education reform in Singapore*. Singapore: Pearson Education.

Times Educational Supplement. (1997, Sept 16). Boost to morale on maths and science. *Times Educational Supplement*, 1.

Torrance, H. (2007). Assessment as learning? How the use of explicit learning objectives, assessment criteria and feedback in post-secondary education and training can come to dominate learning. *Assessment in Education: Principles, Policy and Practice, 14*(3), 281–294.

Trafford, V., & Leshem, S. (2009). Doctorateness as a threshold concept. *Innovations in Education and Training International, 46*(3), 305–316.

Webb, M., & Jones, J. (2009). Exploring tensions in developing assessment for learning. *Assessment in Education: Principles, Policy and Practice, 16*(2), 165–184.

Chapter 7
Assessment Reforms Around the World

Rita Berry

7.1 Introduction

In contrast to the pursuit of evidence at the end of the learning process, which largely defined the twentieth century approach of assessment, the international agenda for assessment in the twenty-first century shows signs of growing recognition of using assessment for learning purposes. There has been widespread call for new ways to think about assessment since high-stakes tests without supportive environments can harm learning (e.g. Black, 1998; Stiggins, 2004; Wiliam, 2006; see Chapter 11 by Scott). The calling has produced varied responses, ranging from a total abolition of high stake testing in some education systems to attempts to strike a balance between classroom and large-scale assessment in a synergistic system. Common to all these visions is the notion of assessment as a positive tool for learning and an interconnected part of teaching and learning. It is a pedagogy that is readily integrated into instructional designs (Berry, 2008). Over the last few decades, there have been waves of assessment reforms around the world. This chapter presents the assessment reforms in different educational contexts in different parts of the world. Selected cases will be presented to illuminate the issues brought to public attention in the reforms with a focus on assessment policies and practices. It examines the tensions and outcomes of assessment reform arising at the interface of policy and implementation and presents the experiences of some countries that turned the challenges into better teaching and learning opportunities.

7.2 The Changing Assessment Landscape in Europe, Americas and Australiasia

In the last half a century, Europe saw a number of education reforms that placed assessment reforms as an important issue on the reform agenda. In *Sweden*, for

R. Berry (✉)
Department of Curriculum and Instruction, Hong Kong Institute of Education, Tai Po, Hong Kong
e-mail: rsyberry@ied.edu.hk

R. Berry, B. Adamson (eds.), *Assessment Reform in Education*,
Education in the Asia-Pacific Region: Issues, Concerns and Prospects 14,
DOI 10.1007/978-94-007-0729-0_7,

example, the first wave of assessment reform began in the 1960s when there was a widespread belief that learning was something which could be quantified and measured. As a result, a norm-referenced grading system was introduced. Over the years of implementation, people constantly raised the question as to how much these grades could actually provide information about learning. With the view of knowledge and learning gradually migrating from positivistic and quantitative to hermeneutic and qualitative, the curriculum had become less focused on detailed knowledge and facts and more on constructs such as critical thinking, cooperation and problem solving. This resulted in the norm-referenced grading system being replaced by a goal-oriented, criterion-referenced one. Four grades were introduced to indicate progression of learning (IG – fail; G – pass; VG – pass with distinction; MVG – pass with special distinction) (Wikström, 2006). The idea is that the students should continue their education until at least a G grade has been reached and that the grade outcome should carry a formative function in addition to its designated summative use. Since the introduction of the criterion-referenced grade system, tests for scale calibration (the National Tests) have been available for the teachers to identify standards so that grades could be comparable. Still, teachers differed in scoring the tests as they had different interpretation of the rubrics (Nyström, 2004).

France initiated the "Haby" reform in 1975 with the goal of identifying and developing students' true talents (Brauns & Steinmann, 1999). Notable among these initiatives was the virtual abolition of all public examinations below the 18+ Baccalauréat level (the final school leaving examination) together with the regular promotion tests during the course of schooling and their replacement with continuous assessment by the teachers (Broadfoot, 1985). French teachers assess their own pupils informally on a regular basis through oral or written exercises in the classroom or through homework. There is formal assessment in the higher forms but the teachers are given free rein on the frequency of the assessment and how they are marked (Bonnet, 1997). The purpose of assessment is to use the information obtained to adapt teaching to the needs of the students. However, the judgments on on-going work are made on the same basis as summative judgments. There is little written feedback of a formative nature (Raveaud, 2004). A large number of the teachers feel the pressure brought about by the implementation of continuous assessment. They are neither committed to, nor prepared for, these responsibilities (Broadfoot, 1985). Given that high-stakes public examinations remained in place for school leavers, students and teachers generally prefer to work to the examinations with teaching and learning more focused on conventional types of knowledge and competence (Bonnet, 1997).

For a long time, *Germany* used a national 6-point marking system (grade 1–6, where 1 is the highest) to monitor students' achievements. Around 1960s, a strong critique of grades emerged because several empirical studies demonstrated that this form of assessment was not helpful for student learning (Ingenkamp, 1971). In addition, during this time, there was a shift in perceptions about learning that are commonly and internationally labelled as the need for "lifelong learning" and "learning-to-learn". Education reformers called for the abolition of grades and for the use of formative assessment. Consequently, several alternative tools for student assessment were proposed, all of which had a more formative focus, for example, in 1970, the Standing Conference of the Ministers of Education and Cultural Affairs of the Federal States of Germany (Kultusministerkonferenz, KMK) decided that marks should be substituted by verbal reports in elementary schools, at least in grades 1 and 2. This decision was intended to base assessment on individual progress instead of social comparisons. Empirical studies of the implementation and practice of verbal reports in elementary schools, however, showed that the reform was not working as hoped. Valtin (2002) and Wagner and Valtin (2003) analyzed the effects of different types of assessment (marks versus verbal reports) on the development of educational outcomes in elementary school. The research comprised 241 children from East and West Berlin who were tested several times, individually or in groups, from grade 2 to grade 4. The outcomes were about attitude toward learning and toward school subjects, academic self-concept, achievement motivation, test anxiety, intelligence, and academic achievement in mathematics and German. Contrary to researchers' predictions, students did not profit notably from verbal reports. One reason for these findings, the researchers reported, might be that the teachers only practiced formative assessment when writing the reports but not in everyday situations in the classroom.

Before the enactment of education reforms between 1981 and 1986, assessment in *Greece* had been very summative-oriented and used mainly for accountability and selection reasons. The assessment approaches varied from end of term to final examinations, using numerical or grading as the main methods of recording and reporting. The overarching aim of the education reform was to make a change to the then traditional pedagogy to a more progressive child-centred one (Ministry of Education 1985). The educational reform agenda included the abolition of formal assessments, examinations and grading and unobstructed promotion from level to level. Mavrommatis (1996) conducted a study to investigate the implementation of assessment in Greek classroom. Twenty teachers were observed and then interviewed to obtain a general picture of the assessment practice the teachers used to assess their students. To enhance understanding of teachers' assessment practices, 360 serving and prospective teachers were invited to complete a questionnaire. The study revealed a number of difficulties that constrained Greek teachers from a full implementation of the assessment reform initiatives. In the Greek classroom, comparisons between students were often found to be an underlying classroom goal although official guidelines advised teachers to avoid this. A few teachers involved in the study did try to use assessment to help individual students learn better. These teachers made an effort to help students see what their learning gaps were and to make them aware what could be done to close the gaps. However, the teachers said that they could only do this occasionally because the constraints of large class size and the time taken up in dealing with many other teaching duties. Other issues revealed by this study included teachers' feedback use and assessment criteria. It was found that feedback was too general and short and therefore most of the students could not work out what kinds of actions they needed to take to improve. The teachers found it hard to achieve a clear understanding of their students' progress as there was a lack of specific written reference criteria reflecting the national standards of prescribed objectives.

Believing that the school system developed for the period of dictatorship (1939–1975) was no longer appropriate for being a democratic member of the European Union, *Spain* initiated an education reforms in 1990 which held formative assessment at their heart. The first initiative in the reforms related to assessment included the abolition of the certification at the end of basic education. There is now only one state examination (*Selectividad*) which serves as the gateway to university education. Other times, assessment is classroom and teacher based. To investigate whether the formative assessment policy made an impact on teachers' assessment practice, Remesal (2007) interviewed fifty Spanish teachers. The results showed that there was a mismatch between the reform intentions and teachers' conceptions of assessment. The teachers, in particularly secondary school teachers, inclined strongly to associate assessment with accountability instead of linking assessment with teaching and learning.

As with Spain, *Portugal* saw the need to revamp its education system after the period of dictatorship. In 1986, the Assembly of the Republic of Portugal approved a four tier education system composing of (i) pre-school education (3–5 years old); (ii) basic education (6–14 years old); (iii) secondary education (15–17 years old); (iv) higher education (18 years old and above). From 1992 onwards, the Portugal government made it explicit in its legislation that formative assessment should prevail in the classroom at all grade levels, with the purpose of improving learning and teaching. According to the legislation, formative assessment should be an integral part of teaching and learning and be related to: (a) self-assessment and self-regulation of learning on the part of pupils; (b) the use of a diverse number of strategies and assessment instruments; (c) the participation of pupils and other intervening persons in the assessment process; (d) the transparency of procedures; (e) the definition of the criteria relative to developing competencies; and (f) the feedback that teachers should provide to their pupils in a systematic way (Fernandes, 2009a). However, Fernandes (2009b) found out in his study that formative assessment was yet to become a norm in teachers' classroom practices. Although most teachers in his study acknowledged the significance of formative assessment in student learning, they were in fact keener on designing tests simulating to those used in the external summative assessments.

Similar challenges have been identified in other countries in Europe and Americas. In *England*, Black and Wiliam (2005) point out that teachers' judgments do feed into national assessments, at 7, 11, 14 and 16, but concerns for reliability and accountability mean that such judgments are made in a way that has little impact on learning (see Chapter 2 by James). The government of *Netherlands* made schools accountable for student learning though it was met by widespread resentment from the teachers. Towards the end of the twentieth century, there was a growing pressure from the Dutch educational officials on schools to implement classroom assessment schemes based on norm-referenced tests. The purpose of the schemes was to systematically chart student learning progress over time. As the tests were standardized, it would be easier for the government to monitor school performance by comparing students' scores across schools. In *Russia,* the main purpose of the assessment reform is to use assessment as a means to promote national standards. The government was determined to prepare the students for the rapidly changing socio-economic conditions in Russia. In 2003, the government introduced a national system of student assessment in the final year of secondary schooling in Russia which aimed at setting minimal standards and providing the much needed credibility to nationally recognized certification. *Denmark* increasingly believes that students need more testing to excel. They think the undesirable results in the international comparisons resulted from a weak assessment culture. The government subsequently set up the Danish Evaluation Institute and is considering establishing a central specification of learning targets with a new marking scale (Egelund, 2005). In the *United States*, multiple demands for accountability lead the country into measuring the amount of learning that has taken place, which provides little insight into how it might be improved. The American vision of long-term stability as a value and a goal associated with education – an evolutionary not revolutionary approach to educational reform appears to have been interrupted by the urgency surrounding the demands of the "No Child Left Behind" Act of 2001 and its mandated thirst for large-scale assessment (Hess & Petrilli, 2006) (see Chapter 3 by Flaitz). Similar situation happened in Latin America where *Brazil* and *Chile* also used assessment as mechanisms to monitor education systems (Carrasco & Torrecilla, 2009; Guimarães de Castro, 2001).

Although the above-mentioned countries undertook different initiatives in their assessment reforms, most of them shared one commonality – advocating the use of assessment for learning. With all these good intentions, the results of the reforms showed that there were tensions between government assessment policies and classroom assessment practices. Teachers were still inclined very strongly to associate assessment with accountability instead of linking assessment with teaching and learning.

Some countries achieved better outcomes in their assessment reforms. In 1968, *Finland* underwent an education reform with continuous assessment being used at the basic school level for guidance and encouragement purposes and on student learning and growth (Frassinelli, 2006). All assessment of student learning is based on teacher-made tests, rather than standardized external tests. The teachers viewed regularly scheduled teacher-made classroom tests as opportunities for learning as much as for assessing student achievement. Grades are prohibited by law and only descriptive assessments and feedback are employed (Sahlberg, 2009). The non-grade approach is to encourage students to become responsible, make their own decisions, and learn to plan their own life (Aho, Pitkänen & Sahlberg, 2006). In recent years, the focus of reform has been on the need for new type of life-long professional training for teachers to include up-to-date research, virtual learning environments and changes in the work force. It is worth noting that Finland relates the success also to their dedicated teachers who are willing to continuously strive for professionalism. Finland related its excellent student results of the Programme for International Student Assessment (PISA) in 2000 and 2003 to the success of its national school reform.

Canada advocated striking a balance between large-scale testing and classroom assessment and to use both to facilitate student learning. Common features among jurisdictions in the Canadian Report prepared by the Council of Ministers of Education in 2005 include:

- providing tools teachers need to develop and implement a well-planned student evaluation program that uses assessment techniques for formative, diagnostic and summative purposes;
- developing achievement standards for subject and grade specific courses that are supported by formative and summative assessment tools;
- promoting alternative approaches to student assessment and the education of educational personnel to adopt and effectively utilize such practices in the classroom;
- providing rubrics and exemplars to teachers as guides to varying levels of student performance;
- developing provincial processes regarding the assessment of learners;
- providing sample assessment strategies for classroom use;
- providing teacher professional development opportunities for all teachers; and
- promoting the use of criterion-referenced evaluation as a means of classroom-based evaluations.
- using the results of large scale assessments in a formative manner to guide academic intervention initiatives and to improve student learning.

(Council of Ministers of Education, 2005)

Beginning in the 1990s, in Canada, province-wide assessment systems were in place in most provinces for measuring and reporting on student achievement in literacy and mathematics at the school, school district and provincial levels (Dunleavy, 2007). In the classroom, the government advised that assessment should make up a large part of the school day, not in the form of separate tests, but as a seamless part of the learning process (Friesen, 2009). An important key to shifting the classroom, school, or district to a stronger learning orientation is to focus professional learning towards a passionate interest in helping learners become more self-regulated, more motivated, and more successful, which many schools across Canada were engaged in helping learners achieve this goal (Kaser & Halber, 2008).

New Zealand, influenced by local and overseas developments, in particular from the United Kingdom (see Chapter 2 by James) and to a lesser extent Australia (see Chapter 5 by Klenowiski), implemented its major curriculum and assessment reforms affecting primary and secondary schools in 1989 (Philips, 2000). From this time, school curricula have been extensively restructured listing achievements objectives by levels (1–8). Criterion-reference (more commonly called "standards-based assessment" locally) was introduced to replace norm-referenced assessment. The main rationale for these changes was to improve student learning through better designed and more focused teaching and assessment programmes. The programmes were seen as helping teachers as they provide them with a more structured system for guiding teaching and monitoring students' learning progress. With the encouragement from the Ministry of Education and the Education Review Office, teachers and schools tried to come to grips with the new system. To implement the assessment initiatives successfully, Crooks (2002) drew teachers and researchers' attentions to some details in assessing students.

- The teacher's judgement might be made on the basis of just one task, yet many tasks could be developed for the objective and students would perform differently on different tasks.
- Children who could do a particular task on 1 day often could not do that task or a very similar one the next day.
- Trying to complete this process for all the achievements objectives in the primary school curriculum for a particular class was overwhelmingly time consuming and threatened the quality of teaching.
- There were major difficulties in summarizing student performance by aggregating across achievement objectives in a curriculum strand or whole curriculum areas, with student performance fluctuating markedly across objectives.
- Teachers differed considerably in the standards they set for judging what an objective had been met or a level achieved.
- The gap between adjacent levels (2 years of normal progress) was too large to give a satisfying sense of progress (pp. 243–244).

7.3 The Assessment Reform Experiences in Asia and Africa

Asia has a long tradition of using examinations to select government officials and to assign people of different talents to different professions. On record, China was the first country that used scholastic achievement tests as a means to select its civil servants (Han & Yang, 2001). From Western Zhou, the first dynasty in China over 2,000 years ago, to Qing Dynasty, the last dynasty in Chinese history, imperial examinations were used frequently for selection purposes (Berry, 2008). The imperial examination system had a far reaching impact on its neighbours, as countries such as Vietnam, Korea and Japan established their own imperial examination system based on the ideas borrowed from China (Wang, 2008). In *Vietnam*, beginning in the eleventh century, the examinations were conducted personally by successive kings who pursued Confucian ideals (Broadfoot, 2009). As with the countries in the western world, Asian countries underwent educational reforms with new policies set for assessing their students. The reforms in *Mainland China, Hong Kong* and *Taiwan* aim at making a change to the examination-oriented education to an education that is aimed at all-round development in students. Teachers are encouraged to use assessment to enhance teaching and learning. However, the findings of a number of studies revealed that there were gaps between intentions and reality. In many classrooms, teaching was still very examination-driven (see Chapter 4 by Berry).

South Korea experienced a widespread expansion of education between 1945 and 1970, when the government decided to establish a national education system that aimed at providing educational opportunities to all school aged children and high quality human resources to the society. The system, highly centralized, is responsible for developing national level standardized tests and diagnostic tests for basic skills of elementary students. The college entrance examination is extremely high-stakes. Most South Korean students spend their entire high school life preparing for this examination. Fierce competition amongst students was overtly encouraged. To achieve good results, students attend privately owned institutions after school. Statistics showed that seven out of ten students receive private tutorial for an average of 6.8 h a week and private expenditure for education accounts for an average 12.7% of household expenses (Na, 2005). In the international comparative tests, South Korean students outperformed many of their counterparts from the resource affluent countries. Given the amount of stress that the students face, the price of success is quite high. South Korean high school students suffer from high rates of depression and suicide cases particularly around times of major examinations.

In *Japan,* the secondary school and university entrance examinations exert considerable influence on assessment practices in the classroom. To prepare students for the examinations, Japanese school teachers have traditionally relied heavily on summative assessment of student learning. Standardized paper-and-pencil tests are the most common form of assessment used in the school. Assessment has been and remains dominated by teacher-centred practices (White, 2009). There were some individual attempts to make assessment serve teaching and learning. Yoshinori and some of his colleagues used extended assessment tasks to facilitate deep thinking. In the process, the educators became aware of what their students needed and used the information to improve teaching (Shimizu & Lambdin, 1997). The major assessment reform agenda in Japan was in higher education in the 1990s with "Outcomes Assessment" as the main reform focus. Universities were required to constantly check their activities and enhance the quality of education by themselves (Kiamura, 1997). It was a response to a twofold interpretation of assessment needs realized in Japan about a decade ago. The interpretation tried to address two issues – "accountability" and "student active learning". Japanese universities had been described as "hard to enter, easy to graduate from" and it was deemed necessary to monitor the quality of tertiary education through outcomes assessment. The change was also a response to a paradigm shift in higher education. When the focus of education moves from "instruction by the teacher" to "learning by the student", it was deemed necessary to understand student learning through outcomes-based assessment. The national survey conducted in Japan however revealed that the assessment used might not have helped improve education (Kushimoto, 2009).

Like most of its counterparts in Asia, *Malaysia* has a very examination-oriented education system. There are four public examinations in the system – the elementary school achievement test (end of Primary 6), the lower secondary examination (end of Form 3), the Malaysian certificate of education (end of Form 5) and the higher education certificate (Form 6). Examination results are determinants of students' progression to higher levels of education or occupational opportunities. Malaysia does have school-based assessment that aims at monitoring students' learning growth. However, pressure on teachers to produce high test performance results in much teaching to the test and designing tests mimicking the centralized examinations. To address the growing societal dissatisfaction over the examination system, the Minister of Education instituted several changes to improve the assessment system including placing assessment for learning as one major focus of change. In 2007, the Malaysian government recommended expanding school-based assessment and alternative assessment to provide more holistic and accurate judgments of student performance. Several challenges were perceived for successful implementation of the reform including resistance to change, the knowledge and skills of the teachers who are the assessors and the resource implications of the change (Ong, 2010).

Education in *Thailand* is centralized with a national curriculum to stipulate educational standards. Traditional paper-and-pencil tests, usually multiple-choice given at the end of learning, are normal assessment practice. The recent 1990 national curriculum states that teaching and learning activities at any level of education must emphasize "learning to think, to do and to solve problems" and that teachers must deliver instruction so as to encourage the integration of learning to know and learning to or to act (Pitiyanuwat, 2007). The Department of Curriculum and Instruction Development (CID) of the Ministry of Education is responsible for conducting a national assessment of learning outcomes at the end of elementary education (grade 6), lower secondary education (grade 9) and upper secondary education (grade 12). The aim of the assessment is to provide information for determining the standard of learning outcomes. In the classroom, teachers are advised to use formative assessment to decide the next steps for teaching, diagnostic assessment to determine what students need to improve on and summative assessment to inform the level of attainment of the students. To understand how teachers integrated assessment into teaching and learning activities, the CID conducted a pilot study in 1994. A number of assessment strategies were used including tests focusing on the skills and concepts of the subject matters and related skills, observation of practical work by the teacher, student written work, student self-assessment, and student report and records. It was found that students worked quite well in this new mode of learning. They became more self-directed. However, the CID noticed that there were some practical issues that needed attention, including providing professional training for teachers in their new roles in assessing as part of teaching, enhancing the collaboration between parents and the schools and taking actions to address large class size and teachers' workload. For the first issue, specifically, the CID advised that teachers should be helped to develop better instructional plans and to give quality advice to students. Teachers also needed training in developing sound authentic performance tests (open-ended paper-and-pencil tests and practical tests) and marking criteria (rubrics) and in recognizing the potential for embedded assessments as part of instruction (Pravalpruk, 1999).

In *Indonesia*, the education system underwent a radical change in the twenty-first century. This reform was marked by the implementation of school-based management, which included redefining the national education objectives, decentralizing management from the government of schools and implementing the 2004 Curriculum. In the past, the Indonesian education system placed a heavy emphasis on cognitive attainment by students (Muhaimin & Ali, 2001). The new curriculum aims at promoting students' ability in applying knowledge in real life situations and calls for teachers' to use classroom-based assessment to support learning.

A widespread feeling is that continuous professional growth of teachers and strong school management leadership are the keys to the successful implementation of the reforms (Raihani, 2007).

In Africa, *Ghana* on the western coast of Africa had their most recent education reforms beginning in 1987 with an aim to address problems including low participation, curriculum dysfunctionality, gender disparity, rural-urban dichotomy etc. (Kwawukume, 2006). The Programme for Free Compulsory Universal Basic Education was passed by parliament in 1995 and now forms the basis of educational planning in the country. Continuous Assessment was introduced, which made the role of assessment become potentially more formative (Pryor & Akwesi, 1998). Akyeampong, Pryor, and Ghartey (2006) conducted a study investigating Ghanaian teachers' understanding of learning, teaching and assessment. It was found that the assessment teachers used was largely summative and suspected that this might result from teachers' lack of confidence and knowledge in using assessment for learning purposes. *Egypt* discussed the curriculum reform in 1993 aiming at moving children away from rote memorization and passive learning through teacher transmission, towards the model of active individual learning. To be in line with the visions of the new curriculum, assessment had to be changed (Ministry of Education, Egypt, 1995). However, the accountability and the unchallengeable rationality of the examination system left most people unable to act freely (Hargreaves, 2001). In *South Africa*, the government used continuous assessment as a means to reduce pressure from teachers and pupils but the opposite was found to be true in many schools. There was evidence to show that teacher produced tests modeling the matriculation examinations to prepare students for this high stakes university entrance examination. This increased the intensity of pressure (Lubisi & Murphy, 2002).

Generally speaking, the countries of Confucian heritage share a deep-rooted examination culture. Mainland China, Taiwan, Hong Kong, South Korea, Japan, Malaysia, Singapore (see Chapter 6 by Tan), Vietnam, Philippines and a number of other Asian countries all have examination systems that serve accountability and selection purposes. As the stakes are extremely high, schools, teachers and parents alike view preparing students for the public examinations as the ultimate goal for education. Recently, many of these countries saw the need to change this to an assessment culture that is aimed at enhancing students' all-round skills, promoting whole-person development and recognizing and developing different talents in students. Owing to their individual social, economic and educational circumstances, the countries in Asia and Africa planned and implemented their assessment reforms in their own distinctive ways but generally found tensions between the assessment reform policies and assessment practices.

7.4 Conclusion and Implications

Over centuries, assessment has been mainly used for selection and accountability purposes in the eastern and western worlds. The social and economical demands in the nineteenth century created an increasing need for trained workers of different trades for which a standardized examination system was identified as being useful for screening and streaming purposes. In time, people became aware of the problems of high-stakes examinations and realized that, other than for selection and accountability, assessment can be used as a tool to support learning and enhance teaching. Most countries embarked on an education reform with a highly emphasised *Assessment for Learning* agenda. The highlights of this agenda include reducing excessive use of tests and examinations, and using assessment to understand and support learning, as well as using student information to improve teaching. Assessment must be consistent with the objectives of what is taught and learnt. Teachers are encouraged to use a variety of assessment strategies and assessment tasks to allow a range of different learning outcomes to be assessed. In the last few decades, there was a shift in perceptions about learning that are commonly and internationally labelled as the need for "lifelong learning", "learning-to-learn" and "whole-person development". Many countries highlighted in their assessment policies the need to promote learner autonomy, a key element of the above mentioned concepts. In their official documents, these governments specified the use of self- and peer-assessment to increase learners' metacognitive abilities so that learners can take control and manage their own learning. As students' diverse needs have got more recognized, teachers are advised to differentiate assessment strategies and tasks to identify learning needs and use them to cater for specific needs. Teachers should use assessment to develop students' potential in different perspectives. The assessment methods and tasks to be used are varied, allowing different perspectives of learning to be facilitated and acknowledged. Basically, teachers are advised to use the information obtained to adapt teaching to the needs of the students and to change the traditional form of assessment to a more child-centred and formative one.

After years of implementation, there was evidence to show that there had been limited changes in classroom assessment practices. In general, there was over-emphasis on the grading function and under-emphasis on the learning function. The international comparison results did little to help establish an assessment for learning culture. In a number of countries, faith in assessment for learning was considerably undermined by unfavourable international comparisons. Some countries held schools and teachers accountable for the performance of their students in the standardized inter-school comparative tests. Consequently, although many teachers acknowledged the significance of formative assessment in student learning, teaching was still very much test-oriented. To help students achieve good results, a common practice was designing tests simulating the high-stakes external examination and on teaching conventional types of knowledge and competence. The above mentioned depicts a rather gloomy picture for advocates of assessment for learning reforms, as the good intentions appear to have been threatened by the worldwide dominance of high stakes summative discourse and the issues of accountability. Assessment for learning may become a major casualty of a heavily centralized education system torn between tradition and change.

The brighter side of the assessment reform movements is that the assessment landscape worldwide is gradually changing and the learning function of assessment is gaining better recognition in many education contexts. Some countries reported success in their assessment reforms. Common to these countries are the values they see in their teachers and emphasized offering life-long professional training for teachers. Many teachers are in fact very enthusiastic about the ideas of using assessment for learning purposes. They are very willing to try out the assessment for learning concepts although generally find it rather hard to fight the examination culture and the pressure of accountability (Berry, 2010). The current problem is the widespread perception of high-stakes public examinations, believing that they are the best vehicle to boost national performances. Reviews (Black & Wiliam, 1998; Crooks, 1988; Natriello, 1987) provide clear evidence that improving the quality of formative assessment was the key to increasing student achievement. Black and Wiliam (1998) found that improvements in the quality of formative assessment resulted in effect sizes of the order of 0.4–0.7 standard deviations (equivalent to doubling the rate of learning). A more recent review of the literature on the effects of feedback and formative assessment in post-secondary education (Nyquist, 2003) found effects of similar magnitude, and, perhaps more significantly, showed that the larger effect sizes were associated with stronger implementations of the principles of assessment for learning. To improve student achievement across the curriculum, it is suggested that improving teacher quality and their capacity to use assessment as central to learning may be the most effective way to attain this goal. To make assessment a useful tool for teaching and learning, it is necessary to empower the teachers with knowledge and skills (Berry, 2011). What the teachers urgently need are, in addition to the overarching assessment policies, guidelines and directives, concrete ideas on how to translate the assessment for learning concepts into classroom actions, including, for example, detailed techniques for implementing assessment for learning in classroom situations (see Chapter 4 by Berry and Chapter 8 by Gardner et al.).

References

Aho, E., Pitkänen, K., & Sahlberg, P. (2006). Policy development and reform principles of basic and secondary education in Finland since 1968. World Bank. http://siteresources.worldbank.org/EDUCATION/Resources/278200-1099079877269/547664-1099079967208/Education_in_Finland_May06.pdf. Accessed 28 July 2010.

Akyeampong, K., Pryor, J., & Ghartey, A. J. (2006). A vision of successful schooling: Ghanaian teachers' understandings of learning, teaching and assessment. *Comparative Education, 42*(2), 155–176.

Berry, R. (2008). *Assessment for learning*. Hong Kong: Hong Kong University Press.

Berry, R. (2010). Teachers' orientations towards selecting assessment strategies. *New Horizons in Education, 58*(1), 96–107.

Berry, R. (2011). Assessment Trends in Hong Kong: Seeking to establish formative assessment in an examination culture. *Assessment in Education: Principles, Policy & Practice, 18*(2).

Black, P. J. (1998). *Testing: Friend or Foe? Theory and practice of assessment and testing*. London: The Falmer Press.

Black, P., & Wiliam, D. (2005). Lessons from around the world: How policies, politics and cultures constrain and afford assessment practices. *Curriculum Journal, 16*(2), 249–261.

Black, P. J., & Wiliam, D. (1998). Inside the black box: Raising standards through classroom assessment. *Phi Delta Kappan, 80*(2), 139–148.

Bonnet, G. (1997). Country profile from France. *Assessment in Education: Principles, Policy & Practice, 4*(2), 295–306.

Brauns, H., & Steinmann., S. (1999). Educational reform in France, West Germany and the United Kingdom: Updating the CASMIN educational classification. *ZUMA-Nachrichtung, 44*, 7–44.

Broadfoot, P. (1985). *Recent Developments in Assessment and Examination Procedures in France.* Paper presented at the Annual Meeting of the American Educational Research Association.

Broadfoot, P. (2009). Foreword. In C. Wyatt-Smith & J. Cumming (Eds.), *Educational assessment in the 21st century: Connecting theory and practice*. London, New York: Springer.

Carrasco, M. R., & Torrecilla, F. J. M. (2009). Learning assessment in Latin America. School performance behaviour and trends of Latin American pupils in primary and secondary education. *Educational Sciences Journal, 9*, 31–46.

Council of Ministers of Education. (2005). OECD Study on enhancing learning through formative assessment and the expansion of teacher repertoires: Canadian Report. http://www.cmec.ca/Publications/Lists/Publications/Attachments/78/OECD_Formative.en.pdf. Accessed 25 July 2010.

Crooks, T. J. (1988). The impact of classroom evaluation practices on students. *Review of Educational Research, 58*(4), 438–481.

Crooks, T. J. (2002). Educational assessment in New Zealand schools. *Assessment in Education: Principles, Policy & Practice, 9*(2), 237–253.

Dunleavy, J. (2007). Public Education in Canada: Facts, Trends and Attitudes. Canadian Education Association.

Egelund, N. (2005). Educational assessment in Danish schools. *Assessment in Education: Principles, Policy & Practice, 12*(2), 203–212.

Fernandes, D. (2009a). Educational assessment in Portugal. *Assessment in Education: Principles, Policy & Practice, 16*(2), 227–247.

Fernandes, D. (2009b). Learning assessment in Portugal: Research and activity theory. *Sísifo. Educational Science Journal, 9*, 87–98.

Frassinelli, L. (2006). Educational reform in Finland. https://www.msu.edu/user/frassine/EAD845%20-%20Educational%20Reform%20in%20Finland.pdf. Accessed 28 July 2010.

Friesen, S. (2009). *What did you do in school today? Teaching effectiveness: A framework and rubric.* Toronto, ON: Canadian Education Association.

Guimarães de Castro, M. H. (2001). Education assessment and information systems in Brazil. *Instituto Nacional de Estudos e Pesquisas Educacionais Anísio Teixeira.* http://www.inep.gov.br/download/internacional/idioma/Education%20Assessment%20and%20information%20systems%20in%20brazil.pdf. Accessed 28 April 2010.

Han, M., & Yang, X. (2001). Educational assessment in China: Lessons from history and future prospects. *Assessment in Education: Principles, Policy & Practice, 8*(1), 5–10.

Hargreaves, E. (2001). Assessment in Egypt. *Assessment in Education: Principles, Policy & Practice, 8*(2), 247–260.

Hess, F. M., & Petrilli, M. J. (2006). *No child left behind.* New York: Peter Lane.

Ingenkamp, K. (1971). *Die Fragwürdigkeit der Zensurengebung*. Weinheim: Beltz.

Kaser, L., & Halber, J. (2008). From sorting to learning: Developing deep learning in Canadian schools. *Education Canada, 48*(5), 56–59.

Kiamura, K. (1997). Policy issue in Japanese higher education. *Higher Education, 34*, 141–150.

Kushimoto, T. (2009). Outcomes assessment and its role in self-reviews of undergraduate education: In the context of Japanese higher education reforms since the 1990s. *Higher Education, 59*, 589–598.

Kwawukume, V. (2006). *Assessment for improving learning*. Paper presented at the 32nd Annual Conference of the International Association for Educational Assessment (IAEA), Singapore.

Lubisi, R. C., & Murphy, R. J. L. (2002). Assessment in South African schools. *Assessment in Education: Principles, Policy & Practice, 9*(2), 255–268.

Mavrommatis, Y. (1996). Classroom assessment in Greek primary schools. *Curriculum Journal, 7*(2), 259–269.

Ministry of Education, Egypt. (1995). *Mubarak's national project.* Cairo: MoE.

Ministry of Education: Law 1566. (1985) Nomos Plaisio yia tin paidia no 1566. (Education Act, 1566). Athens: OEDB.

Muhaimin, S. A., & Ali, N. (2001). *Paradigma Pendidikan Islan: Upaya Mengefektifkan Pendidikan Agama Islam di Sekolah*. Bandung: Rosda Karya.

Na, J. (2005). The Asian Craze for Education. http://gunsandbutter.blogspot.com/2005/05/asian-craze-for-education.html. Accessed 28 July 2010.

Natriello, G. (1987). The impact of evaluation processes on students. *Educational Psychologist*, *22*(2), 155–175.

Nyquist, J. B. (2003). *The benefits of reconstruing feedback as a larger system of formative assessment: A* meta-analysis. Unpublished master's thesis, Vanderbilt University, Nashville, TN.

Nyström, P. (2004). *Rätt mätt på prov: om validering av bedömningar i skolan* [Validation of educational assessments] (Umeå, Umeå University, Department of Education).

Ong, S. L. (2010). Assessment profile of Malaysia: High-stakes external examinations dominate. *Assessment in Education: Principles, Policy & Practice*, *17*(1), 91–103.

Philips, D. (2000). Curriculum and assessment policy in New Zealand: Ten years of reforms. *Educational Review*, *52*(2), 143–153.

Pitiyanuwat, S. (2007). School assessments in Thailand: Roles and achievement of ONESQA. *Educational Research for Policy and Practice*, *6*(3), 261–279.

Pravalpruk, S. W. (1999). Learning and assessment in the science classroom in Thailand. *Assessment in Education: Principles, Policy & Practice*, *6*(1), 75–82.

Pryor, J., & Akwesi, C. (1998). Assessment in Ghana and England: Putting reform to the test of practice. *A Journal of Comparative and International Education*, *28*(3), 263–275.

Raihani. (2007). Education reforms in Indonesia in the twenty-first century. *International Education Journal*, *8*(1), 172–183.

Raveaud, M. (2004). Assessment in French and English infant schools: Assessing the work, the child or the culture? *Assessment in Education*, *11*(2), 193–212.

Remesal, A. (2007). Educational reform and primary and secondary teachers' conceptions of assessment: The Spanish instance, building upon Black and Wiliam (2005). *Curriculum Journal*, *18*(1), 27–38.

Sahlberg, P. (2009). A short history of educational reform in Finland. http://192.192.169.112/filedownload/%E8%8A%AC%E8%98%AD%E6%95%99%E8%82%B2/A%20short%20history%20of%20educational%20reform%20in%20Finland%20FINAL.pdf. Accessed 28 July 2010.

Shimizu, Y., & Lambdin, D. V. (1997). Assessing students' performance on an extended problem-solving task: A story from a Japanese classroom. *Mathematics Teacher*, *90*, 658–664.

Stiggins, R. (2004). New assessment beliefs for a new school mission. *Phi Delta Kappan*, *86*(1), 22–27.

Valtin, R. (2002). *Was ist ein gutes Zeugnis? Noten und verbale Beurteilungen auf dem Prüfstand*. Weinheim: Juventa.

Wagner, C., & Valtin, R. (2003). Noten oder Verbalbeurteilungen? Die Wirkung unterschiedlicher Bewertungsformen auf die schulische Entwicklung von Grundschulkindern. *Zeitschrift fürEntwicklungspsychologie und Pädagogische Psychologie*, *35*, pp. 27–36.

Wang, D. (2008). On the international influence of the Chinese imperial systems. *Hubei Normal University Journal (Educational Science Issue)*, *10*(1), 71–74 (in Chinese).

White, E. (2009). Student perspectives of peer assessment for learning in a public speaking course. *Asian EFL Journal*, *33*, 1–36.

Wikström, C. (2006). Education and assessment in Sweden. *Assessment in Education: Principles, Policy & Practice*, *13*(1), 113–128.

Wiliam, D. (2006). Formative assessment: Getting the focus right. *Educational Assessment*, *11*(3/4), 283–289.

Part II
Issues in the Spotlight

Chapter 8
Engaging and Empowering Teachers in Innovative Assessment Practice

John Gardner, Wynne Harlen, Louise Hayward, and Gordon Stobart

8.1 Introduction

As our understanding of the role of assessment in learning increases, assessment by teachers has taken on new importance in schools and indeed in education systems as a whole. External testing has created a situation, especially in England (see Every Child Matters (Department for Children & Schools and Families, 2004)) and the USA (see No Child Left Behind (US Department of Education, 2002); see Chapter 3 Flaitz), in which schools are forced continuously to improve their performance and that of their students by striving for externally imposed targets and standards. The problems that arise include "... teaching to the test, narrowing the curriculum and focusing disproportionate resources on borderline pupils" (House of Commons, 2008, p. 93). Problems of meaning, validity and reliability have also dogged such systems with Stobart (2008), Mansell (2007) and Harlen and Deakin Crick (2003) taking particular issue with the negative impacts of testing. External testing will always be a feature of most education systems and when they are carried out and used appropriately they are perfectly acceptable. However, the Assessment Reform Group (Harlen, 2007) have clearly demonstrated in their Assessment Systems of the Future project, that the complementary and currently under-developed role of assessment by teachers holds out the promise of assessment being much more integrated into the classroom and learning context in the future. One of the challenges in achieving this potential is to find the best means to engage and empower the teachers involved.

Across the UK, a number of research and development projects have considered how to engage teachers more formally in assessment in schools. These projects have been initiated in response to renewed interest in the role of teachers not only in using assessment *for* learning (AfL), where the assessment is integrated into classroom teaching, but also in assessment *of* learning, where teachers make dependable assessments of students' learning for reporting to the students or other stakeholders.

J. Gardner (✉)
School of Education at Queen's University, Belfast, Northern Ireland, UK
e-mail: j.gardner@qub.ac.uk

R. Berry, B. Adamson (eds.), *Assessment Reform in Education*,
Education in the Asia-Pacific Region: Issues, Concerns and Prospects 14,
DOI 10.1007/978-94-007-0729-0_8,

Yet some of these initiatives have had less success than might have been expected in implementation on a wider scale despite having considerable influence on those involved in their development.

The Analysis and Review of Innovations in Assessment project (ARIA, funded by the Nuffield Foundation over an 18 month period from 2006 to 2008) set out to explore these initiatives and to glean from them the key issues for the effective promotion of assessment by teachers. To focus closely on these factors, ARIA selected 13 initiatives (listed in the Appendix) from all four countries of the UK: England, Wales, Scotland and Northern Ireland. A variety of aspects relating to two key questions were explored[1]. These were:

1. How can assessment by teachers be improved for formative and summative purposes? ARIA aimed to provide insights into professional development approaches that enable teachers to ensure their formative and summative assessments are effective.
2. What facilitates the dissemination of improved practice in assessment by teachers? ARIA sought to identify the factors that facilitate or hinder the successful uptake of assessment by teachers and schools, leading to improved learning and raised standards.

The research design chosen for the project was a "Consultation with Experts" study. This process involves the gathering of empirical research reports and related publications from the selected initiatives and then analyzing them to reveal their key features. These are then subjected to discussion and development by experts, to seek a convergent view on their relative importance and how improvement or progress may be advanced. The sequence is set out below:

- Published and other written materials relating to the initiatives were sourced and reviewed by the research team.
- Synoptic overviews of each initiative were developed and circulated for internal project discussion.
- The overviews were used to create working papers for discussion by over 200 experts in invitational seminars held in each of the four UK countries.
- The early seminars involved key people from the initiatives (project leaders, teachers, evaluators etc) and experts drawn from the practitioner, professional support, academic and policy making communities.
- As a result of new insights gained from each seminar, the initial working papers were further developed and new working papers on emerging themes were commenced. In parallel, an interview survey of 35 participants across the initiatives was undertaken to deepen the empirical base for the work.

[1] A third key question, not reported upon here, related to how policy on assessment by teachers needs to change at system level to ensure there is a productive balance between accountability in terms of standards and the quality of student learning.

- Towards the end of the project the seminars were used to challenge and refine the emerging conclusions, informing and culminating in the project group's agreed findings and implications.

One of the main benefits of this approach to examining developments in the classroom and schools is that it can aim to establish a degree of consensus across cognate (i.e., education-related) but differently focused groups such as practitioners, policy-makers and academics. That is not to say, however, that the conclusions of this study attract the endorsement, in whole or in part, of each member of each seminar or initiative. Rather it is a synthesis developed by the project group itself. The chapter is structured in two main parts: *Review of Innovations in Assessment Initiatives across the UK* and *Insights from the Expert Seminars.*

8.2 Review of Innovations in Assessment Initiatives Across the UK

There were a number of common findings in the reviews of the various initiatives, identified through interviews with participants and through existing written reports and evaluations of the projects involved. For example, in almost all cases, the interviewees expressed their reasons for participating as being related primarily to improving students' learning. Another common observation was the beneficial effect of increased engagement by the students in the learning and assessment processes. However, the initial observations and findings were focused on three main areas: *Professional Learning*, *Dissemination* and *Sustainable Development.* These formed the basis of three working papers, which were then developed on a continuous basis as a result of discussions and expert inputs in subsequent seminars. An additional working paper, on the concept of *Innovation* in assessment, was developed to assist with discussions and, as we will discuss later, three additional dimensions, namely *Warrant*, *Impact* and *Agency,* were developed as a result of the expert seminars. The particular case of *Self- Agency*, is a crucial indicator of a successful handing over of responsibility for personal professional development to the teachers themselves.

8.2.1 Professional Learning

Accounts of attempts to bring about change in assessment invariably emphasize the role of professional development (for example, see James & Pedder, 2006). One outcome of the research led us to prefer the term *professional learning*, as it was clear in some of the initiatives that attempts to change assessment practice were prone to a superficial adoption of techniques rather than an increased understanding. In essence, the term *professional learning* implies the process of teachers developing their own understanding of the processes involved. Without this understanding, the evidence indicated that innovative practice soon waned in the face of the more familiar, established practices.

There are many different forms that professional learning can take and, as demonstrated by all of the initiatives reviewed, there are several key issues to consider. These include the balance between what has been described as top-down and bottom-up approaches and the tension between theory-based and technique-based models. In these debates there are shades of what Sfard (1998) has called the *acquisition* versus *participation* metaphors of learning. Applied to professional learning, the distinction implies a choice between designing participative practical experiences that lead to reflection and deeper assimilation of the principles, and an acquisition approach in which the teachers are relatively passive and are simply required to adopt the practices they have been shown. In extreme cases of the latter, teachers are told what to do; with the hope, perhaps, that practice will instil understanding. The research literature offers no dependable conclusions on the debate as to which is better, and in a large majority of the cases studied in ARIA the process was considerably more organic, with the different issues and approaches being blended according to circumstance and opportunity.

The *King's Medway Oxfordshire Formative Assessment Project, KMOFAP* project (see Hodgen & Marshall, 2005; Black & Wiliam, 2006) is an example of an approach which was essentially bottom-up, reflecting a view that participation in developing new procedures or materials is a most effective way of encouraging commitment to change. The project showed how groups of teachers can learn from each other, combine ideas, achieve ownership of the emerging practices and work with researchers to be creative and experimental in a "safe" environment. With the addition of opportunities to reflect and develop understanding of principles underlying the change, this experience can be a most effective form of professional learning. But it is also very demanding of resources, time in particular, and clearly cannot be extended to large numbers of teachers in an economic fashion.

An alternative approach, in which teachers are not expected to develop techniques but are to try out ready-made approaches, was illustrated in the *Portsmouth Learning Community: Assessment for Learning Strand* project (Blanchard, Collins, & Thorp, 2003). Two teachers from each of 13 primary schools in Portsmouth attended training on such strategies as sharing learning intentions, identifying success criteria, "no-hands-up" questioning and comments-only marking. These strategies, and others such as "traffic lights", wait time and "two-stars-and-a-wish" mentioned later in the text, are sometimes termed "Assessment for Learning strategies" as they are techniques used by teachers to secure students' participation in the assessment of their own learning. Such techniques promote meaningful feedback, self and peer-assessment, and the sharing of learning outcomes, which are key dimensions of the formative use of assessment (i.e., assessment *for* learning). Following the training, the Portsmouth teachers put the strategies into practice in their classes and subsequent evaluations indicated that positive use was made of them, with classroom practice changed as intended. However, there was evidence of confusion about the purpose of some strategies, probably resulting from using the techniques without understanding the underlying principles, as we have argued above. Teachers have to make decisions about their use of assessment and the project demonstrated that they will be uncertain about how to do it unless they have a clear understanding of the benefits and educational rationale.

The most important findings on professional learning were related to time, ownership and understanding. These are set out briefly below, illustrated by comments from participants in the initiatives.

8.2.1.1 Time

- Teachers need time to reflect and to adjust their teaching to take on board new practices. *(I went to conferences and heard about people making it happen in 6 weeks which I thought absolutely doesn't work. It took us a year and a half and even now we have to say: remember to do... remember to do..."* – Teacher).

  Professional development is best spread over time with opportunities for trying out ideas between sessions. ("*Absolutely crucial*" – Local authority advisor).
- Teachers find it very helpful to talk to other teachers to share experiences and planning should allow time for this form of professional learning. (*"Fantastic CPD* [continuing professional development] *for staff...* [involves] *conversations about pedagogy... focus on learning in school... sharing/visiting one another's classrooms"* – Teacher).

8.2.1.2 Ownership

- "Bottom-up" approaches are more likely than "top-down" approaches to lead to ownership and understanding of new procedures, but teachers need to be clear about the direction in which they should be trying to move and need to have feedback on their progress. ("*It's not quite as simple as somebody at the bottom having an idea and passing it all the way up. It is like opening up a debate at all levels and making time to do it properly"* – Local authority advisor).

8.2.1.3 Understanding

- Some teachers may prefer to start by following techniques for change rather than understanding reasons for change, but unless they eventually reach this understanding, techniques are likely to be followed mechanically and be easily abandoned. (*"Some people still see it as traffic lighting... So for example, you know the teacher hasn't got it if they ask you to come on a Wednesday afternoon to see their AfL lesson... whereas if the teacher says come in any time you know you are going to see the principles* [in operation] *at any point*" – Teacher).

As Holmes, Gardner, and Galanouli (2007) would argue, planning for successful professional learning demands a focus on teachers' values and the utility of the innovation. It also requires planned opportunities to try out the activities themselves and sustained support during the period after any formal professional development intervention and as the process of embedding the changes proceeds.

8.2.2 Dissemination

When the aim is to reach large numbers of teachers, to make changes nationally rather than locally, the approach to professional development needs to be scaled up. The solution often adopted is one of "cascade" training (see for example, Stobart & Stoll, 2005), where those who have been trained are in turn expected to disseminate the "message" further in their schools or authorities. The Assessing Pupils' Progress (APP) (partly reported in Qualifications and Curriculum Authority, 2006) and Monitoring Children's Progress (MCP) projects for ages 11–14 and 7–11 respectively were concerned with assessment for summative purposes and were intended to change practice nationally across England. Resource materials arising from the APP were developed to help teachers make judgments in relation to their students' levels of achievement. During the development and trialling of the materials, two teachers from each participating school attended training sessions and two summer conferences. From this relatively small coverage of the school and teacher population (around 70 schools, 140 teachers over 2 years), the cascade model was designed to disseminate the techniques to all schools through local authorities and school-based work. In such an approach there may be little opportunity to tailor experiences to enable teachers to engage within the context of their own needs. However, the worst effects of the "top-down" structure can be ameliorated by ensuring opportunities for discussion, reflection and contextualized action in the schools themselves. In this manner, the top-down policy and guidance aligns more closely with a model that aims to empower and engage both teachers and schools to take matters forward in a bottom-up development.

8.2.2.1 Transmission Model

Many of the approaches to dissemination described in the selected initiatives were based on the transmission of ideas to teachers and schools from such sources as policy-makers and academic researchers. Most commonly, practice perceived to be good was promoted by government and local authorities and then shared across the practice communities. Sophisticated models of this approach encouraged practitioners to tell their own stories of practice and to make explicit the process of change, identifying problems faced and issues addressed. For example, the Learning How to Learn project (James, Black, McCormick, Pedder, & Wiliam, 2006; Pedder, James, & MacBeath, 2005) is arguably best viewed as a collection of good learning practices. The selection of these practices was based on the potential to promote students' autonomy in learning.

All of the initiatives that used this "shared good practice" approach reported problems with "pilot and roll out". It became clear that a major distinction could be drawn between the pilot phases, which often successfully involved teachers in developing the ideas and practices, and the "roll out", where the model changed from the *engagement* of the teachers in developing new practice (the pilot teachers) to *telling* the new batches of teachers what to do. We have described this as a failure to recognize that dissemination must adopt the same professional learning approach for the last person trained as was successful for the first.

8.2.2.2 Transformation Model

This was a crucial finding but it was also recognized by planners of the most recent initiatives who based their ideas more on a process of transformation, that is, the need for professional learning and dissemination to transform practice. That said, it was also acknowledged that successful dissemination could not rely on any single strategy. In Wales, for example, schools involved in the two initiatives: the Programme for Developing Thinking and Assessment for Learning, and the Assessment Programme for Wales: Securing Key Stage 2 and Key Stage 3[2] Teacher Assessment (DCELLS, 2008) attended dissemination conferences while a virtual discussion forum also provided a searchable database of resources and lesson plans.

In Scotland the Assessment is for Learning Programme (see for example, Condie, Livingston, & Seagraves, 2005; Hutchinson & Hayward, 2005; Hayward, 2007; see Chapter 2 James) had brought together policy-makers, academic researchers and practitioners right from its inception. The national plan was for all teachers to be involved in thinking and action on formative assessment over time rather than having one group of teachers who developed ideas for others to put into practice. Rather than simply transmitting good practice, the underlying and potentially much more effective approach, is the full engagement of teachers in transforming their own practice.

8.2.3 Sustainable Development

A strong conclusion from the work of the project was that it was inappropriate to conceive of sustaining any new assessment practice in some kind of unchanging state itself. Sustainable development of new practices is therefore a dynamic process, itself prone to updating and change. This was amply demonstrated by the experience of the Assessment for Learning project in Northern Ireland. Classroom activities, which were at one time new and useful, e.g. the "traffic lights", wait time and "two-stars-and-a-wish" strategies (see Council for the Curriculum & Examinations and Assessment (CCEA), 2007, for a description of these), soon became drab routine for some teachers and no longer met the ever-changing needs of the classroom. In an evaluation of the initiative (CCEA, 2006), over one third of

---

[2]The national curricula of England, Wales and Northern Ireland have the same basic structure set out in "key stages" with, for example, Key Stage 3 covering the education of students in the approximate age range 11–14 years.

the 69 teachers responding to a survey felt that AfL approaches were not suitable for all students and over half displayed "some resistance" to the initiative. The evaluation indicated that communication was a problem, with many of the teachers being unaware of the potential benefits of, or reasons for, using formative assessment. The conditions for sustaining change were not in place but when the teachers were encouraged to engage with the underlying processes this AfL initiative achieved much greater success.

Change in education is both an individual and a collective process within communities as diverse as schools and nations. However, changing the assessment practice of individual teachers, or even schools, is not enough to maintain change in a whole system. For this, changes may well be needed in teacher education programmes, in policies, in criteria used in school evaluation by schools themselves and by inspectors, in funding arrangements, and so on. Where policy arrangements are not consistent, the potential for innovation to be sustained may be compromised. Successful innovation in assessment involves sustaining a climate of development where policy-makers, academic researchers, schools and teachers seek collectively to improve learning. Most importantly, it involves engaging teachers and schools in a culture of reflection and review, to ensure that change is properly planned and actioned.

The main conclusions to be drawn on sustainability from the various initiatives may be summarized as follows:

- Sustainable development in assessment is a dynamic process and must feature as part of every teacher's approach to their practice (*"You can't let it off the agenda if you want to keep it alive"* – Teacher).
- Teachers must be enabled to maintain good practice through continuous review and reflection. (*"Embedding it in your core purposes... re-visiting it... sharing what works regularly"* – Local authority advisor).
- Sustainable development involves sustaining ideas, practices and people. Teachers and schools must share a sense of common, worthwhile purpose ("*There is a real commitment among a core of staff that we keep the commitment to AfL really high and don't lose that at all because I think it's something that we've been proud of, that has been developed in the school*" – Teacher).
- Sustainable development involves sustaining a learning culture where policy-makers, researchers and practitioners use evidence to adapt practice – in effect, not unlike the process of formative assessment.

8.3 Insights from the Study

Analysis of the publications and reports relating to the initiatives, in combination with the expert seminar discussions, led to two major conclusions from the study. The first related to the lack of comprehensive planning ("under-designing") of many of the initiatives and the second related to perceptions of what constituted quality assessment practice.

8.3.1 Planning for Change in Assessment Practice

The story of each initiative was predominantly one of success; innovations in practice were successfully piloted and for those that intended wider dissemination appropriate attempts to promote wider adoption were undertaken. In essence, however, analysis of the initiatives pointed to the observation that planning for the post-pilot phase in most of the initiatives was invariably ad hoc. No overall blueprint was available from the beginning for addressing all of the key dimensions that arguably form the change process. The various discussions and literature searching identified these dimensions as being those set out in Fig. 8.1:

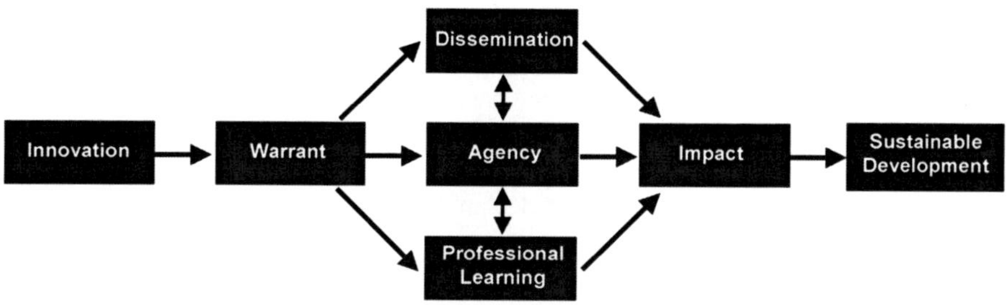

Fig. 8.1 Key dimensions of assimilating change in schools

Our analysis suggested that planning for the evaluation of *Impact* and for *Sustainable Development* was absent from all but a couple of the initiatives. Instead, as perhaps suggested by the [false] sense of linear sequencing[3] in Fig. 8.1 above, these dimensions tended to be addressed towards the end of the process (if at all) rather than as part of a holistic design approach from the beginning. The conclusions reached on the issue of *Impact* argued the importance of ensuring that the effects of an innovation were systematically monitored. An innovation seeks to make a difference, so something should change. For most of those involved in the initiatives, improvement in student learning was seen in broad terms; it was about changed attitudes, better understanding and more learner autonomy. Only two initiatives provided evidence of attempts to "measure" the impact of the innovations through monitoring students' performance in tests and examinations. Most respondents talked instead about changes to the classroom climate, different ways of teaching and improved attitudes to learning. The use of teacher perceptions was the dominant form of evidence and what emerged was a strong sense of teacher belief that the innovations in assessment, especially the formative assessment developments, had benefited both teaching and learning. A key issue here, especially for

[3]It must be emphasized that the dimensions of change outlined in this figure should not be considered as part of a linear sequence, though it does represent the general direction of travel. The process of changing assessment practice may begin with a specifically identified innovation and (ideally) end with the establishment of sustained practice, but the processes in between are highly inter-related and inter-dependent.

policy-makers and those engaged in school evaluation, is that improved learning might be reasonably expected to lead, at some point, to improved test or examination results. We would not wish to undermine the importance of teachers' personal observations but the consensus of those taking part in the seminars would be to pursue a more systematic collection of evidence.

There was also evidence that acceptance of the specific *Innovation* in assessment practice, and its *Warrant* from the literature and work undertaken elsewhere, was a relatively passive process. There was a general acceptance that the innovation was desirable. The validity of its potential benefits was more or less taken for granted and there was no detailed conceptualization or critical evaluation of its nature. This was not a particularly serious issue across the initiatives, and least of all in those with evidence pointing to the positive effects of AfL, but taking efficacy for granted has proven more problematic in the context of the many fads that have assailed Education in recent years. However, what can be much more problematic, as demonstrated in some of the initiatives, is an ad hoc approach to *Professional Learning* and *Dissemination*.

For the most part, the initiatives did plan for these two interrelated and major activities but this planning was generally not in place from the beginning. It was in this sense that some of the initiatives could be described as being "under-designed". It was clear from the study that the planning and design for successful and embedded changes in assessment practice must address all of the key dimensions (Fig. 8.1) from the beginning.

8.3.2 Self-Agency of Teachers

Another important feature of the initiatives was that the relatively traditional top-down approach, which was widely used, did not specifically seek to identify and exploit the key agents of change (*Agency*). A variety of key agents may be identified including senior school managers, peer influences and even students. However, it was clear throughout that the commitment and understanding of the teachers themselves was crucial and that the key approach to sustaining change in assessment practice was the self-agency of the teachers. As Dadds (1997, p. 34) put it "When the formal CPD [continuing professional development] course has ended, professional judgement in the classroom goes on, often without continuing support. So the learning has to be made personal for it to be used independently."

Professional learning, in which teachers act as their own agency of change, might come about through the teachers' interest being stimulated by conversations with colleagues, ideas promoted at traditional professional development courses or from reading about the potential benefits of changes in practice. Self-agency is a powerful device in fostering change because it draws on self-motivation. What appeared strongly to be the case throughout the selected initiatives was that unless teachers are committed to any particular innovation in assessment, the prospects for successful changes in practice are likely to be slim. Self-agency is therefore considered to be a powerful element in ensuring the successful development of teacher assessment in schools. Schools and others must strive to cultivate and capture this self-agency if the changes are to be assimilated into sustainable practice.

8.3.3 Principles and Standards

The second major conclusion from the study developed from the observation that there was not a consistent view of what "good" assessment is for any particular purpose. The many voices in the initiatives and the early seminars appeared to be talking about the same issue (improvement in assessment practice) while using almost as many definitions of that issue as there were voices. Ultimately such a situation can create a melee of jargon describing different types of assessment, different uses of assessment and different perceptions of what is considered to be acceptable quality in assessment practice. Addressing this issue therefore became a second key focus for the work of the project.

Cross-cutting the components in the process of change, represented in Fig. 8.1 and discussed earlier, is the notion of quality in assessment practice. The ARIA project identified a set of principles (see Gardner, Harlen, Hayward, Stobart, & Montgomery, 2009), which attracted the endorsement of a wide variety of teachers, academics and support professionals through both the expert seminars and a series of dissemination events. They are:

- Assessment of any kind should ultimately improve learning.
- Assessment methods should enable progress in all important learning goals to be facilitated and reported.
- Assessment procedures should include explicit processes to ensure that information is valid and is as reliable as necessary for its purpose.
- Assessment should promote public understanding of learning goals relevant to students' current and future lives.
- Assessment of learning outcomes should be treated as approximations, subject to unavoidable errors.
- Assessment should be part of a process of teaching that enables students to understand the aims of their learning and how the quality of their achievement will be judged.
- Assessment methods should promote the active engagement of students in their learning and its assessment.
- Assessment should enable and motivate students to show what they can do.
- Assessment should combine information of different kinds, including students' self-assessments, to inform decisions about students' learning and achievements.
- Assessment methods should meet standards that reflect a broad consensus on quality at all levels from classroom practice to national policy.

The last principle introduces a previously unidentified issue: the need to have standards by which assessment practices can be judged, just as there are standards of practice in other areas of professional and personal conduct. Note that our use of the word "standards" differs from that commonly assumed in education, where standards are often taken to mean normative levels of achievement as measured by test scores or examination grades. Here we are using standards in relation to assessment in a more general sense, reflecting reasonable expectations about, for instance, the range of learning outcomes included in assessment, the impact of the process of assessment on students, teachers and the curriculum, and how assessment policy is formulated. The intention is that these suggested standards can be used to help

Table 8.1 Standards for classroom assessment practice

Assessment generally	Formative use of assessment	Summative use of assessment
1. The assessment uses a range of methods that enable the various goals of learning and progression towards them to be addressed 2. The methods used address the skills, knowledge or understanding being assessed without restricting the breadth of the curriculum 3. Teaching provides students with opportunities to show what they can do through tasks that address the full range of goals of learning 4. Teachers use evidence from their on-going assessment to: • help students' learning; • summarise learning in terms of reporting criteria; • reflect upon and improve their teaching 5. Teachers develop their assessment practice through a variety of professional learning activities including reflecting upon and sharing experiences with colleagues	1. Teachers gather evidence of their students' learning through questioning, observation, discussion and study of products relevant to the learning goals 2. Teachers involve students in discussing learning goals and the standards to be expected in their work 3. Teachers use assessment to advance students' learning by: • adapting the pace, challenge and content of activities; • giving feedback to students about how to improve; • providing time for students to reflect on and assess their own work 4. Students use assessment to advance their learning by: • knowing and using the criteria for the standards of work they should be aiming for; • giving and receiving comments from their peers on the quality of their work and how to improve it; • reflecting on how to improve their work and taking responsibility for it	1. Teachers base their judgments of students' learning outcomes on a range of types of activity suited to the subject matter and age of students, which might include tests or specific assessment tasks 2. Assessment of learning outcomes is based on a rich variety of tasks that enables students to show what it means to be "good" at particular work 3. Teachers take part in discussion with each other of students' work in order to align judgments of levels or grades when these are required 4. Students are aware of the criteria by which their work over a period of time is judged 5. Students are aware of the evidence used and how judgments of their learning outcomes are made 6. Students are helped to use the results of assessment to improve their learning

various groups to identify good practice where is already exists, to show what needs to be changed where it does not, and to help to ensure that key aspects of assessment procedures are and continue to be in place.

Four sets of standards were developed and aimed at the key groups: Teachers, School Management, Inspection and Advice Services, and Policy-makers (see Gardner et al., 2009). Focusing on engaging teachers, Table 8.1 presents the proposed standards for classroom assessment practice (there is not scope in this chapter to develop the remaining three categories of standards). They are set out as general standards in the first column and separately as standards for formative and summative assessment in the other columns.

It is important to stress that these standards should be viewed as a first attempt, derived from the views of experts (including teachers), to express a consistency in perception of what counts for quality assessment practice by teachers. As such, they are presented here to be endorsed, adapted and refined, or indeed challenged, by teachers.

8.4 Concluding Remarks

The ARIA study showed that many initiatives in developing assessment by teachers, an innovation in many schools, are under-designed, that is, they do not begin by planning for the whole change process (from innovation to sustainable development). There is also considerable uncertainty about defining quality in assessment practice and the first steps towards developing a common language of quality in assessment by teachers have been proposed.

Across the four nations of the UK, the key findings included the identification of potentially successful approaches to professional learning and dissemination, for example by ensuring that teachers are empowered to play a meaningful and participative role in the developments. A balance needs to be struck between introducing theory (what ultimately needs to be known and understood) and practice (what skills and strategies need to be learned). The adoption of innovative practice is a dynamic and complex process that requires commitment from teachers and appropriate support from policy-makers, researchers and educational support professionals.

Common weaknesses in assessment initiatives were identified as not actively pursuing appropriate dimensions of teachers' self-agency as a key instrument of change, not undertaking systematic monitoring of the impact of changes made and inadequate attention to how changes in practice might be sustained into the future, for example, through developing a culture of readiness to engage dynamically with changing and new assessment practices.

Finally, the study's findings highlight the power of enabling teachers to play a role in the design and conduct of professional learning opportunities, thereby engaging them in their own professional learning rather than simply telling them what they ought to be doing.

Appendix

A List of the Main Projects Reviewed Under the Auspices of ARIA

- Assessment is for Learning (Learning and Teaching Scotland and the Scottish Government)
- Assessing Pupils' Progress (Key Stage 3) and Monitoring Children's Progress (Key Stage 2) (Qualifications and Curriculum Authority with the Primary and Secondary National Strategies)
- Assessment for Learning in the Northern Ireland Revised Curriculum (Council for Curriculum, Examinations and Assessment (CCEA), Northern Ireland)
- Consulting Pupils on the Assessment of their Learning (Queen's University, Belfast)
- Programme for Developing Thinking and Assessment for Learning (Department for Children, Education, Lifelong Learning and Skills, Welsh Assembly Government)
- Assessment Programme for Wales: Securing Key Stage 2 and Key Stage 3 Teacher Assessment (Department for Children, Education, Lifelong Learning and Skills, Welsh Assembly Government)
- Project e-Scape. Goldsmiths, University of London
- Jersey Actioning Formative Assessment (JAFA) (King's College London and the Education Department of Jersey)
- King's Oxfordshire Medway Formative Assessment Project (KMOFAP) (King's College, London, Oxfordshire LA and Medway LA)
- King's Oxfordshire Summative Assessment Project (KOSAP) (King's College, London and Oxfordshire LA)
- Learning How to Learn (University of Cambridge)
- Portsmouth Learning Community Assessment for Learning Strand (Portsmouth LA)
- Summative Teacher Assessments at the End of Key Stage 2 (Birmingham and Oxfordshire LAs)

References

Black, P., & Wiliam, D. (2006). Assessment for learning in the classroom. In J. Gardner (Ed.), *Assessment and learning* (pp. 9–25). London: Sage.

Blanchard, J., Collins, F., & Thorp, J. (2003). Portsmouth assessment for learning project. University of Sussex. Accessed July 22, 2010, from http://www.aaia.org.uk/pdf/Portsmouth%20Assessment%20for%20Learning%20Project.pdf

Condie, R., Livingston, K., & Seagraves, L. (2005). Evaluation of the assessment is for learning programme. Final report. University of Strathclyde: Quality in Education Centre, http://www.scotland.gov.uk/Publications/2005/12/0792641/26428

Council for the Curriculum, Examinations and Assessment (CCEA) (2006). *Assessment for learning project: Final report May 2006 council for curriculum, examinations and assessment.* Belfast: CCEA Research and Statistics.

Council for the Curriculum, Examinations and Assessment (CCEA) (2007). Assessment for learning for key stages 1 & 2. Council for Curriculum, Examinations and Assessment. Belfast: CCEA. Accessed July 22, 2010, from http://www.nicurriculum.org.uk/docs/assessment_for_learning/training/AfL-Guidance-KS12.pdf

Dadds, M. (1997). Continuing professional development: Nurturing the expert within. *British Journal of In-service Education, 23*(1), 31–38.

Department for Children, Education, Lifelong Learning and Skills (DCELLS) (2008). *Programme for developing thinking and assessment for learning and the assessment programme for wales: Securing key stage 2 and key stage 3 teacher assessment.* Cardiff: Department for Children, Education, Lifelong Learning and Skills.

Department for Children, Schools and Families (2004). Every Child Matters: Change for Children in Schools. London: Department for Children, Schools and Families. Accessed June 28, 2009, from http://www.everychildmatters.gov.uk/_files/07CD1E89BFFA749324DC47F707DD5B7F.pdf

Gardner, J., Harlen, W., Hayward, L., Stobart, G., & Montgomery, M. (2009). *Developing teacher assessment.* London: McGraw-Hill.

Harlen, W. (2007). *Assessment of learning. London: Sage.*

Harlen, W., & Deakin Crick, R. (2003). Testing and motivation for learning. *Assessment in Education, 10*(2), 169–208.

Hayward, L. (2007). Curriculum, assessment and pedagogies in Scotland: The quest for social justice 'Ah kent yir faither'. *Assessment in Education, 14*(2), 251–268.

Hodgen, J., & Marshall, B. (2005). Assessment for learning in mathematics and English: A comparison. *The Curriculum Journal, 16*(2), 153–176.

Holmes, B., Gardner, J., & Galanouli, D. (2007). Striking the right chord and sustaining successful professional development in ICT. *Journal of In-Service Education, 33*(4), 389–404.

House of Commons (2008). *Testing and assessment: Third report of session 2007-08*, House of Commons Children, Schools and Families Committee (Vol. 1). Norwich: The Stationery Office.

Hutchinson, C., & Hayward, L. (2005). The journey so far: Assessment for learning in Scotland. *The Curriculum Journal, 16*(2), 225–248.

James, M., Black, P., McCormick, R., Pedder, D., & Wiliam, D. (2006). Learning how to learn in classrooms, schools and networks: Aims, design and analysis. *Research Papers in Education, 21*(2), 101–118.

James, M., & Pedder, D. (2006). Professional learning as a condition for assessment for learning. In J. Gardner (Ed.), *Assessment and learning* (pp. 27–43). London: Sage.

Mansell, W. (2007). *Education by numbers: The tyranny of testing*. London: Politico's.

Pedder, D., James, M., & MacBeath, J. (2005). How teachers value and practise professional learning. *Research Papers in Education, 20*(3), 209–243.

Qualifications and Curriculum Authority (2006). Monitoring pupils' progress in English at key stage 3 Final report on the 2003-5 pilot. London: Qualifications and Curriculum Authority. Accessed June 20, 2009, from http://www.qca.org.uk/libraryAssets/media/qca-06-2324-monitoring-pupils-progress-research-report.pdf

Sfard, A. (1998). On two metaphors for learning and the dangers of choosing just one. *Educational Researcher, 27*(2), 4–13.

Stobart, G. (2008). *Testing times: The uses and abuses of assessment*. Abingdon: Routledge.

Stobart, G., & Stoll, L. (2005). The key stage 3 strategy: What kind of reform is this? *Cambridge Journal of Education, 35*(2), 225–238.

US Department of Education. (2002). No Child Left Behind (2002). No Child Left Behind Act. The White House. Accessed July 22, 2010, from http://www.ed.gov/policy/elsec/leg/esea02/107-110.pdf

Chapter 9
Teachers' Feedback to Pupils: "Like So Many Bottles Thrown Out to Sea"?

Eleanore Hargreaves

9.1 Introduction

> ... part of the feedback given to pupils in class is like so many bottles thrown out to sea. No one can be sure that the message they contain will 1 day find a receiver... (Perrenoud, 1998, p. 86)

Philip Perrenoud's words in the quotation above raise the issue of when teacher feedback really does help pupils in their learning. Perrenoud goes on to remind us that "... some of the messages which the teacher conceives as feedback do not in fact play this role for the pupil". Within the discourse of Assessment for Learning (AfL), classroom feedback is assumed to have a beneficial influence on pupils' knowledge construction, but the chain of events leading from feedback to successful learning is complex and has not yet been adequately described despite substantial research (Kluger & DeNisi, 1996; Mason & Bruning, 2001; Mory, 2004; Narciss & Huth, 2004; Hattie & Timperley, 2007; Shute, 2008). Most teachers are familiar with the frustration of spending many hours writing feedback comments on pupils' work, only to discover that pupils have no better understanding the next time, and seem to have taken little notice of meticulously crafted feedback comments. In his seminal and much quoted article of 1989, Sadler similarly describes the

> common but puzzling observation that even when teachers provide students with valid and reliable judgements about the quality of their work, improvement does not necessarily follow. Students often show little or no growth or development despite regular, accurate feedback (p. 119).

Many previously reported research studies of feedback have been conducted in experimental conditions, rather than natural settings such as classrooms, and several major studies have related to computer-generated feedback (e.g. Azevedo & Bernard, 1995; Narciss & Huth, 2004) or non-educational settings (e.g. Kluger & DeNisi, 1996), many of which take insufficient account of social, personal or

E. Hargreaves (✉)
Institute of Education, University of London, London, UK
e-mail: E.Hargreaves@ioe.ac.uk

R. Berry, B. Adamson (eds.), *Assessment Reform in Education*,
Education in the Asia-Pacific Region: Issues, Concerns and Prospects 14,
DOI 10.1007/978-94-007-0729-0_9,

classroom dimensions in understanding feedback. Pollard (1990, p. 242) suggests, "... the lack of an integrated analysis, comparable to the integrated nature of experience, denies the validity and thus the credibility of the academic account". This chapter therefore aims to draw not only on existing research, but also on teachers' perceptions of feedback, in order to throw further light on the role feedback plays in supporting learning within the setting of classroom realities. The question it explores is: What can teachers and researchers tell us about important factors affecting feedback's role in promoting individuals' knowledge construction?

9.2 Research Design

This chapter draws on a recently conducted survey of 88 teachers as to how feedback becomes effective. The majority of respondents were teachers in the UK. There were also English speaking participants from Chile, Greece and USA among others, all of whom were studying education at the Institute of Education, in London, UK. Data were collected between November 2007 and November 2008. The 88 teachers were invited, without conferring with others, to complete the sentence, "Feedback becomes effective when. . . ." They submitted their responses anonymously.

In order to supplement and illustrate some of the teachers' written comments, seven primary pupils aged 9–10 years, were interviewed for at least 45 min each, about feedback they receive from their teachers (four pupils from a London school and three from a Surrey school, in the south-east of the UK). These supplementary interviews were carried out during January and February 2008.

Using my own previous experience of the range of perceptions about feedback that teachers might hold, I then grouped together perceptions that seemed to have a common emphasis. The groups of perceptions also reflected various emphases I had noticed in different types of academic literature about feedback. The teachers' responses provide a basis for the discussion presented in this paper, with a scattering of pupil examples intended to provide additional insights. Verbatim comments written by the teachers in the sample are listed and indented. Pupil comments are given, mainly within the text, but italicized.

9.3 Teacher Perceptions of Effective Feedback

9.3.1 Social and Personal Factors Affecting Feedback

The 88 teachers in this sample indicated an acute awareness of how social and personal factors affected the usefulness of feedback in learning. Their comments did not just focus on the form, or even the content of the feedback but to a great extent on the interactions between pupil and teacher, the learning environment, the values of the pupils and the readiness of pupils to respond to feedback.

One group of the teachers described the feedback process as necessarily involving interaction between pupil and teacher. For example, they believed that feedback became effective:

- When you [the teacher] include yourself in the discussion and discuss as "we" with an open attitude.
- On the spot in the classroom in a two-way thought developing process. Less beneficial is the notes on the students' work as it is not a two way process.
- When the pupil and teacher work together building motivation and the feeling that anything is achievable by the child.

Where feedback was seen as such an interactive process, teachers in the sample perceived that the teacher, as feedback giver, would be a learner too. Askew and Lodge (2001) describe how two-way feedback can simply be a "ping pong" of discrete ideas between teacher and learner; but more richly it can be a set of "interactive loops" in which increasingly complex knowledge is constructed collaboratively by teacher and learner:

- The result becomes useful to both the teacher and the learner in the teaching-learning process.
- It helps the person who gave the feedback to take something out of the experience.

A few teachers in the sample went further to suggest that feedback not only came through interaction between pupil and teacher, but also from "all members of the learner's inner circle". This resonates with Allal and Mottier Lopez's (2005) conception of formative assessment as interactive regulation "based on the interactions of the student with... the teacher, with other students and/or with material allowing self-regulated learning" (p. 245). These views feed into the further discussion about feedback from a range of agents, but this is the subject for another paper.

Teachers in the sample perceived that feedback would only be fruitful when the learning environment was comfortable for pupils, where:

- The child is confident and happy to continue learning.
- When the child is in a play-like situation. If feedback were given using children's creative minds, their lingo, their level of understanding of things, or whatever interested them like computers or lego, then that feedback would stick and take effect irrespective of the particular learning intention.

The most important factor facilitating a supportive learning environment for feedback was pupils' trust in the giver of feedback. Feedback is only effective when:

- The feedbacker's opinion is respected/valued.
- Pupils trust what has been said to them and know it is in their interests to act.
- It comes from people who really care about you.
- It is honest – not false.

This point was illustrated in interview with a primary pupil about her teacher's feedback. Pupil Lucy described receiving insincere feedback on her mathematics work. Her teacher had said, "I know you're very good at maths, so you've got to try harder!" and "You're a very bright little girl!" Lucy told us she was not sure if they were true as she did not think of herself like that. "I'm more of a sporty, artistic little girl", she said, "and I prefer other lessons than maths". She thought the teacher "might say it just to make me feel better if I was finding it really tough". In other words, the praise made her feel better in the moment, but also confused her because she could tell that it did not make sense.

These views emphasize the futility of focusing purely on the feedback message without paying heed to the relationship within which it is given. They also expose the sensitivity of the feedback receiver. Kluger and DeNisi (1996) confirm that computer-generated feedback can be more effective than teacher feedback; and one analysis of this could be that the computer is perceived to be neutral, and this makes its feedback more palatable than feedback given by a teacher who is feared or not respected by pupils. Although practice in classrooms may not always reflect the belief, teachers in the sample suggested that, because of the vulnerability of pupils, feedback should avoid being personal and should certainly never be unfair or humiliating. Feedback becomes effective when:

- It doesn't affect the learner's feelings.
- It is not critical of one's character.
- It is just, so the student will accept it and take it in.
- The children realize it is given to help them, and does not humiliate them or degrade them.

Hattie and Timperley (2007) and Kluger and DeNisi's extensive reviews (1996) stress the dangers of using feedback focused on "self", which, they suggest, may distract attention away from learning and onto the ego. An illustration of the complex emotional factors involved in responding to negative feedback, was given during an interview with a primary pupil called Len. It showed how aroused emotions could become barriers to further learning for some pupils. He told us that:

> Different pupils respond differently to [negative] feedback because children have different minds and are brought up differently. If they have "soft" parents, then they might be "soft" themselves, but if someone's father is "tattoo man" then they would not care much. So some people might completely ignore negative feedback; someone else might be quiet for the rest of the day; some people might be annoyed; and others might take it out on their mum at home.

A perception was evident among our teachers that even if the learning environment was conducive to learning, and pupils trusted the feedback provider, if they did not value the actual feedback, then it would not be effective. As Ryan and Deci (2000) suggest, for pupils to be most highly motivated to act, they need to have integrated and internalized for themselves, teachers' external directives. Teachers suggested that pupils need to recognize that feedback is there to help, not criticize, them, and it needs to be in keeping with their own goals rather than in conflict with them or alien to them (Butler & Winne, 1995). Teachers in this sample said that feedback would be most effective when:

- You agree with the feedback (danger of shrugging it off if you don't agree).
- It is sought (even sub-consciously) by the learner.
- It is about something one wishes to be fed back on.

Stobart (2008) has described the lengths to which children will go in order to gain self-feedback about a skill they value such as skateboarding. His point is that feedback is sought and acted on with speed and enthusiasm when the learner sees feedback as the route to achieving a much valued goal, in contrast to an externally imposed one. In similar vein, one teacher drew from the sports world when he described feedback as "the breakfast of champions", meaning that champions become champions by being constantly open to feedback. Phillipe Perrenoud (1998, p. 86) reminded us that 'the intention [of feedback] can only be effective if a window is found into the cognition system of the learner. There is no point in sending him or her messages if they are treated as noise or redundancy'...

In addition to (a) the right interaction between pupil and teacher, (b) the right learning environment and (c) recognition of the pupils' values, teachers suggested that feedback would only be effective if they timed it right. Readiness for feedback was a theme teachers in the sample found important. Feedback would be effective if:

- It is at a time when it can be contemplated and explored.
- You find (create) the moment when you can exchange ideas with students, so you can reinforce what is being taught.
- It is given during the activity or task so that the child can use the feedback while it is still fresh in their mind. This way it can become embedded in the child's understanding.
- It is little and often.
- There is an appropriate balance between immediate or delayed, written or oral responses that suits the purpose of the feedback.

Teachers are here acknowledging the need for sensitivity as to the most appropriate time for feeding back. The international research on the timing of feedback is inconclusive (Shute, 2008), although there are some indications there that immediate feedback is most effective for "difficult" tasks and for the retention of procedural or conceptual knowledge, and delayed feedback for "relatively simple" tasks and to promote transfer of learning (p. 32). In the pupil interviews whose aim was to illuminate our understanding of these issues, pupil Lucy described wanting assistance in the moment of learning. She needed "someone right by my side, telling me what I've done wrong and helping me". However, another pupil, Len, found it useful to revisit work the day after he had done it, in time dedicated for pupils to read feedback comments. He said, "I like little comments. It gives me something to do!" However, Len also told us that the most effective feedback was comments his teacher might make casually in the playground, such as, "You need to improve on this" or occasionally, "You're very good at that".

9.3.2 The Focus of Effective Feedback

Once the crucial effects of social and personal factors have been acknowledged, the actual focus of the feedback message needs to be examined. The 88 teachers in this sample described the following five focuses for feedback as most effective: Learning objectives and assessment criteria, Motivating learning and reinforcing positive achievements, Deepened understanding, Action and improvements, and Reflection and learning processes.

Tunstall and Gipps (1996a, 1996b) proposed that feedback could be categorized as either evaluative or descriptive. Evaluative feedback refers to self and includes value judgments, while descriptive feedback relates directly to learning objectives and assessment criteria. While this distinction does not cover a full range of possible purposes for feedback (the purpose of provoking thought, for example), it is useful in its emphasis on feedback that provides information to the learner about what made learning good, not just whether it was good. Tunstall and Gipps suggest that while evaluative feedback can be helpful in changing behaviour, descriptive feedback is more effective for learning (see also Hargreaves, McCallum, & Gipps, 2000). This suggestion was affirmed by teachers in the sample. They perceived that feedback was most effective when:

- The person receiving it is told why [work/learning] was good or bad.
- It is directly related to the learning objective. If [pupils] don't know about the goal, they don't know how to interpret the feedback.
- There is recognition of criteria met.

However, given the discussion above of social and personal factors affecting feedback, in particular the need for pupils to value the feedback given and play an active role in constructing it, reference to learning objectives and assessment criteria within feedback needs to be further analysed. As Tunstall and Gipps (1996b) stress, objectives and criteria can be "givens" or can be negotiated. Torrance (2007) has drawn attention in the post-16 sector to how the use of objectives and criteria can actually take over from learning rather than encourage it, where feedback is very directive in relation to "criteria compliance". Torrance's research found that teaching could become reduced to getting students to meet criteria, rather than helping students learn. Pryor and Crossouard (2008) suggest that the negotiation of objectives and criteria is perhaps the fertile ground for learning rather than pupils' compliance to them. Therefore, the process of using and of deciding on valued objectives and criteria, must be considered before their benefit as effective feedback can be assured. This may be a challenge for teachers in an educational climate where externally imposed "objectives" are championed. However, some teachers clearly find ways of negotiating valuable criteria whilst still "covering" required curricula.

A much expressed view among the teachers in our sample was that feedback should be positive. It would be effective when:

- It acknowledges positive aspects/things that work.
- There is a clear understanding of what you have done well so that you can repeat the success again and again. If the feedback suggests failure it is important to understand what can be done to change quickly so that success follows the improvement or change.
- Praise is given for what was done but also giving it a way to move forward to make progress.

This view mirrors Kluger and DeNisi's (1996) finding that negative feedback does not improve achievement. However, a distinction needs to be made between feedback whose purpose is to motivate, and feedback whose purpose is to indicate successful learning, perhaps in relation to valued learning objectives or assessment criteria. The comments given above stress the latter purpose, in which the pupil's own achievements act as models for future successful learning.

Comments whose main purpose is to motivate (an "evaluative" purpose) come with more cautions. Teachers may assume praise to be crucial for raising the self-esteem of their pupils. However, Pryor and Torrance (1998) have painted a vivid picture of a teacher who wholeheartedly wanted to improve his pupils' self esteem, but his praise only exacerbated the pupil's belief that good learning was learning that others praised, without giving her any clues as to how she could choose to improve her own learning. Henderlong and Lepper's (2002) review of the benefits of praise is inconclusive, suggesting that praise plays an ambivalent role in learning. However, the recognition that feedback should be encouraging rather than discouraging is important within the AfL framework and the teachers in the sample suggested how praise might encourage future learning, when:

- We give them [pupils] support, tools, knowledge and strategies to feel more self confident.
- The learner is motivated to complete a task in achieving his or her goals.
- It gives the learner confidence to repeat the activity and try to improve their own capabilities.
- [Feedback] praised risk-taking and praised children for saying when they did not understand.

Pryor and Torrance (1998) have identified a spectrum of assessment approaches from "convergent assessment" at one end to "divergent assessment" at the other end, where convergent assessment demands correct answers from pupils and divergent assessment explores what pupils can and cannot do and how they make connections between ideas. Feedback within a convergent framework focuses on the elicitation of correct answers and identifies errors in a pupil's performance (see also, Black and

Wiliam's "directive" feedback, 1998) while within a divergent framework, feedback is "exploratory, provisional or provocative" (Pryor & Crossouard, 2008, p. 4), often encouraging pupils to reconstruct their thinking about the subject domain or learning process (see also, Black and Wiliam's "facilitative" feedback, 1998). There were teachers among the 88 in the sample who believed that for feedback to be effective, it needed to operate divergently, leading to deeper and more sophisticated thinking which was sustained over time. These teachers had sustained such a belief despite current pressure in schools to produce quick, measurable results. For these teachers, feedback became effective when:

- It assists students with the immediate task at hand but also promotes life-long learning (future application of feedback).
- It changes/reinforces/stimulates the learner for the future.
- The recipient uses it to alter their learning in a positive way.
- It was provocative in helping students to think more critically.

The unifying idea underlying AfL is that formative assessments lead to learning action rather than being an end in themselves (Black & Wiliam, 2006). Many of the 88 teachers in this sample stressed the importance of teacher feedback promoting future action in pupils. This action might be particular behaviour that the teacher hopes will aid pupil learning, or it might be improving on weaknesses pointed out by teacher feedback. Feedback promoting action or improvement might also be criteria related, positive and motivating and should support extended understanding:

- It provokes a reaction.
- It empowers.
- It asks for evidence that the person given the feedback has made changes/ improvement.
- The teacher has successfully been able to communicate to the pupil, and the pupil has successfully understood and is able to implement the advice that was given.

Teachers described effective feedback particularly as promoting improvement in pupils' learning, sometimes by pointing out their weaknesses using critical, but constructive, feedback:

- It is delivered in a positive way with suggestions for improvement.
- It encourages students to try again using the correct method.
- It highlights the areas of development the learner should take and how they should go about it.
- It is specific about how to improve.

The specificity of the "advice" given requires further thought. Some teachers mentioned the importance of feedback advice being realistic and achievable. However, if the aim of feedback is extended, even life-long understanding by a learner who is the owner of her/his own learning, then provocative rather than prescriptive comments may promote a more meaningful response in pupils. For example, rather than telling the pupil what s/he should do to improve a piece of work, the teacher might invite the child to make her/his own suggestions. In similar spirit, she might ask her/him to write down what s/he thought her own general target was for improvement in a given subject.

A sense of ownership of learning, which stems from the pupil's power to direct her/his own learning, is the ultimate aim for feedback within the discourse of AfL, and is more widely considered to be central to successful learning and its sustainability (Dennison & Kirk, 1990; Murnane & Levy, 1996). Successful learning therefore comprises the development of subject domain knowledge and metacognitive knowledge about the learning processes, the latter helping the learner to construct the former (cf. Biggs & Moore, 1993; Butler & Winne, 1995; Watkins, 2003).

Self-assessment is therefore not an added luxury but a fundamental tenet of AfL, and a constituent element of learning from constructivist perspectives (Dann, 2002, calls it "assessment as learning"). However, "self-monitoring" (Sadler, 1989) does not happen automatically, but has to be learned by pupils and supported by teachers' feedback. This view was reflected in teachers' emphasis in this sample, on the need for feedback to support pupils' reflection on their own learning. This reflection was on (a) what a pupil was learning and (b) the effectiveness of their own learning processes. For feedback to be effective, they believed firstly with reference to reflection on domain content:

- It allows the learner to reflect on their work.
- It helps you to reflect on and develop your understanding.
- It makes the learner aware of what s/he is learning.

Secondly, teachers recognized that powerful feedback was feedback that assisted pupils in giving themselves feedback, or self-monitoring. For example,

- The individual learns to self check their work and provide internal feedback.
- It makes students think about the way something was done and how they could improve.
- [It] encourages [pupils] to find out what worked for them and share good strategies with peers by demonstrating them in class.
- It develops self-regulation.

Hattie and Timperley's (2007) extensive review of feedback concluded that when teachers' feedback focused on how pupils went about processing tasks and on how they managed or regulated their processes, this was most effective for transferring skills to future tasks and for deeper and more sophisticated thinking which is sustained over time. That focus contrasted with feedback about the self as a person, or feedback to pupils on how to complete a one-off task: neither of these, they claimed, had sustained effects. This perspective implies that when feedback suggests actions and improvements, these need to be related to pupils monitoring their learning processes as well as to immediate subject domain criteria. An example of such feedback, described during interviews with pupils, was of pupil Len's teacher who fed back to the children in the form of a plenary using process questions such as: "What did you find easy today?" and "Did anyone find anything difficult? How did you overcome the difficulty?" He allowed children to talk in pairs and took individual answers from children. Finally he asked, "Who or what helped you?" and "What strategies did you use today?" and "If you were to learn this again, what would you do differently?"

9.3.3 The Message Form, for Effective Feedback

Teachers in our sample recognized that the right context for feedback and the appropriate focus were not enough to guarantee its positive effect. The form of the feedback message was also important 'to mediate understanding... to enable the student to appreciate and effectively access the communication and feedback.'

Although prescriptive advice may not help the learner develop ownership of learning, clarity and consistency in the feedback message were seen as fundamental requirements by teachers and in the research literature (Hattie & Timperley, 2007). Even when the message is clear, other factors may intervene, but the feedback receiver cannot possibly act appropriately on a message whose actual content is not accessible. Clarity of purpose is important as well as clarity of meaning. Feedback can only be effective when:

- The learner can crack the message's code.
- The receiver understands what they have been told and understands ways to implement methods to achieve their next step.
- The learner understands the purpose of the feedback and how to apply it to himself/herself in order to benefit from it.

9.4 Summary and Concluding Comments

Perceptions of effective feedback taken from across the 88 teacher respondents in this research project, can be summarized as follows.

1. Feedback becomes effective when social and personal factors are supportive to learning, especially when there are trusting relationships between feedback giver and feedback receiver; in fact, this notion of giver and receiver is less useful than one of negotiation and co-construction between teacher and learner. Feedback becomes effective when pupils feel comfortable in their learning environment, where feedback does not distract them into thinking about their own self-worth but rather focuses on learning itself. Feedback becomes effective when pupils want to receive it because it accords with their own values and goals; and when pupils are ready to take it on board.

2. Feedback becomes effective when the focus of feedback is appropriate, for example: when valued learning objectives or assessment criteria are addressed or negotiated through it; when positive achievements, past and future, are stressed; when feedback aims to promote sustained changes in pupils' thinking, rather than "quick fixes" of immediate tasks; when it encourages pupils to take action to continue or improve current progress; and when it allows pupils to reflect on their own learning and so take control over it.
3. Feedback becomes effective when the form of its message makes it clearly accessible to the learner.

This chapter has illustrated how teachers' perceptions accord with or add to existing research about feedback. The special contribution of teachers' perceptions on feedback is their classroom base and, at the same time, their far-reaching scope: unlike some existing research, teachers draw heavily on day to day practicalities, and on experience of many curriculum subjects and many learners, often over many years. Research evidence, on the other hand, can offer teachers insights into their own feedback practice too, because it is drawn from large samples of learners surveyed systematically for their feedback responses. The outcomes of such research can sometimes challenge everyday assumptions. Children's perceptions also have a special, yet largely untapped, potential to give us insights into the processes of feedback. This is an important area for further research work not drawn on in this survey, but the few examples of children's words presented here do illuminate some feedback issues from the unique perspective of the feedback respondent.

The range of teachers' perceptions described in this research reflects the range of emphases portrayed in existing research reviews (see for example, Shute, 2008). Clearly, there are no "one-size-fits-all" prescriptions for effective feedback, but rather a combination of factors that teachers and pupils must bear in mind. However, teachers in this sample put particular emphasis on the social and personal aspects of feedback processes, while existing research into feedback has sometimes focused on the form and content of the feedback message. Teachers suggested that feedback messages thrown by teachers "out to sea" are more likely to find a receiver if the situation in which pupils come across them is supportive to learning, is a situation where relationships are trusting, where pupils feel comfortable and focused on learning, and where pupils' own values and goals drive the agenda. In other words, pupils are more likely to make constructive meaning out of feedback messages when teachers recognize the influence of social and personal factors as well as of the content and form of feedback.

Such a conclusion accords with Michelle Boekaerts' dual processing theory (1993), portrayed by Wiliam (2007). Wiliam describes how, in Boekaerts' model, it is assumed that students who are invited to participate in any learning activity use three sources of information to form a mental representation of the task-in-context and to appraise it:

(1) current perceptions of the task including the environmental, social, and learning context within which it is embedded;

(2) their existing knowledge and metacognitive strategies related to the task; and
(3) personal beliefs about motivation, including beliefs about their competence, interest and effort (Boekaerts, 2006).

Boekaerts suggests that, following this initial appraisal of the task, the student begins to act along one of two pathways. If the task appraisal is positive, the student begins activity along the "growth pathway" where the goal is to increase competence. If, on the other hand, the task appraisal is negative, attention shifts away from the learning task and towards the pathway of trying to maintain well-being. The student then becomes focused on self-appraisal rather than task appraisal, concentrating on preventing threat, harm or loss. This form of self-regulation is triggered by cues in the environment, rather than by learning goals. Boekaerts' theory therefore emphasizes the role that social and personal factors play in facilitating or hindering learners' engagement.

Sadler's "common but puzzling observation" about the ineffectual nature of teacher feedback becomes less puzzling when these social and personal factors which contribute to feedback's effectiveness are taken into account. As this chapter has indicated, teachers simply providing students with "valid and reliable judgements about the quality of their work" (in Sadler's words, 1989, p. 119), does not pay sufficient heed to the complexity of factors affecting feedback's role in learning, in particular to social and personal factors. If AfL is "a framework of social mediation that fosters the student's increasing capacity to carry out more autonomous self-assessment and self-regulated learning" (Allal & Mottier Lopez, 2005, p. 252), feedback is the key player in this social mediation. It is the essentially social and personal nature of this mediation, based on individuals' relationships, interactions, values, experiences and feelings, as well as academic knowledge, that may supply a missing piece to Sadler's puzzle.

Acknowledgements Many thanks are due to Professors David Scott, Gordon Stobart and Dylan Wiliam for their extremely helpful comments on earlier drafts of this chapter.

References

Allal, L., & Mottier Lopez, L. (2005). Formative assessment of learning: A review of publications in French. In J. Looney (Ed.), *Formative assessment: Improving learning in secondary classrooms* (pp. 241–264). Paris: OECD.

Askew, S., & Lodge, C. (2001). Gifts, ping-pong and loops – linking feedback to learning. In S. Askew (Ed.), *Feedback for learning* (pp. 1–18). London: Routledge.

Azevedo, R., & Bernard, R. (1995). A meta-analysis of the effects of feedback in computer-based instruction. *Journal of Educational Computing Research, 13*(2), 111–127.

Biggs, J., & Moore, P. (1993). *The process of learning*. Englewood Cliffs, NJ: Prentice Hall.

Black, P., & Wiliam, D. (1998). Assessment and classroom learning. *Assessment in Education: principles, policy and practice, 5*(1), 7–75.

Black, P., & Wiliam, D. (2006). Assessment for learning in the classroom. In J. Gardner (Ed.), *Assessment and learning* (pp. 9–25). London: Sage.

Boekaerts, M. (1993). Being concerned with well being and with learning. *Educational Psychologist, 28*(2), 149–167.

Boekaerts, M. (2006). Self-regulation and effort investment. In K. A. Renninger & I. E. Sigel (Eds.), *Handbook of child psychology*, Child psychology in practice (Vol. 4, 6th ed., pp. 345–377). New York: Wiley.

Butler, D., & Winne, P. (1995). Feedback and self-regulated learning. *Review of Educational Research, 65*(3), 245–281.

Dann, R. (2002). *Promoting assessment as learning: Improving the learning process*. London: RoutledgeFalmer.

Dennison, B., & Kirk, R. (1990). *Do, review, learn, apply: A simple guide to experiential learning*. Oxford: Blackwell.

Hargreaves, E., McCallum, B., & Gipps, C. (2000). Teacher feedback strategies in primary classrooms: New evidence. In S. Askew (Ed.), *Feedback for learning* (pp. 21–31). London: RoutledgeFalmer.

Hattie, J., & Timperley, H. (2007). The power of feedback. *Review of Educational Research, 77*(1), 81–112.

Henderlong, J., & Lepper, M. (2002). The effects of praise on children's intrinsic motivation: A review and synthesis. *Psychological Bulletin, 128*(5), 774–795.

Kluger, A., & DeNisi, A. (1996). The effects of feedback interventions on performance: A historical review, a meta-analysis, and a preliminary feedback intervention theory. *Psychological Bulletin, 119*(2), 254–284.

Mason, B., & Bruning, R. (2001). Providing feedback in computer-based instruction: what the research tells us. Accessed July 22, 2010, from http://dwb4.unl.edu/dwb/Research/MB/MasonBruning.html

Mory, E. (2004). Feedback research review. In D. Jonassen (Ed.), *Handbook of research on educational communications and technology* (pp. 745–783). Mahwah, NJ: Erlbaum Associates.

Murnane, R., & Levy, F. (1996). *Teaching the new basic skills*. New York: Free Press.

Narciss, S., & Huth, K. (2004). How to design informative tutoring feedback for multi-media learning. In H. Niegemann, R. Brunken, & D. Leutner (Eds.), *Instructional design for multimedia learning* (pp. 181–195). Munster: Waxman.

Perrenoud, P. (1998). From formative evaluation to a controlled regulation of learning. Towards a wider conceptual field. *Assessment in Education: Principles Policy and Practice, 5*(1), 85–102.

Pollard, A. (1990). Towards a sociology of learning in primary school. *British Journal of Sociology of Education, 11*, 241–256.

Pryor, J., & Crossouard, B. (2008). A socio-cultural theorisation of formative assessment. *Oxford Review of Education, 34*(1), 1–20.

Pryor, J., & Torrance, H. (1998). Formative assessment in the classroom: Where psychological theory meets social practice. *Social Psychology of Education, 2*, 151–176.

Ryan, R., & Deci, E. (2000). Self-determination theory and the facilitation of intrinsic motivation, social development and well-being. *American Psychologist, 55*(1), 68–71.

Sadler, D. (1989). Formative assessment and the design of instructional systems. *Instructional Science, 18*, 119–144.

Shute, V. (2008). Focus on formative feedback. *Review of Educational Research, 78*(1), 153–189.

Stobart, G. (2008). *Testing times: The uses and abuses of assessment*. Abingdon: Routledge.

Torrance, H. (2007). Assessment as learning? How the use of explicit learning objectives, assessment criteria and feedback in post-secondary education and training can come to dominate learning. *Assessment in Education, 14*(3), 281–294.

Tunstall, P., & Gipps, C. (1996a). Teacher feedback to young children in formative assessment: A typology. *British Educational Research Journal, 22*(4), 389–404.

Tunstall, P., & Gipps, C. (1996b). 'How does your teacher help you make your work better?' Children's understanding of formative assessment. *Curriculum Journal, 7*(2), 185–203.

Watkins, C. (2003). *Learning: A sense-maker's guide*. London: ATL.

Wiliam, D. (2007). Keeping learning on track: Classroom assessment and the regulation of learning. In F. K. Lester, Jr. (Ed.), *Second handbook of mathematics teaching and learning* (pp. 1053–1098). Greenwich, CT: Information Age Publishing.

Chapter 10
Assessment for Learning in Language Classrooms

Alice Chow and Pamela Leung

10.1 Introduction

In recent years, there have been numerous reform initiatives in different contexts around the world aimed at improving educational planning and practices. For the success of these reforms, teachers play a crucial role in conceptualizing, interpreting and modifying them in ways that have significant impact on the kinds of learning that take place in the classroom. This chapter examines how the educational environments within which a reform initiative is undertaken shape the challenges teachers have to contend with for a sustainable and wider use of assessment for learning (AfL) strategies. It describes an assessment project undertaken by one secondary school in Hong Kong to improve student learning of languages through classroom-based assessment for learning (AfL) strategies.

10.2 The Language Situation in the Hong Kong SAR

The policy of promoting "biliteracy and trilingualism" announced in 1998 by the Chief Executive of the first Hong Kong Special Administrative Region (HKSAR) Government gives recognition to the roles that Putonghua, Cantonese and English play in the political, cultural and economic arenas of Hong Kong. Ethnically, more than 96% of the population of 7 million are of Chinese descent, of whom 88.7% speak Cantonese, a Chinese dialect, as the usual language (Bacon-Shone & Bolton, 1998), and 1.3% are native speakers of English (Tsui, 2004). Clearly cultural loyalties of its people belong to China, with all important aspects of their lives, including education practices, reflecting Chinese traditions and influences (Chow & Mok-Cheung, 2004). Nevertheless, English has always played a very important role in Hong Kong during and beyond its 150 years of British colonial rule until 1997 when

A. Chow (✉)
Department of English, Hong Kong Institute of Education, Tai Po, Hong Kong
e-mail: alice@ied.edu.hk

R. Berry, B. Adamson (eds.), *Assessment Reform in Education*,
Education in the Asia-Pacific Region: Issues, Concerns and Prospects 14,
DOI 10.1007/978-94-007-0729-0_10,

its sovereignty was returned to the People's Republic of China (PRC). Before the political handover, when both Chinese and English were the official languages in Hong Kong, the language situation was described by Lai (2005) as "largely biliterate and bilingual", characterised by the use of modern standard Chinese and English in writing, and Cantonese and English, the two main spoken languages, for different functions.

The status of English has always been high, attributable not only to Hong Kong's British colonial history, but also to its drive for internationalization in an increasingly globalized world. The fact that English had been perceived as the language of power and prestige led to a predominance of English medium secondary schools in the early 1980s, outnumbering Chinese medium secondary schools by nine to one. Though the Mother Tongue Education Policy mandated by the first HKSAR Government reversed the situation, and led to a drastic drop in the percentage of English medium schools to 25% in 1998 (Chow, Tse-tso, & Li, 2005), this lasted for only a period of 10 years until 2009 when the "fine-tuning" of the medium of instruction policy revived the supreme role of English as a gatekeeper to higher education, a means for upward and outward mobility and a marker of internationalization (Lai & Chow, 2010). The role that the English language plays in the schooling of Hong Kong students has always been as significant as that of Chinese.

10.3 Reforms in Language Education and Assessment

In order to enable Hong Kong to continue as a thriving metropolis in Asia, the HKSAR Government believes that a steady and abundant supply of bilingual workers with proficiency in Chinese and English is needed (Cheng, 2004), and therefore, the two languages have always been two of the core subjects that students must take from primary one to senior secondary three (from 6 to 18 years of age). A two-track system in the medium of instruction is adopted in the majority of primary and secondary schools in which Cantonese is the teaching medium for oral communication, while standard modern Chinese (which has significant differences from Cantonese in terms of grammar and vocabulary) is adopted for written communication.

To raise the standard of Chinese and English, and to enhance the use of the two languages in the territory, the syllabuses of the two languages have undergone several revisions in different stages over the years (Lord & Cheng, 1987; Lee, 1995). For the subject of Chinese, the integrationist view emphasizing the integration of language learning with the nurture of Chinese cultural and ethical values shaped the Chinese curriculum in the 1950s (Tse et al., 1995). From the late 1960s onwards, it was replaced by the separationist view which argues that the acquisition of effective communication skills and thinking abilities should be the primary objective of Chinese language education (Tse, 2009). In line with the large-scale education reforms at the macro level, the new Chinese curriculum (Curriculum Development Council (CDC), 2001b, 2002b) now has an open and flexible framework which features a learner-focused approach (Tse, 2009), aiming at motivating students to learn and enhancing the teaching effectiveness of the subject through authentic learning activities and diversified learning materials (CDC, 2001b).

The revisions in the English Language Syllabuses and associated curriculum guides over the years have been numerous. They share a common aim to give pupils more opportunities to use English as a tool for communication, and to ensure that their proficiency is adequate for further studies and future employment (e.g., CDC, 1999, 2002a). It was hoped that with these revisions English language teaching approaches practised in the Hong Kong classrooms would also be reformed. For instance, the emphasis, in the English Language Syllabus, on enabling students to master the formal structure of the language in the 1970s was shifted to preparing students to develop linguistic functional competences in the 1980s (CDC, 1983), and then to enhancing the all-round developments of every child through integrated tasks in the 1990s (CDC, 1999). A major reform initiative which involved both Chinese and English in the 1990s was the Target Oriented Curriculum (TOC) initiative which advocated an integrated approach to teaching, learning and assessment.

At the classroom level, attempts have been made, over the years, to align educational processes with the student-centred pedagogy advocated in the published curriculum guides. With regard to curriculum implementation, while some studies conclude that the new Chinese Language curriculum has been successfully implemented (e.g., Wong, 2000; Wong & Lee, 2006), the research findings of other studies suggest that there is still room for improvement (e.g., Ho, 2003). Research studies investigating the process and outcomes of the TOC initiative enacted at the classroom level suggest that it failed as a curriculum and assessment renewal endeavour because of the lack of corresponding support measures in the external domain (Clarke & Hollingsworth, 2002), which, in the case of Hong Kong, includes the cultural settings in which assessment is perceived and utilized as a means for measurement, quality control and selection. The examination-driven nature of the Hong Kong education system has constrained assessment innovations such as the TOC initiative (Adamson & Davison, 2003; Berry, 2008; Carless, 2005). The incompatibility between the espoused learning theories of Hong Kong teachers and the constructivist approaches advocated in the TOC initiative was also cited as another reason for its downfall (Cheung, 1996; Morris, 2000; Morris, Lo, & Adamson, 2000; Adamson & Davison, 2008). It was also pointed out by Adamson and Tong (2008) that teachers do not just implement the curriculum, they adapt and modify the innovation to form a "hybrid version" of the reform.

The backwash effect of major changes in high-stakes examinations on teaching is best illustrated by the changes in classroom processes instigated by the introduction of a spoken component in the Use of English examinations and Advanced Supplementary Level Examination in Chinese Language and Culture in Hong Kong in 1990s. These changes led to a substantial increase in class time being devoted to speaking activities, and to an increase in spoken fluency noted in the subject of English (Allison, 1999). Recent assessment reforms in particular for the subjects of Chinese and English include the introduction of school-based assessment (SBA) in high-stakes examinations such as the Hong Kong Certificate Education

Examination (HKCEE) (for pupils aged 18) (HKEAA, 2005; CDC, 2007a), which aim to promote a wider use of AfL strategies in the secondary school classrooms. The Territory–wide System Assessment (TSA) (for pupils aged 9–15) implemented in the subjects of both Chinese and English since 2004 is another policy intended "to enable participating teachers to understand the key process involved in making sense of the (assessment) data and facilitate teachers' effective use of TSA results to inform learning and teaching" (TSA, 2009).

Situated within an educational context which has a history of failed educational renewal initiatives, but increasing concerted efforts at all levels to revamp the educational processes and assessment practices – for example, through the introduction of TSA and the SBA component in the HKCEE, both of which emphasize the "analysis, feedback and reflection cycle" (Coome, Folse, & Hubley, 2007, p. 13) – the AfL Project reported in this chapter might provide insights into the possibilities and challenges involved in the application of learning-oriented assessment strategies for improving learning and teaching at the classroom level. The design and perceived outcomes of the project will be outlined in the following sections.

10.4 Design of the Project

Guided by the fundamental concepts of AfL in the literature (e.g., Assessment Reform Group, 1999, 2002; Black & Wiliam, 1998a; Torrance & Pryor, 1998; Watkins, Carnell, Lodge, Wagner, & Whalley, 2002) and the CDC curriculum guide (CDC, 2007a, 2007b), one secondary school in Hong Kong undertook a 12-month investigation in 2006–2007 into the use of AfL strategies in its junior Chinese and English language classrooms for students aged 13–15.

The project involved two teams of language teachers in the school: the Chinese language subject team consisting of the Head as well as ten members of the Chinese Department, and the English subject team comprising two English language teachers and the Head of the English Department. The project teams experimented, in junior secondary language classes and in two action cycles, with the use of AfL strategies, namely questioning, sharing of criteria and standards, provision of feedback, and peer and self assessment. These AfL strategies were tried out in a total of 10 Chinese language classes, i.e., five Secondary One (S1) and five Secondary Two (S2) classes for students aged 13–14 and 14–15 respectively, and two Secondary One (S1) English language classrooms for students aged 13–14. While the Chinese language teachers focused on the use of AfL strategies in promoting the development of oral presentation skills of students in both action cycles, the English language teachers explored their use in the development of students' writing skills in the first action cycle, and then in their oral presentation skills in the second action cycle. Four faculty members from the Hong Kong Institute of Education served as facilitators and academic subject consultants in supporting the teachers' efforts. The process and outcome of the initiative were captured through various methods of data collection. Recordings were made of the project meetings, lessons in which

AfL strategies were tried out, and semi-structured interviews with project teachers, students and the Principal of the school about their evaluation of the project. Project teachers' reflections on their experiences were recorded in open-ended questionnaires.

The following section describes the use of AfL strategies by the two subject teams. Materials used by the teachers in conducting classroom assessments, and lesson extracts are included for illustrative purposes. The perceived impacts of the project on student learning and teacher development are also reported to highlight the successes achieved and challenges encountered by the teachers in their attempts to enact AfL in their classrooms.

10.5 Use of AfL Strategies

The project teachers were introduced to the notion of AfL through a pre-project seminar conducted by the Institute's faculty members, during which the importance of the following AfL strategies were highlighted:

(1) the use of questioning in language classrooms;
(2) the notion of criteria-sharing for enhancing students' knowledge and awareness of the critical areas in which their performance would be assessed;
(3) the provision of constructive effective feedback; and
(4) the use of peer- and self-assessment for equipping students with the knowledge and skills for making judgments on their own as well as their classmates' performance.

10.5.1 The Use of Questioning

AfL is premised on the notion of communicative interaction in the classroom between teachers and students, through which students are guided to understand what is expected of them with respect to their learning and achievement. The following is a lesson extract illustrating the use of questioning by the teachers as a technique to raise students' awareness of the critical areas in which their performance would be assessed.

Lesson extract 1 CT7 – 2nd cycle (original in Chinese)

CT7: What do we need to pay attention to when reading aloud?
STD 1: We should avoid repetitive reading [*not repeating the same word or sentence so as to enhance fluency]...........*
STD 2: Voice should be loud enough.
CT7: What do you mean by loud enough?
STD 2: You must project your voice.
CT7: Anything else do we need to pay attention to when reading aloud?
STD 3: We need to have correct pronunciation.

CT7: Correct pronunciation, I have mentioned some initial sounds which you need to pay special attention to, don't mix them up, and also avoid slurring.
STD4: You need to put in more emotions.
CT7: Putting in more emotions. Please take some time to look at the following paragraph, can you tell me, how to put in emotions? What do you need to pay attention to?
STD5: When we read text that portrays a happy mood, we need to read louder [read in ways that convey that mood].
CT7: Can you give some examples?
STD6: For example, I got 100 marks for my exam today [saying this very loudly].
CT7: Experiencing something happy or successful, you need to have a clear and resounding tone. How about the opposite? Being criticized or when you experienced failure, what sort of tone is appropriate?
STD7: The tone needs to be lowered.
CT7: Other than these, anymore?
STD8: You need to have eye contact.

....

CT7: (teacher demonstrated reading aloud a passage)

Note: CT7- Chinese Language teacher 7; STD- Student

The above extract shows the ways in which the Chinese language teacher facilitated and elicited a recap of pertinent assessment criteria which were relevant to the assessment of the reading aloud task at hand. The ultimate aim of reading aloud in the curricular subject of Chinese language is to enhance comprehension and appreciation of various types of texts. Students are required to read fluently and clearly with appropriate pausing and intonation, making very few or no pronunciation mistakes. By asking the right questions, the teacher (CT7) has successfully drawn the students' attention to the assessment criteria such as accuracy, fluency, appropriateness of intonation and awareness of audience.

10.5.2 Criteria Sharing

To share assessment criteria with students, the project teachers devised task-specific assessment checklists and feedback forms listing areas of criteria for assessment for use by both teachers and students (in teacher, peer- and self-assessment) in recording observations, and assessing student performances in the assessment tasks. Samples of checklists and assessment forms used for oral assessment tasks are provided below (Figs. 10.1 and 10.2).

The first sample (Fig. 10.1) was used in Chinese lessons for assessing students' performance in a speaking task which required students to read a text aloud. For this task, there were only two training goals for students to accomplish. The first one was volume control, and the second one fluency, and to achieve the second

Name: ______________________ Date: ______________________

Learning Objectives: Good volume, no repetition Unit 2 Textbook Session 2.36

Self-assessment

Description	Accomplished ✓ / to be improved △
1. I can finish reading 60 words in 1 minute.	
2. I have repeated less than 2 times in a 1-minute presentation.	
3. I think my voice is loud enough.	

Give 3–5 examples of inaccurate pronunciation you made in this task ____________________

Peer-assessment 1 ______________________ (Name of Student Assessor)

Description	Accomplished ✓ / to be improved △
1. S/he can finish reading 60 words in 1 minute.	
2. S/he repeated less than 2 times in a 1-minute presentation.	
3. I think his/her voice is loud enough.	

I think his/her overall performance is (Please ✓ the appropriate box)

☐ good ☐ very good ☐ excellent

Give 3–5 examples of inaccurate pronunciation your classmate just made in this task: ____________

Peer-assessment 2 ______________________ (Name of Student Assessor)

Description	Accomplished ✓ / to be improved △
1. S/he can finish reading 60 words in 1 minute.	
2. S/he repeated less than 2 times in a 1-minute presentation.	
3. I think his/her voice is loud enough.	

I think his/her overall performance is (Please ✓ the appropriate box)

☐ good ☐ very good ☐ excellent

Give 3–5 examples of inaccurate pronunciation your classmate just made in this task: ____________

Fig. 10.1 Checklist 1: Assessment form for reading aloud in Chinese

Teacher assessment

Description	Accomplished ✓ / to be improved Δ
1. S/he can finish reading 60 words in 1 minute.	
2. S/he repeated less than 2 times in a 1-minute presentation.	
3. I think his voice is loud enough.	

I think his/her overall performance is (Please ✓ the appropriate box)

☐ good ☐ very good ☐ excellent

3–5 examples of inaccurate pronunciation this student just made in this task : ______________

Fig. 10.1 (continued)

goal students were discouraged from repeating sentences in which they had made some minor mistakes. The clearly defined goals helped focus students' attention on specific aspects of the task, and specific indicators, such as the number of words read within a 1-min presentation, provided students with a more objective reference when they undertook self-assessment and peer-assessment. Of course, students' experience in doing assessment may not be comparable to teachers' professional judgment. Nevertheless, one of the characteristics of AfL is that through the process of self- and peer-assessment students are expected to study the assessment criteria repeatedly and refine their judgment with the support of teacher feedback. One of the key features of the use of checklists in the project is that both teachers and students used the same checklists for teacher, and student self- and peer-assessments. This design reduces the difference in expectations between students and teachers.

Checklist 2 (Fig. 10.2) is a generic assessment form used in English lessons for assessing students' performance in speaking tasks. Analytical scoring, as opposed to holistic assessment, was adopted, whereby the performance was judged against each of the assessment criteria specified for the task (see Chow & Li, 2008 for analytic and holistic assessment). Key domains, such as content, command of language and communicative strategies, were identified as aspects of oral performance which would be observed and evaluated. Additional criteria were added to focus on textual and skill-based features that characterized a particular assessment task.

As an essential AfL strategy that helped illustrate and elucidate the meanings of the assessment criteria and facilitate the development of abilities of discernment in students, exemplars illustrating different levels of performance in related assessment tasks were devised, and were also accompanied by focused training, in the form of performance analysis, led by the teacher, on samples of student work. The following Lesson extract 2 illustrates one such attempt by one teacher to help students

Presenter' s Name:______________ Class:_______ Assessor's Name: ____________ Class: _______

Task: Picture Description

A. Content (Relevance, coherence and interest of ideas)

1 = Very Weak 2 = Below Average 3 = Average 4 = Above Average 5 = Outstanding

Content	Self Evaluation	Peer Evaluation	Teacher Evaluation
1. Express ideas with details and examples			
2. Elaborate on ideas by giving reasons and results			
3. Draw on own or others' experiences			
4. Describing feelings			
Other Useful Ideas:			
5. Make good use of cues provided			
6.			

B. Command of Language and Pronunciation

1 = Very Weak 2 = Below Average 3 = Average 4 = Above Average 5 = Outstanding

1. Use a good range of vocabulary and accurate grammar			
2. Speak fluently with accurate pronunciation			
3. Use voice well to draw audience's attention			
4. Use good intonation to express ideas			
Other Functional or Notional Requirements:			
5.			
6.			

C. Communication Strategies

1 = Very Weak 2 = Below Average 3 = Average 4 = Above Average 5 = Outstanding

1. Show appropriate awareness of audience (e.g. eye contact, smiling and body language)			
2. Use coherent linkers effectively (e.g. although, then, and, but, first, when, while, however, this, there, that, those)			
Other Specific Requirements:			
3. Ask questions to enhance communication			
4.			

D. Overall Feedback

Strengths and Improvements

Fig. 10.2 Checklist 2: Generic assessment form for English speaking tasks

understand one of the assessment criteria of oral presentations, which focused on the richness of the contents.

Lesson extract 2 CT3 – 1st cycle (original in Chinese)

CT3: Please indicate which presentation, the one made by student A or student B in the video, has a rich content. When you hear a beeping sound,. . . . [it means] the students went over time. (*Teacher showed a video*)
Which presentation has a richer content? Please raise your hand if you think Student A has a richer content (*students raised their hands*). Please raise your hand if you think student B has a richer content (*students raised their hands).* Why do you think B has a richer content?

STD 1: The content covered more places for sightseeing.

CT3: How about A? What do you think of the places that A introduced? He talked about a fair bit of history, Stanley and the Airport. If you were a tourist, what would you think about his recommendations on the sites for sightseeing? Are they interesting?

STD 2: They are not interesting.

CT3: Compared with B, Student A's recommendations were not as interesting. Other than whether it interests you, what other suggestions can you give him?

STD 3: Recommend more places.

CT3: Student A had a fair bit of time left, whereas Student B went overtime and had the timer set off.....

Note: CT3- Chinese Language teacher 3; STD- Student

Besides using videos for performance analysis, the teachers also used sample student writings in class to illustrate to students the assessment criteria, and different levels of performance in a particular writing task.

10.5.3 Peer and Self Assessment

Ample opportunities were provided in the project for students to assess the performance of their fellow classmates as well as their own performance, for facilitating the application of the criteria, and for promoting self-regulation and self-directed improvement. The following extract from a project lesson illustrates one such attempt by a teacher to promote the practice of peer and self-assessment.

Lesson extract 3- CT3-1st cycle (original in Chinese)

CT3: Before I assess the presentations, I would like you all to select two of the best presentations by your classmates (listed the different presentations on board). Please raise your hand if the first classmate's presentation was interesting...., the second......

STD 1: The first student used a lot of formal phrases, the second used more informal language, and had a bit of pronunciation problems.

CT3: Any suggestions on how to improve?

STD 2: Talk in front of a mirror.
STD 3: ......
STD 4: My self-reflection is that my own time management wasn't good enough.
CT3: Ok, you have done some self-reflection, any more comments? Ok, it's my turn to give some feedback. When you do a presentation, you need to attract the audience's attention, your voice needs to be loud, and you must have a rich content. There is one thing most classmates didn't pick up on, it is that some of you forgot to address the audience before making the presentation, this [greeting the audience] is to let your audience and yourself get ready for the start of the presentation, and also this is a gesture of politeness. And today, you have been very serious and engaged about the speaking task, this is excellent.

Note: CT3- Chinese Language teacher 3; STD- Student

Table 10.1 Overview of classroom assessment: practice of individual speech

Class: 1A
Topic: individual speech
No. of students: 40
Duration: about 35 min
Using "a piece of memorable news" or "a memorable TV programme" as a topic, the teacher guides students to prepare a 1-min speech at home before the lesson.

Time (minute)	Lesson flow	Remark (AfL strategies)
5	Introduction – explaining the requirement of the activity (focusing on "content" and "volume");	Questioning, Sharing the assessment criteria
	Teachers' demonstration – "a piece of memorable news";	
	Distributing assessment forms;	
3	Students practise the speech they have prepared at home on their own. Then every one of them fills in the self-assessment part of the assessment form;	Self-assessment
12	Students work in pairs and take turns to talk on prepared topics. Then they fill in the peer-assessment part of the assessment forms;	Peer-assessment 1 & 2
1	Teacher briefly concludes the activity;	–
12	The teacher picks 3 students to demonstrate to the whole class;	Peer-assessment
	When each student finishes, the teacher invites other students to comment on the performance;	Questioning
	The teacher fills in assessment forms and gives feedback to the students who have just given a speech to the class;	Feedback (peer + teacher)
2	Conclusion – the teacher stresses the learning objectives and asks students to tidy up their assessment record;	–

The above extract, as well as lesson extract 4, also shows the provision of feedback by the teacher on students' performance. As illustrated, the teacher's feedback focused on the presentation content, language use and strategies for oral communication. This practice was prevalent in many other lessons. Table 10.1 illustrates an overview of lesson procedures in which AfL strategies were incorporated in classroom assessments.

Lesson extract 4- CT1 – 2nd cycle (original in Chinese)

CT1: Although this student was reading off her speech due to nervousness at first, once she got used to it, she had lots of eye contact, she put in emotions well, had used adverbs like last but not least etc, she used evidence to back up her argument. Here is the third presentation.
(Another student presents)

CT1: All three students did very well. For the third presentation, although the student was 4 seconds short of the 1:15 mark, his pace was pretty fast. His content was rich, his voice was loud and clear, his eye contact...... (students interrupted).

STD1: His voice was loud enough, his content was rich. He projected his emotions well; he had used evidence and also adverbs.

Note: CT1- Chinese Language teacher 1; STD- Student

Table 10.1 illustrates an overview of lesson procedures in which the above AfL strategies were incorporated in classroom assessments.

10.6 Impact on Student Learning

One of the valuable outcomes of this project was a notable cultural shift from a pervasive tradition of formal and standardized examinations in schools, where evaluative judgment was exclusively in the hands of teachers with students given limited information about the basis of the judgment or opportunities for self-assessment, to a classroom environment where assessment was experienced as a learning event with students developing an expanded awareness of achievement standards, and enriched capacities for self- and peer-evaluation, and for qualifying such evaluation with constructive feedback in relation to the set achievement goals. Through learning-oriented assessment procedures of co-construction of achievement goals, assessment criteria-sharing, provision of quality feedback and student assessment, students acquired the knowledge, confidence and capabilities to assess their performance, monitor progress, and regulate and take ownership of their learning. To critics such as Torrance (2007) who lamented the use of explicit learning objectives, assessment and criteria as promoting instrumentalism, the cultural shift, albeit to a limited extent, in the classroom assessment practices would seem to have been a welcome change. Black & Wiliam (1998b) and Berry (2005) point out that through self- and peer- assessment, students learn how to monitor their own learning, develop the ability to evaluate their own and their peer's work, as well as think about what to do next. What should be applauded as a commendable effort in this project was the increase in student engagement in the process of assessment which helped to close the achievement gap, and boost the self-confidence of under-achieving students.

Both the teachers and students in the project reported improvements in students' performance in skill areas selected as foci of investigation. Following the AfL practices, both teachers and students found the contents of students' speaking in Chinese, and both speaking and writing in English richer. Some teachers also reported that the improvements in the performance among weaker students were more noticeable than among the more capable students, but in the long run, they believed that all students would benefit from a sustained and wider implementation of AfL.

> *Very impressive, never thought that their improvement would be so great. Their improvement in speaking was most noticeable. Through AfL, their confidence in speaking was strengthened to a great extent. When they have the confidence, they are more motivated to continue. This is what we wished to achieve through AfL, because you need to motivate them to become active learners. First of all, they need to be confident in learning English. Therefore, [the results] were quite impressive.* (Interview- English teacher A)

Self-assessment was perceived to be useful in that it enabled students to identify their own strengths, and peer-assessment alerted them to the weaknesses that they were not aware of. Specifically they mentioned that students benefited from peer assessment and teacher-guided performance analysis of exemplars showing different levels of student performance in key domains of assessment.

> *In fact the students' English was not very bad, but their organizational skills were weak. That is, they had a lot to say, but couldn't organize [their ideas].... Through AfL, they saw how well others did in the presentation tasks, what was meant by a composed performance, and then how ideas were expressed.... Through analyzing the use of linking words, we showed them how to organize ideas, how paragraphing is done in compositions, their organizational skills have improved. When they know what they are saying, they rely less on cue cards. They began to have eye contact with the audience, they did better in all areas, this was most noticeable in my class....*
>
> *[Peer assessment] benefits students, because they are their peers, i.e., when they saw May performed at level 5, [and they knew that] they performed at level 4, they would think that they could do better.* (Interview- English Teacher A)

To the surprise of this teacher, some of her students were able to point out ways in which they did well, and ways in which they would improve on in their next performance.

> *That's already very impressive. I thought they would say "bad", or" ok", but I never thought that they could say what was wrong with their performance; they were only S1 students, shy, possibly not knowing much, but some were brave enough to say they were good....* (Interview- English Teacher A)

This was corroborated by students who were interviewed about their experiences in the AfL project.

> *My friends commented [through peer assessment] that I provided a lot of useful details in my essay, and that I was fairly clear in expressing my ideas.* (Interview-1E Student 2)

Similar points were made in all the interviews with the students who highlighted the learning they gained through the AfL practices.

> *Through peer-assessment, we knew about our strengths and weaknesses. We also learnt from our classmates through observing their performance.* (Interview-2B Student 1)
>
> *My friends suggested that I should improve in ways that I organized my ideas.* (Interview-1E Student 3)

Many students attributed improvements in their performance to the assessment criteria and performance analysis provided by the teachers.

> *We also understood the goals of the oral presentation task through the assessment criteria [provided by the teacher].* (Interview-1E Student 2)
>
> *I like the AfL project, because through self-, peer- and teacher assessment, I understand more about my performance.* (Interview-1B Student 2)

As described above, performance analysis was part of the teachers' attempt to share assessment criteria with students, and this enabled students to tell what the next higher level of performance for them would be like. With enhanced understanding of the basis of assessment, some students were found to have developed stronger abilities to monitor their own performance.

> *Besides, after I had tried it for half a semester, after the first writing task when I assigned the second writing task and distributed the evaluation form, students were already very much on task, noticing problems in their writing, even when they were in the process of writing. Therefore, I feel that they did benefit from it.* (Interview- English Teacher A)

10.7 Impact on Teacher Development

The teachers felt that they had benefited from the project in the following ways:

1. They now had an expanded teaching repertoire to include new strategies such as criteria-sharing, the use of exemplars for illustrating different performance levels, and the use of peer and self assessment with students. One teacher mentioned her attempt in applying the strategies with students in other classes at senior secondary level, which though proved to be less effective owing to lack of teacher preparation, yet was worthy of further exploration.

   > *Perhaps it's easier to implement AfL in junior classes, because in senior classes, we had to finish the syllabus..... AfL emphasizes the importance of the process of development, the learning process........, it's worth giving it a try.* (Interview- English Teacher A)

2. They had developed enhanced techniques in providing students with feedback on their performance with clear focus and specificity, and using questioning techniques to encourage deeper and reflective thinking and analysis.

   > *In some of the lessons, after the presentations, I noted down some of the mistakes, and then let the whole class do some practice. I think that's a kind of feedback for the whole class..... With practice with the whole class, they are aware of their problems, and will do better next time.* (Interview- English Teacher A)

> *Through assessment, I see what they have done well, and know whether certain strategies are okay or not. And then we [teachers] have the confidence to explore other things, and then realize how some other things don't work. [We]don't give up.* (Interview-English Teacher B)

3. They were now using assessment to inform and structure future teaching to address areas of difficulties in student learning, and students' needs.

> *In regard to teaching, I have learned a lot from my colleagues and even from my students. They might tell me what they wanted to learn and how they liked to learn. I then could work to meet their abilities. I think this is very useful for teaching.* (Interview-Chinese Teacher B)

4. They had strengthened their skills in curriculum design through improving the linkage between teaching, learning and assessment.

> *[H]onestly, I might not gain similar experiences in other schools. Through this project, I realize that I can progressively make use of self- and peer-assessments. The students would be more serious too. Telling them the procedures can let them understand our requirements......Although it was quite time-consuming, knowing how to do this systematically is good.* (Interview-Chinese Teacher A)

10.8 Conditions for Sustained and Wider Use of AfL

Despite the many benefits cited as the positive impacts of the project on student learning and professional development, the teachers did have to contend with the following challenges.

First of all, although the school had obtained external funding for employing a teaching assistant for the project, her role was limited to providing logistic support such as lesson recording and questionnaire administration. It would therefore be more useful if additional resources and staffing could be provided for assisting the project teachers with materials development as well as reducing the teaching load of these teachers, so that educational initiatives would not be viewed as simply more work for the teachers.

The second challenge related to the professional development needed to equip the teachers with both the skills and confidence for designing and enacting AfL strategies (see Fontana & Fernandes, 1994) in the following areas in particular:

1. the use of high-level, reflective questions to gauge students' understanding of assessment criteria;
2. ways to help students to get to a higher level of performance which required pedagogical tact;
3. transfer of assessment skills from one skill area to another;
4. adapting the AfL strategies for use in public examination classes, which was perceived by project teachers to be particularly challenging, as these classes had a very packed teaching syllabus to ensure the students were adequately prepared for public examinations;

5. the use of peer and self- assessment with less capable students particularly in grammar-focused assessment tasks which generally demanded a relatively higher level of grammatical knowledge for students to be able to identify their and others' grammatical errors.

Several suggestions were put forward by the project teachers for creating a conducive environment and support for enhancing the use of AfL strategies:

1. Implementing small-class teaching (the teachers currently have more than 40 students per class) with relevant, corresponding pedagogical techniques would enable teachers to monitor student progress and provide feedback on individual students' performances in assessment tasks;
2. Involving more teachers in the subject departments for wider and sustained implementation, lest when the project teachers leave the school, AfL can continue and be further embedded into the regular practices of the teachers;
3. Changing school based assessment policies by incorporating continuous assessment but reducing summative assessment, so that students take their daily tasks for formative assessment more seriously, and allowing more time and space for practising AfL.

The third recommendation listed above is particularly relevant to the contexts which have a strong examination culture and where most teachers and students consider only formal examination to be "assessment" and therefore take other forms of assessment less seriously. In Hong Kong, many schools rely heavily on using paper-and-pencil tests for summative purpose and the papers are designed in a way that memorization of facts is made an obvious focus (Pong & Chow, 2002; Berry, 2010). This AfL reform was situated within a culture which has a strong tradition of didactic pedagogy in which classroom teaching is mostly expository, and sharply focused on preparation for external examinations which are highly competitive and exert excessive pressure on teachers and students (Morris, 1992, 1995). In Hong Kong, in addition to large-scale public examinations at the end of secondary schooling, there are the TSA at the levels of Primary 3, 6 and Secondary 3 (at the age of 8, 11 and 15 respectively) and the Pre-Secondary 1 Hong Kong Attainment Test at the end of Primary 6. In addition to these examinations, every year, the student has to take at least two school-based examinations and numerous tests and quizzes, which in some schools are held weekly.

The Head of the English Department was keenly aware of the concerns of the school's academic development team, which was responsible for quality assurance, and which might want to maintain formal, summative assessment, believing that such assessment would make teachers do their jobs properly, providing repeated examination "drills" for students, and make students concentrate on studying for high-stake public examinations.

> *I think they [academic development team] would be worried. They would like to have some control, they think that it's necessary… to get students to study their books.… Besides, it's for control, for administration, for monitoring.… and for fairness.* (Interview- Head of English Department)

It would take the academic development team great courage to implement changes when the school had a good reputation for doing well in public examinations. Without corresponding changes in school assessment policy and mechanism – for instance making student participation in AfL contributory to their actual academic results – it would be difficult to persuade his teachers and students that it was worth exploring new teaching and learning initiatives.

Given the critical impact that examination cultures have on the pedagogical and assessment practices in Hong Kong as an Asian city, the pockets of success reported in this chapter could be read alongside the cultural sensitive view of Kennedy, Chan, Fok, and Yu (2008), who argued that if formative assessment (or AfL) is to be taken up in Asian cultural contexts, it may need to be indigenized in order to match more readily with local needs and priorities.

Appendix

Form 1 English: Writing – An Event That Happened in My Secondary School

Student Exemplar 1

1 Last week, Karen had a school camp with Tiffany. "Karen, we go to camp now" Karen and Tiffany shouted happily.

3 At night, they reached the camp site with teachers and other students. It was very dark with some breeze. It was very spooky. Tiffany and Karen went to their room. "Oh, this room is very old" Karen exclaimed. That room was very old and dirty. The things were all broken or old. Nothing is new. They felt very unhappy.

7 At twelve o'clock. Tiffany woke up in a sudden and asked Karen "I want to go to the toilet, can you accompany me?" Karen answered "Of course".

9 They went to toilet. But they felt something wrong. Because no any body in the toilet but have some water sound. "I think there is a monster in the toilet" said Tiffany. Karen answered, "Don't scare me, please." "Ah" They screamed. They felt very scared and ran out the toilet. They ran very fast than before. They quickly rushed into their bedroom and slept.

13 They wouldn't go to camp anymore, because after this camp. They were scared.

Text Analysis

Time Indicator	L1 Last week L7 At twelve o'clock	L3 At night L12 quickly

Direct Speech	L1 "Karen, we go to camp now." L4 "Oh, this room is very old." L7 "I want to go to the toilet, can you accompany me?"

	L10 "I think there is a monster in the toilet."		
	L11 "Don't scare me, please."		
Past Tense	L1 had	L3 reached	L5 were
	L6 felt	L7 woke	L9 ran
	L12 rushed	L13 were	L13 wouldn't go

Speaking Verbs	L2 shouted	L5 exclaimed	L7 asked
	L8 answered	L10 said	L11 screamed

References

Adamson, B., & Davison, C. (2003). Innovation in English language teaching in Hong Kong primary schools: One sep forwards, two steps sideways. *Prospect, 18*, 27–41.

Adamson, B., & Davison, C. (2008). English language teaching in Hong Kong primary schools: Innovation and resistance. In *Planning change, changing plans. Innovations in second language teaching* (pp. 11–25). Michigan: The University of Michigan Press.

Adamson, B., & Tong, S. Y. A. (2008). Leadership and collaboration in implementing curriculum change in Hong Kong secondary schools. *Asia Pacific Education Review, 9*(2), 181–190.

Allison, D. (1999). *Language testing and evaluation*. Singapore: Singapore University Press.

Assessment Reform Group (1999). *Assessment for learning: Beyond the black box*. Cambridge: School of Education.

Assessment Reform Group (2002). *Assessment for Learning: 10 Principles*. Cambridge: University of Cambridge Faculty of Education.

Bacon-Shone, J., & Bolton, K. (1998). Charting multilingualism: Language censuses and language surveys in Hong Kong. In M. Pennington (Ed.), *Language in Hong Kong at century's end* (pp. 43–90). Hong Kong: Hong Kong University Press.

Berry, R. (2005). Entwining feedback, self and peer assessment. *Academic Exchange Quarterly, 9*(3), 225–229.

Berry, R. (2008). *Assessment for Learning*. Hong Kong: Hong Kong University Press.

Berry, R. (2010). Teachers' orientations towards selecting assessment strategies. *New Horizons in Education, 58*(1), 96–107.

Black, P., & Wiliam, D. (1998a). Inside the Black Box: Raising standards through classroom assessment. *Phi Delta Kappan, 80*(2), 139–144.

Black, P., & Wiliam, D. (1998b). Assessment and Classroom Learning. *Assessment in Education: Principles, Policy & Practice, 5*(1), 7–74.

Carless, D. (2005). Prospects for the implementation of assessment for learning. *Assessment in Education, 12*, 39–54.

Cheng, N. L. (2004). Hong Kong SAR. In K. W. Ho. & R. Wong (Eds.), *Language policies and language education: The impact in East Asian countries in the next decade* (pp. 100–114). Singapore: Eastern Universities Press.

Cheung, W. W. (1996). The implications of implementing the Target-Oriented curriculum (TOC) for teacher education. *Journal of Primary Education, 6*(1–2), 37–44.

Chow, A., & Li, B. (2008). Task-based Assessment. In A. Ma (Ed.), *Practical guide to task-based curriculum planning and assessment* (pp. 102–127). Hong Kong: City University Press.

Chow, A., & Mok-Cheung, A. (2004). English language teaching in Hong Kong SAR: Tradition, transition and transformation. In W. K. Ho & R. Wong (Eds.), *English language teaching in East Asia today. Changing policies and practices* (pp. 150–177). Singapore: Eastern Universities Press.

Chow, A., Tse-tso, Y. W., & Li, B. (2005). Learning English or learning through English: Evaluating an English enrichment programme in post-colonial Hong Kong. In S. May, M. Franken, & R. Barnard (Eds.), *LED2003: Refereed conference proceedings of the 1st international conference on language, education and diversity*. Hamilton: Wilf Malcolm Institute of Educational Research, University of Waikato.
Clarke, D., & Hollingsworth, H. (2002). Elaborating a model of teacher professional growth. *Teaching and Teacher Education, 18*(8), 947–967.
Coome, C., Folse, K., & Hubley, N. (2007). *A practical guide to assessing English language learners*. Michigan: University of Michigan.
Curriculum Development Council (1983). *Syllabuses for secondary schools: English (Secondary 1-5)*. Hong Kong: Education Department.
Curriculum Development Council (1999). *Syllabuses for secondary schools. English language secondary 1-5*. Hong Kong: the Printing Department.
Curriculum Development Council (2001b). *Syllabuses for secondary schools. Chinese language secondary 1-5*. Hong Kong: The Printing Department.
Curriculum Development Council (2002a). *English language education. Key learning area curriculum guide (Primary 10- Secondary 3)*. Hong Kong: The Printing Department.
Curriculum Development Council (2002b). *Chinese language education. Key learning area curriculum guide (Primary 10- Secondary 3)*. Hong Kong: The Printing Department.
Curriculum Development Council (2007a). *Chinese language education key learning area English language curriculum and assessment guide (Secondary 4-6)*. Hong Kong: The Printing Department.
Curriculum Development Council (2007b). *English language education key learning area English language curriculum and assessment guide (Secondary 4-6)*. Hong Kong: The Printing Department.
Fontana, D., & Fernandes, M. (1994). Improvements in mathematics performance as a consequence of self-assessment in Portuguese primary school pupils. *British Journal of Educational Psychology, 64*, 407–417.
Ho, M. S. (2003). *A critical review of Hong Kong Chinese language education reform at the turn of the century*. Hong Kong: Cultural Education Publishing (In Chinese).
Hong Kong Examinations and Assessment Authority (2005). 2007 HKCE English language examination. In *Introduction to the school-based assessment component*. Hong Kong: Hong Kong Examinations and Assessment Authority.
Kennedy, K. J., Chan, K. S. J., Fok, P. K., & Yu, W. M. (2008). Forms of assessment and their potential for enhancing learning: Conceptual and cultural issues. *Educational Research for Policy and Practice, 7*(3), 197–207.
Lai, M. L. (2005). Language attitudes of the first postcolonial generation in Hong Kong secondary schools. *Language in Society, 34*(4), 363–388.
Lai, M. L., & Chow, A. (2010, June). Medium of instruction policies in postcolonial Hong Kong – the national or international agenda? In *The international conference on who needs languages? Micro and macro perspectives into language education policies*. (pp. 7–10). Finland: University of Jyväskylä.
Lee, K. S. (1995). The trend of Chinese language teaching in the 90's. *Modern Education Bulletin, 19*, 46–49.
Lord, R., & Cheng, H. (Eds.) (1987). *Language education in Hong Kong*. Hong Kong: The Chinese University Press.
Morris, P. (1992). Preparing pupils as citizens of the special administrative region of Hong Kong: An analysis of curriculum change and control during the transition period. In G. Postiglione (Ed.), *Education and society in Hong Kong: Towards one country and two systems* (pp. 117–145). Hong Kong: Hong Kong University Press.
Morris, P. (1995). *The Hong Kong school curriculum*. Hong Kong: Hong Kong University Press.
Morris, P. (2000). The commissioning and decommissioning of curriculum reforms: The career of the target-oriented curriculum. In B. Adamson, T. Kwan, & K. K. Chan (Eds.), *Changing the*

curriculum: The impact of reform on Hong Kong's primary schools (pp. 21–40). Hong Kong: Hong Kong University Press.

Morris, P., Lo, M. L., & Adamson, B. (2000). Improving schools in Hong Kong: Lessons from the past. In B. Adamson, T. Kwan, & K. K. Chan (Eds.), *Changing the curriculum: The impact of reform on Hong Kong's primary schools* (pp. 245–262). Hong Kong: Hong Kong University Press.

Pong, W.Y., & Chow, J.C.S. (2002). On the pedagogy of examinations in Hong Kong: *Teaching and Teacher Education, 18*(2), 139–149.

Territory–wide System Assessment (TSA) (2009). Accessed August 3, 2009, from http://www.systemassessment.edu.hk/sec/eng/index_eng.htm/

Torrance, H. (2007). Assessment *as* learning? How the use of explicit learning objectives, assessment criteria and feedback in post-secondary education and training can come to dominate learning. *Assessment in Education, 14*(3), 281–294.

Torrance, H., & Pryor, J. (1998). *Investigating formative assessment*. Buckingham: Open University Press.

Tse, S. K. (2009). Chinese language education in Hong Kong: Twenty five years of educational research in Hong Kong. *Educational Research Journal, 24*(2), 231–255.

Tse, S. K., Chan, W. S., Ho, W. K., Law, N., Lee, T., Shek, C., et al. (1995). *Chinese language education for the 21st century: A Hong Kong perspective*. Hong Kong: Faculty of Education, University of Hong Kong.

Tsui, A. B. M. (2004). Medium of instruction in Hong Kong: One country, two systems, whose language? In J. J. W. Tollefson & A. B. M. Tsui (Eds.), *Medium of instruction polices: Which agenda? Whose agenda?* (pp. 97–116). Mahwah, NJ: Lawrence Erlbaum Associates, Publishers.

Watkins, C., Carnell, E., Lodge, C., Wagner, P., & Whalley, C. (2002). Effective learning, ISIN. *Research Matters, 17*, 1–8.

Wong, H. W. (2000). *In search of the knowledge base of curriculum design and teaching*. Hong Kong: Institute of Educational Research, the Chinese University of Hong Kong. (in Chinese).

Wong, H. W., & Lee, Y. Y. (2006). *Developing student potentials in a collaborative culture: A case study of implementing the newly revised Chinese language syllabus for secondary schools*. Hong Kong: Institute of Educational Research, the Chinese University of Hong Kong. (in Chinese).

Chapter 11
Assessment Reform: High-Stakes Testing and Knowing the Contents of Other Minds

David Scott

11.1 Introduction

Michel Foucault (1979) in his brief and only direct reference to education argued that the introduction of the examination into society had three consequences. It transformed the economy of visibility into an exercise of power; introduced individuality into the field of documentation; and constructed each individual as a case. All three of these consequences impact on the workings of a range of educational and social mechanisms, not least, those that relate to high-stakes testing and knowledge of the contents of other people's minds. This is the focus of this chapter.

The argument that I will be making is as follows. Two forms of knowledge can be identified (let us call them K_a and K_b). K_a represents those knowledge sets, skills, and dispositional states of a person, collectively known as capacities. K_b represents those knowledge sets, skills and dispositional states which allow this person to do well in tests, and, in particular, high-stakes tests. K_a and K_b have different characteristics. If an education system introduces high-stakes testing, that is, testing in which there are significant rewards attached to success in the test both for the individual and the institution in which she works, then there are two consequences. The first is that K_b becomes the dominant form of knowledge in the curriculum and the second is that K_a over time is transformed so that it becomes more like K_b, that is, it has more of its characteristics. Testers commonly conflate K_a and K_b, and in doing so make a number of false assumptions about knowledge and its assessment, with the consequence that these two forms of knowledge become indistinguishable in the minds of policy-makers, educational practitioners, students and other stakeholders.

The default position taken by those working within this psychometric tradition of knowing other minds is that the individual has a number of capacities (i.e., knowledge sets, skills, dispositions), which we can describe as the contents of that person's mind, and which subsequently we can characterize using the methods of

D. Scott (✉)
Institute of Education, University of London, 20, Bedford Way, London WCIH OAL, UK
e-mail: d.scott@ioe.ac.uk

R. Berry, B. Adamson (eds.), *Assessment Reform in Education*, Education in the Asia-Pacific Region: Issues, Concerns and Prospects 14,
DOI 10.1007/978-94-007-0729-0_11,

experimentation and testing. There is therefore potentially a true score for a person, and this true score represents in symbolic terms her capacity in the particular domain being tested. For a variety of reasons, errors may occur in the process of constructing that true score, but these are corrigible, i.e., they can be corrected by using different (and thus by implication better) methods and approaches. Errors may occur because the wrong type of instrument is chosen for determining the person's true score or because that person's emotional and affective states are such that she gives a false impression of her capacities. In contrast, I want to suggest that there are a number of false assumptions being made here, perhaps best expressed as false beliefs.

11.2 False Beliefs

The first is that a person has a knowledge, skill or dispositional set, which is configured in a particular way (i.e., it has a grammar), and it is this knowledge, skill or dispositional set, or at least elements of it, which is directly assessed when that person is tested. This is to be contrasted with a view which suggests that any testing that is carried out with the purpose of determining whether these attributes are held, not held, or even partially held by an individual, always involves an indirect process of examination, where the additional element is a conjecture, logical inference or best guess. Furthermore, the required performance elicited during the test is specifically related to the testing technology, so, for example, if a multiple-choice test is chosen, the correct answer and therefore the correct construction of the problem are framed to fit this technology. In order to obtain a true measure of that person's capacity (i.e., K_a), and not, it should be noted, a comparative measure of the construct being tested at the individual or group level (i.e., K_b), then a retroductive mode of inference would need to be used to identify what must have been the case in order to bring about the observed event (i.e., the testee answering a multiple-choice question in a standardized test).

A second false belief is that this grammar is organized into elements, there are relations between those elements, and each element can be scaled, so a person may have more or less of that element, which can then be investigated. This can be contrasted with a position which suggests that, in the application of the knowledge, skill or dispositional set, whether for the purposes of testing or for use in everyday life, a range of other knowledge elements, skills and dispositions are called upon, which we might want to call background material. However, cognitive psychologists and test constructors presume that these background elements are not relevant to the assessment of the performance during the test, or even to a different type of performance outside it. This should not be conflated with the argument that the contents of the curriculum cannot be disconnected for the purposes of testing, leading to a belief in property holism (cf. Curren, 2006, for a refutation). What, in contradistinction, is being asserted here is that in the application of a knowledge set, skill or disposition, whether for the purposes of testing or otherwise, a range of other types of knowledge and skill are needed, and the testee may not have sufficient knowledge of these matters or be sufficiently skilful in relation to them. As a result, if a judgment is made about that person's capacity in relation to the construct, it may be incorrect because its construct validity is weak.

A third false belief is that in the use of a knowledge-set, or in the performance of a skill, or in the application of a disposition, no internal transformation takes place. (In fact, both internal and external transformations are neglected within traditional psychometric accounts.) In contrast, within a person's mind two knowledge sets are being activated. The first is the original knowledge set (K_a); and the second is the transformed set (K_b). Further to this, K_b is not just the result of a causal mechanism at work but may also at different points in time influence and transform K_a; that is, it has the capacity to bend back on itself and act recursively to change its original form.

There is also an external transformative process at work, and thus a fourth false belief is that testing a person's knowledge, skills and aptitudes has no washback effects on either K_a, the original knowledge construct, or K_b, the internally transformed knowledge set ready for testing. In contrast, the well-documented process of washback works in just this way, so that instead of the assessment acting merely as a descriptive device, it also acts in a variety of ways to transform the construct it is seeking to measure, either exogenously or endogenously. Washback effects work on a range of objects and in different ways. So, for example, there are washback effects on the curriculum, on teaching and learning, on the capacity of the individual and more fundamentally on the structures of knowledge, though these four mechanisms are frequently conflated in the minds of educational stakeholders.

Micro washback effects work directly on the person, whereas macro washback effects work directly on institutions and systems, which then subsequently have an impact on individuals within those institutions and systems. For example, at a global level, as in the international comparative system of testing known as the Programme for International Student Assessment (PISA) (OECD, 2000, 2001), policy enactments may lead to changes in national curricula and national systems of testing, which in time will lead to changes in curriculum and assessment at the level of schools and thence to changes in what is learnt and what an individual considers to be performative knowledge. What is considered to be appropriate performative knowledge has therefore changed as a result of changes at global, national and school levels. Washback effects do not work in a deterministic way, since there are a large number of activities that have to be coordinated during the sequence of events to achieve the desired result, and mechanisms such as these have emergent properties because they operate in open systems (cf. Bhaskar, 1989).

The argument is therefore made by cognitive psychologists and test constructors that no internal or external processes of transformation occur when the knowledge, skills, or dispositions of the person are tested; i.e., that person knows A or has skill B or disposition C, and that in the act of displaying that knowledge or using that skill or allowing that disposition to be realized, no change occurs to the original knowledge construct, or skill set or disposition, in order for that person to respond in the appropriate manner to the situation confronting them. In contrast, it is argued that there is a transformative process and it may take a number of forms, i.e., accretion and thus retention of the original knowledge domain, skill or disposition, or subsumption, where the original knowledge domain is subsumed into a new domain and thus loses its identity, or subtraction so that parts are discarded to accommodate the contingencies of the new setting. What this also points to is that in the process of determining whether a person knows this, or can do this, or has the necessary disposition, an inferential process is required so that the observer can move from evidence, i.e., the test result, to state of being. The assumption is made that if this person can do X in the test situation, then they can also do it in different situations; or if that person knows something in the test situation, then they also know it in other situations. It is, in short, the problem of transfer (from T_1 to T_2 or from C_1 to C_2, where T refers to a moment in time and C refers to a context of application), and it is problematic because it is prospective and morphogenetic. A measure of predictive success to determine whether a person or group of people can do X in other settings outside the testing environment can be developed; however it is an unreliable measure for two reasons. Events, happenings and unplanned occurrences during the interval between the two time points (T_1 – the test setting and T_2 – the application setting) cannot be controlled for; and the two different activities are not comparable.

A fifth false belief is that the process of testing works in a unidirectional linear fashion. For example, a person knows X, that person is subjected to a test which is designed to test for traces of X in a population of knowers with similar characteristics, and a score in relation to that construct is recorded indicating that the person either knows it, doesn't know it or knows it to some extent. No consideration is given to bidirectionality, incorporating forward and backward flows, so that the taking of the test and the recording of the mark impact on and influence the original knowledge construct. This changes the structure (both quantitatively and qualitatively) of the construct, and its affordances, making the original determination of it and them unreliable.

A sixth false belief is that different types of knowledge, including those at different levels of abstraction, can be tested using the same algorithmic process. For example, testing a knowledge of facts and testing a capacity to synthesize basic facts are different processes. And this is because in the former case the test item refers directly to the construct being tested, whereas in the latter case it refers to an example of the construct, and successful mastery of the construct has to be inferred from successful mastery of the example. This latter process therefore additionally has to satisfy criteria such as relevance, quality and probative force for that inferential relationship between example and construct to be considered valid.

A seventh false belief is that the performance on the test represents to a greater or lesser extent (given that the person may have been distracted or constrained in some way or another) what the testee can do or show, rather than there being a qualitative difference between the performance on the test and the construct, skill, or disposition of the testee. An individual may have to reframe their knowledge set to fit the test, and therefore the assessment of their mastery of the construct is not a determination of their capacity in relation to the original construct, but a determination of whether the testee has successfully understood how to rework their capacity to fit the demands of the testing technology.

An eighth false belief is that a test can be constructed which is culture-free or free of those issues which disadvantage some types of learners at the expense of others. This mechanism works in a number of ways: test constructors may use background material which is unfamiliar to some testees but familiar to others; test items may have been taught in different ways to different groups of testees, that is, they have been given different values, or taught in a different order, or even not taught at all; and the testing technology may be unfamiliar to them because of factors which are peripheral to the articulation or use of the particular construct, but central to the testing technology used to assess it.

If no incentive is attached to the taking of a test, i.e., personal benefit such as gaining entry to a higher education institution, or monetary reward, or furtherance of a student's learning trajectory, or national advantage, then the student is not likely to treat it very seriously. The value that she attaches to it is always a matter of perception, rather than designation, and this means that different types of students will be motivated to do well to different degrees. Cognitive psychologists and test constructors argue that these individual characteristics of test takers are accounted for at the level of the group, and the argument is then made that these characteristics, i.e., propensity to lose concentration in a test or not give a true account of their capacities because the examination technology offers them no incentive to do well, or having a presentational style which is at variance with the affordances of the examination technology, are randomly distributed amongst members of any group, and therefore do not effect scores at the group level. As a result, groups can be reliably compared with each other. However, the assumption that these characteristics of group members are evenly distributed is false, and in addition, this is a measure of reliability rather than construct validity. Furthermore, these characteristics may be the defining characteristics of the group.

As an example, let us take a multiple choice test. The technology only allows a limited range of answers, therefore there is a high probability of false negative and false positive errors (Wood & Power, 1987), despite misleaders being inserted as questions to allow reliability checks to be performed. Only a limited range of knowledge items and processes can potentially be tested because correct answers are being asked for, and those answers are framed in ways that do not allow discursive, equivocal responses. As a result, this technology has the effect of widening the gap between the capacity of the individual and her performance (both internally and externally), because the test is constructed so that it has few of the characteristics of the original knowledge construct and potentially its application. There is in short a limited discretion given to the person being tested and therefore in principle at least, multiple-choice testing has a greater propensity to washback onto the curriculum. Furthermore, the characteristics of the technology used for multiple-choice testing favour some groups in comparison with others, i.e., boys may have an advantage over girls.

A contrasting example might be the use of a free-ranging essay format to determine the comparative capacity of a group. A wide discretion is given to each candidate, though marker unreliability effects may be high. The assessment is not focused on discrete facts but on general competencies, i.e., the ability to sustain an argument. Thus in principle it may be better able to measure higher level skills. Validity may be high if this is understood as an alignment between the knowledge, skills and dispositions of the person and the description that is made of them. Because marker discretion is high and because the candidate is allowed more latitude in how she frames her answers, then the possibility of a significant washback effect is reduced.

A test is always a performance. The taker of the test frames their response to the test in terms of what they perceive to be the correct answer. This operates at the unconscious level, and it is unremarkable. When we have a conversation with another person, we frame our responses and our mode of responding to how we think our messages are going to be received. With regards to testing, there is a further element, which is that the testee frames their answers in terms of their perception of what they consider to be the correct response. If for example, there is some ambiguity in the question, the testee asks herself the question: what type of answer should I give which is likely to result in the award of the maximum amount of marks? Test constructors aim to write questions or construct problems to be answered with as little ambiguity as possible. This is achieved (though rarely successfully) by reducing the scope of either the question/problem to be solved or by reducing the response that the testee is required to make, and this involves a reformulation of the knowledge construct, though it may still contain residues of its original form.

11.3 Symbol-Processing Views of Mind

Cognitive psychologists and test constructors implicitly adopt a computational or symbol-processing view of mind. Learning (i.e., the process by which the social actor gains access to the external world), and the assessment of this learning (i.e., the process of giving an account of it), are understood as inputting coded unambiguous information about the world, which is then sorted, stored, retrieved and managed in the same way that a computer processes data. Information is inputted into this device, and this information consists of pre-digested facts about the world which map the way the world works. The mind, in the act of learning, processes that information, assimilates the new information into the store of facts and theories that it already holds, and then adjusts that worldview in the light of this new information. This is a mechanical process, and it has within it an impoverished view of the role interpretation plays in learning. Interpretation is now reduced to the assimilation of new information and the subsequent reformulation of the mind-set of the individual. Here, the individual is treated as a passive reflector of the way the world works and correct or incorrect views of the world are understood as a function of the efficiency with which these processes are conducted.

This viewpoint separates out language from reality, mind from body and the individual from society (cf. Bredo, 1999). The first of these is the separation of language from reality. As a result, learning and assessment processes are understood in terms of four principles. Knowledge of the contents of another person's mind is determinate (there is a certain truth that can be known), rational (there are no contradictory and even alternative explanations), impersonal (the more objective and the less subjective the better), and predictive (assessment is the making of knowledge claims in the form of generalizations from which predictions can be made, and events, people and phenomena controlled). Cognitive psychologists and test constructors follow a pre-specified path or protocol which allows them to access reality. The only domain of inquiry is the empirical one, and therefore empirical verifiability is achieved through measurement of various kinds. Causality is based on associations between covariant variables, and thus causal mechanisms are reduced to associational relationships or correlations established between pre-specified variables. Using experimental and quasi-experimental test designs (more suited to closed systems than the open systems which educational phenomena, including assessment processes, operate within), they control reality by isolating certain variables. If as many as possible cause-variables can be shown not to correlate with the effect-variable, they can have greater confidence in the relationship they have established between the cause- and effect-variables that have not been isolated, and this allows them to make a claim about a causal relationship, over and above a mere associational one. This produces a model of learning and assessment which comprises: accessing the outside world, receiving sensory inputs into existing conceptual schema, assimilating those external stimuli through processes of selection/negotiation/rearrangement and the like, and in the process creating new conceptual frameworks, which can then subsequently be described.

The most important of the points made above is the idea that facts about a person's capacity, that are free of the value assumptions of the assessor, can be collected. These facts constitute unequivocal and true statements about her. Assessment or testing comprises discovering what they are and developing adequate models to explain them. However, this faithful representation of reality implies that the world is fixed by language, with language acting as a transparent medium. This notion of representational realism then, for Taylor (1995), misrepresents the process of how human beings act in relation to stimuli from their environment, and how an account can be given of this process.

Symbol-processing approaches to cognition also suggest a further dualism, between mind and body. This separation of mind and body locates learning and cognition in the mind, as it passively receives from the bodily senses information which it then processes. The mind is conceived of as separate from the physical body and from the environment in which the body is located. Learning is understood as a passive process of acquiring information from the environment and thus this view of cognition supports didactic approaches to teaching and learning, and psychometric approaches to knowing the contents of other people's minds. Situated-cognitionists argue that learning involves close and interactive contact with the environment, and this contributes to further understanding for the individual, and changes or transforms the environment itself. Knowledge is not understood as a passive body of facts about the environment but as an interactive process of reconstructing meanings.

Finally, it is important to identify a third dualism which Taylor (1995) and other critics of symbol-processing approaches have suggested is problematic. This is the separation of the individual from society. The individual/societal distinction which is central to a symbol-processing view of cognition separates out individual mental operations from the construction of knowledge by communities of people and this leaves it incomplete as a theory of learning, and suggests a partial view of knowledge construction. The symbol-processing or computational view of learning can be compared with learning theories which emphasize cultural elements which are situated or embedded in society. Symbol-processing or computational models for epistemic construal or for assessment then, are deficient as explanations of the contents of other people's minds and the way these contents change. This set of relationships therefore cannot act as a sufficient descriptor of learning and assessment.

11.4 Creating the Case

At the beginning of this chapter, I referred to Foucault's work on examinations in Discipline and Punish: The Birth of the Prison (Foucault, 1979), and suggested that it is relevant to the various forms of learning and the various modes of assessing capacity that I have discussed above. His remarks, in summary, are intended to surface the common sense discourse which surrounds these matters by showing how they could be understood in a different way. Previously, the test was thought of as a progressive mechanism for combating nepotism, favouritism and arbitrariness, and for contributing to the more efficient workings of society. The test was considered to be a reliable and valid way for choosing the appropriate members of a population for the most important roles in society. As part of the procedure a whole apparatus or technology was constructed that was intended to legitimize it. This psycho-metric framework, though continually in a state of flux, has served as a means of support for significant educational programmes in the twentieth century, i.e., the establishment of the tripartite system in the United Kingdom after the Second World War, and continues to underpin subsequent educational reforms throughout the world.

For Foucault (1979, p. 184) the test:

> combines the techniques of an observing hierarchy and those of a normalizing judgment. It is a normalizing gaze, a surveillance that makes it possible to qualify, to classify and to punish. It establishes over individuals a visibility through which one differentiates them and judges them.

The test therefore does not only describe the contents of a person's mind, but allows society to construct that person in a particular way. This has the effect of binding individuals to each other, embedding those individuals in networks of power, and sustaining mechanisms of surveillance which are all the more powerful because they work by allowing individuals to police themselves. The test, according to Foucault, introduced a whole new mechanism which both contributed to a new type of knowledge formation and constructed a new network of power, all the more persuasive once it had become established throughout society.

This mechanism works in three ways: firstly, it transforms "the economy of visibility into the exercise of power" (ibid., p. 187); secondly, it introduces "individuality into the field of documentation" (ibid., p. 189); and thirdly it makes "each individual a 'case'" (ibid., p. 191). In the first instance, disciplinary power is exercised invisibly and this contrasts with the way power networks in the past operated visibly, through perhaps the naked exercise of force. This invisibility works by imposing on subjects a notion of objectivity which acts to bind examined persons to a truth about that test, a truth which is hard to resist. The test therefore works by "arranging objects" (ibid., p. 187) or people in society. In the second instance, the test allows the individual to be archived by being inscribed in a variety of documents which fixes and captures them, even if the rhetoric suggests that the implementation is progressive and benign. The third of Foucault's modalities then, is when the individual becomes an object for a branch of knowledge:

> The case is no longer, as in casuistry or jurisprudence, a set of circumstances, defining an act and capable of modifying the application of a rule; it is the individual as he (sic.) may be described, judged, measured, compared with others, in his very individuality; and it is also the individual who has to be trained or corrected, classified, normalized, excluded, etc. (ibid., p. 191).

One final point needs to be made about the examination or test, as Foucault understood it, and this is that for the first time the individual can be scientifically and objectively categorized and characterized through a modality of power where difference becomes the most relevant factor.

Hierarchical normalization becomes the dominant way of organizing society. Foucault is suggesting here that the test itself, a seemingly neutral device, acts to position the person being tested in a discourse of normality, so that for them to understand themselves in any other way is to understand themselves as abnormal and even as unnatural. Whereas Foucault is writing here about individuals, it also applies in equal measure to nations.

References

Bhaskar, R. (1989). *Reclaiming reality*. London: Verso.

Bredo, E. (1999). Reconstructing educational psychology. In P. Murphy (Ed.), *Learners, learning and assessment*. London: Sage Publications.

Curren, R. (2006). Connected learning and the foundations of psychometrics: A rejoinder. *Journal of Philosophy of Education, 40*(1), 17–29.

Foucault, M. (1979). *Discipline and punish: The birth of the prison*. New York: Vintage.

Organization for Economic Cooperation and Development (OECD) (2000) Manual for the PISA 2000 Database, Paris, OECD.

Organization for Economic Cooperation and Development (OECD). (2001). Knowledge and skills for life: First results from PISA, Paris, OECD.

Taylor, C. (1995). Overcoming epistemology. In C. Taylor (Ed.), *Philosophical arguments* (pp. 1–19). Cambridge, MA; London: Harvard University Press.

Wood, R., & Power, C. (1987). Aspects of the competence-performance distinction: Educational, psychological and measurement issues. *Journal of Curriculum Studies, 19*(5), 409–424.

Chapter 12
Assessment of Significant Learning Outcomes

Richard Daugherty, Paul Black, Kathryn Ecclestone, Mary James, and Paul Newton

12.1 Introduction

The nature and quality of the outcomes of learning are central to any discussion of the learner's experience, from whichever perspective that experience is considered. For those outcomes to be assessed it is also necessary to articulate in some way the constructs on which such judgments are based. The relationship between the intended outcomes of learning and the outcomes as evidenced through assessment is typically conceptualized in terms of the alignment of assessment to curriculum or of congruence between them (Baker, 2005; Porter, Smithson, Blank, & Zeidner, 2007; Beck, 2007; Biggs & Tang, 2007). In principle, for the assessment of outcomes to be valid the inferences drawn from the evidence of learning should be in line with the intended learning outcomes. In practice, the way in which learning outcomes are defined and assessed varies greatly within and across systems of education (European Centre for the Development of Vocational Training, 2008).

The project that is reported here suggests that the relationship between assessment and curriculum is more multi-dimensional and multi-level than the terms "alignment" or "congruence" would imply. That project, "Assessment of Significant Learning Outcomes" (ASLO), was a seminar series funded by the Teaching and Learning Research Programme (TLRP) of the UK Economic and Social Research Council (ESRC) – http://www.tlrp.org/themes/seminar/daugherty/index.html. Five case studies were chosen to illuminate the relationship of assessment to curriculum in different educational contexts:

- A school subject: mathematics education in England.
- Learning to learn: a European Commission project to develop indicators.
- Workplace learning in the UK.
- Higher education in the UK.
- Vocational education in England.

R. Daugherty (✉)
School of Social Sciences, Cardiff University, Wales, UK
e-mail: daughertyr@cardiff.ac.uk

R. Berry, B. Adamson (eds.), *Assessment Reform in Education*,
Education in the Asia-Pacific Region: Issues, Concerns and Prospects 14,
DOI 10.1007/978-94-007-0729-0_12,

In each of the context-specific seminars in the ASLO series the participants analyzed the terms in which the alignment of assessment procedures to learning outcomes was discussed in that context. This involved exploring how, and by whom, control over programmes of learning is exercised as well as how those who are engaged in the discussions perceive and express the issues involved. The overall aim was to identify insights that may have applications beyond the context from which they emerged rather than to develop an overarching conceptual framework that could be applicable to any context.

12.2 Background

The roots of the ASLO project can be found in the work of the Assessment Reform Group (ARG) and in TLRP's Learning Outcomes Thematic Group (LOTG).

Since its inception as a response to the policy changes in curriculum and assessment brought in by the Education Reform Act 1988, the ARG has reviewed the implications for policy and practice of research on assessment. It has taken a particular interest in the relationship between assessment and pedagogy (Gardner, 2006) and between assessment and curriculum, especially through its work on enhancing quality in assessment (Harlen, 1994). In recent years the assessment/pedagogy interaction has been a prominent focus of the Group's work (for example ARG, 2002).

The ARG has argued, for example in the Assessment Systems for the Future project (Harlen, 2007), that assessment regimes that rely only on test-based measures of attainment may be insufficiently valid to be educationally acceptable. Implicit in that critique are such questions as:

- What are the significant learning outcomes that are not being assessed in a system that relies wholly on test-based assessment procedures?
- What are the indicators of student performance which have been/could be developed in relation to such learning outcomes?
- What are the assessment procedures that do not rely on testing but do give/could give dependable measures of student performance in relation to those indicators?

Consideration of validity is the natural starting point for the assessment dimension of the project, drawing on the work of Crooks, Kane, and Cohen (1996), Stobart (2008) and others. There are recurring themes concerning the technical aspects of validity that can be traced across diverse contexts. It is also clear that a focus on "consequential validity" (Messick, 1989) or, alternatively, on the "consequential evidence of validity" (Messick, 1995), necessarily raises questions such as "what consequences?" and "consequences for whom?"

The project also drew on work done by the TLRP, the remit of which was to sponsor research "with the potential to improve outcomes for learners". In 2004, a grounded analysis by the Programme's LOTG of the outcomes mentioned in the first thirty TLRP projects to be funded, led it to propose seven categories of outcome:

- *Attainment* – often school curriculum based or measures of basic competence in the workplace.
- *Understanding* – of ideas, concepts, processes.
- *Cognitive and creative* – imaginative construction of meaning, arts or performance.
- *Using* – how to practise, manipulate, behave, engage in processes or systems.
- *Higher-order learning* – advanced thinking, reasoning, metacognition.
- *Dispositions* – attitudes, perceptions, motivations.
- *Membership, inclusion, self-worth* – affinity towards, readiness to contribute to the group where learning takes place.

(James & Brown, 2005, pp. 10–11)

However, this list was insufficient to capture the range of theoretical perspectives on learning underpinning these projects. Therefore another categorization was based on the metaphors of learning represented in project outputs. A matrix was devised with the classification of learning outcomes on one axis and the metaphors of learning (drawing on Sfard, 1998, distinction between acquisition and participation metaphors), underpinning the construction of those learning outcomes, on the other.

It was evident that the TLRP projects had had difficulty in conceptualizing learning outcomes to take full account of dimensions of learning such as: surface and deep; process and product; individual and social; intended and emergent. James and Brown (2005) pointed out that a reconceptualization of learning outcomes would present considerable challenges:

> The first challenge would be to convince stakeholders that the existing models no longer serve us well; the second would be to convince them that alternatives are available or feasible to develop. Alternatives would also need to be succinct, robust and communicable... (p. 20).

It is to these challenges that the ASLO project was a response.

12.3 Contexts

The educational environment within which current policies and practices have evolved has inevitably shaped the way in which learning outcomes, and the assessment of them, are conceptualized. But the influence of the wider social, economic and political context on the prioritization of learning outcomes and on the approach taken to assessment is also clearly evident in the project's five case studies. The evidence reviewed here relates to the case study contexts at the time the seminars took place, between January and October 2007.

12.3.1 Case Study 1: National Curriculum Mathematics in England

Consideration of school mathematics was particularly relevant to our enquiry, because it is subject to an unusual set of pressures. One critic can claim that all the mathematics the average citizen needs is covered in Key Stage 2 (for students from age 7–11), another that the increased mathematization of our culture makes advanced understanding crucial, whilst an academic has asserted that real understanding of mathematics only begins at the level of an undergraduate course.

Ernest (2000) characterizes the many different stakeholders in terms of five categories:

- industrial trainers;
- technological pragmatists;
- old humanist mathematicians;
- public educators;
- progressive educators.

The views of each of these groups differ, over the aims of mathematics education, over the teaching needed to secure these aims, and over the means to assess their achievement. The operational meaning of their aims is often not clear, and the means are often ill thought-out and ill-informed. The ascendant tendency at present in the UK is to focus on "numeracy", or "application of number", or "quantitative literacy" or "functional mathematics" and on attempts to bring these into working practice (Wake, 2005).

Such groups exert pressures in contrary directions, so it is hardly surprising that many describe the school scene as fractured and unsatisfactory. Some align in approach with Ernest's "old humanist mathematicians". They will typically be well-qualified but have a limited approach to teaching and learning, giving priority to algorithmic capacity to solve well-defined mathematical problems. Others will have a similar vision, but, being less well-qualified and/or confident, will be more narrowly dedicated to teaching to the test; many see the latter as a particularly weak characteristic of mathematics education (Advisory Committee on Mathematics Education, 2005). Such teachers will find it hard to be clear about what counts as being good at mathematics, i.e. they will not have a clear concept of validity. Those practitioners who are "progressive educators" will have clearer views about validity, usually at odds with the aims reflected in the formal tests.

A consequence of this situation is that many pupils have an impoverished experience of the subject, in ways pointed out by Schoenfeld (2001), who wrote of his experience as:

- mainly consisting of the application of tools and techniques that he had just been shown;
- being mainly "pure" and lacking opportunity to be involved in mathematical modelling;
- not involving real data;
- not being required to communicate using mathematics.

The fault line which runs through much of this is between mathematics, seen as the performance of routine algorithms, and mathematics seen as a tool to tackle "everyday" or "real world" problems. The former leads to assessment of achievement with well-defined exercises, which have a single right answer, with learners inclined to think of achievement as arriving at that answer. The latter looks for evidence of a capacity to tackle the rather messy contexts which are characteristic of every-day problems, problems for which there is no right answer, and where explanation of the way the problem has been defined and of the approach adopted, including justification for the methods used, are as important as the "answer" itself. Such work is much more demanding to guide, and harder to mark. Yet pupils taught in this way achieve as well in the General Certificate of Secondary Education (GCSE) as those taught in more traditional methods, will take more interest in the subject, will be better able to see mathematics as useful in everyday life and will be better able to tackle unusual problems (Boaler, 1997).

The National Curriculum in mathematics in England gives prominence, in Attainment Target 1 (AT1), to "using and applying mathematics". There are clear statements about different levels of competence in tackling problems, but no mention of the nature or context of such problems, so no guidance on "textbook" versus "everyday" choices. The other three ATs are about the formal content of mathematics. Teachers see this curriculum as overcrowded; this in part is due to the atomistic approach to the formulation. The ACME (2005) report recommended that "The Government should reduce the overall volume and frequency of external assessment in mathematics", and reported the general belief in the mathematical community that "many of the negative effects of external assessment are serious". The 2007 revision has reduced the content to focus on a few "big ideas", but teachers seem to be misinterpreting the text as broad statements which still imply that all the content has to be "covered".

The testing system is of course of crucial importance here. With time-limited tests to cover a very full curriculum, any activity which involves much more time than that in which a single examination answer can be given is ruled out, thus ruling out realistic problems. There was teacher based/coursework assessment for AT1, but teachers saw this as stereotyped and providing little opportunity for interesting activities or for ways to assess them. For such activities, the right-answer approach does not work, and it is difficult for teachers to work with the inevitable ambiguities (Morgan & Watson, 2002).

There is thus an invalidity block, which could in principle be cleared by strengthening the use of teachers' own assessments in national tests and public examinations. That these can achieve validity with an acceptable level of reliability has been argued in general terms by the ARG (ARG, 2006). Nevertheless, the current coursework assessment at GCSE is unpopular: a consultation by the Qualifications and Curriculum Authority (2006) showed that mathematics teachers "thought that existing coursework did not provide a reliable and valid assessment for the subject" and it has been abandoned. At the same time, the experience of the King's Oxfordshire Summative Assessment Project project (Black, Harrison, Hodgen, & Serret, 2006a, 2007) is that mathematics teachers can develop their own summative assessment in ways that they find rewarding and which can produce dependable results, but that such development will be hard to achieve.

In summary, whilst the National Curriculum could be interpreted to reflect a valid representation of mathematics, the testing system does not realize this potential. However, to repair this mis-alignment would require changes which would demand extensive professional development for teachers, and a consensus about the aims of mathematics education which does not at present exist.

12.3.2 Case Study 2: Learning to Learn

The seminar on the assessment of "learning to learn" (L2L) drew on evidence from three UK projects and from the European Union (EU) Learning to Learning Indicators (Fredriksson & Hoskins, 2007). The papers revealed, more clearly than any of the other project case studies, the significance for the way assessment and learning are conceptualized of the contexts in which the constructs involved are developed. As McCormick argued in his commentary on the EU project (McCormick, 2007), it is essential to understand the *purposes* of measuring L2L as well as the *views of learning* underpinning its conceptualization.

The work of James and her colleagues (James et al., 2007) in England on "learning how to learn" (LHTL), has primarily focused on the development of pupils' learning practices. An early attempt to devise instruments to assess learning to learn "competence" encountered two obstacles. One was the dependence of the outcomes on the nature and context of the task. The second was that the project team could not agree on what the tasks were measuring. A deeper consideration of the concept of "learning to learn" (Black, McCormick, James, & Pedder, 2006b) led to the conclusion that "learning to learn" is not an entity, such as a unitary disposition or mental trait, but a family of *practices* that promote autonomy in learning. Thus the "how" in the project's preferred terminology was considered important, as was the close relationship between "learning how to learn" and learning per se. The implications are that LHTL practices can only be developed and assessed in the context of learning "something" in substantive domains; they are not easily, validly or comprehensively assessed by instruments similar to IQ tests or by "self report" inventories.

Thus, assessments of LHTL are likely to require sustained observation of how learners develop learning strategies for learning within domains – an argument for most emphasis to be placed on assessment by teachers in authentic learning contexts. The conceptualization of "learning to learn" and "learning how to learn" that emerged here (Black et al., 2006b) was not shaped by policy considerations and, if taken seriously, would call into question the appeal of these popular ideas as expressions of assessable learning outcomes.

Claxton and his colleagues at the University of Bristol were also interested in "learning to learn" for "lifelong learning" and how this might be assessed. They state the aims of their work as:

> ... firstly, to seek to *identify* the elements that define a good learner. Secondly.... to devise an instrument that could be used to assess where an individual [is] located in relation to those elements at any given time and in any particular context. (Deakin Crick, Broadfoot, & Claxton, 2004, p. 248)

Their intentions, however, were not to develop a measure of "learning to learn" attainment that could be used in the policy arena, but to develop instruments for formative and diagnostic use by learners and their teachers. To this end they developed a self-report instrument, the Effective Lifelong Learning Inventory – ELLI, which focuses on "learning power", argued as being concerned with quality of learning (rather than with learning competences) and defined as:

> A complex mix of dispositions, lived experiences, social relations, values, attitudes and beliefs that coalesce to shape the nature of an individual's engagement with any particular learning opportunity. (http://www.ellionline.co.uk/research.php – accessed 26 July 2010).

Seven dimensions of "learning power" were identified, and scales for each were developed. These were described as: changing and learning, meaning making, curiosity, creativity, learning relationships, strategic awareness and resilience. Although these constructs are much more broadly defined than those to which conventional assessments of attainment are related, the "self-report" nature of the tools meant that they were relatively easy to construct. The instrument developers saw no need to devise tasks and contexts in which these dispositions and behaviours could be demonstrated. There are, of course, questions about whether respondents' answers to the questions are realistic, even if they strive to be honest, and whether the statements apply in all contexts, but the problems encountered by James and her colleagues (Black et al., 2006b), concerning the operationalization of constructs, were avoided.

The important point to be made here is that the origins and purposes of an instrument are crucial for understanding and judging its value. The ELLI project team wanted to develop measures of their constructs for diagnostic and formative purposes. Self-report instruments may be valid for at least some of these purposes though their validity, in relation to the constructs and to the particular uses of evidence from the instruments, is potentially problematic. If, however, the intention is to find measures of learning to learn for evaluation and decisions on matters of public policy, then their validity and reliability for those purposes may come more into question.

In contrast to these projects the work of Hautamäki and his colleagues in the University of Helsinki has been overtly linked to a declared purpose associated with national policy. Although the original purpose was to develop tools for school self-evaluation, it has been used to evaluate the outcomes of education in Finland and judge the "effectiveness" of the national system of education. Since 1995 the National Board of Education in Finland has sponsored work in the University of Helsinki to develop tools to assess learning to learn, one of five aspects of system effectiveness. School development is claimed to be the "first and foremost" purpose of the "learning to learn" assessment instruments although the assessment places the school on a national scale thereby directly comparing individual schools with national norms.

According to the researchers in Helsinki, "learning to learn" is defined as:

> the competence and the willingness – here referred to as beliefs – to adapt to novel tasks. Competence refers to the generalized knowledge and skills that develop by studying

> different subjects at school and which is needed for learning new things. Beliefs and attitudes direct the use of these competencies in new situations. (http://www.helsinki.fi/cea/english/opiopi/eng_opiopi.htm – accessed 26 July 2010).

Learning competencies are assessed as generic skills demonstrated in specific contexts, for example, the ability to identify salient points in an argument developed in the context of a literature task, or the ability to use evidence in a science task. The assessment of beliefs and attitudes is based on self-report questionnaires similar to the ELLI instruments. The resulting 40 scales are described as an "easy to execute and cost effective measure", although the learning competences scales are vulnerable to the challenges that James and her team encountered, and the self-report scales have some of the limitations of the ELLI instruments.

These might not matter much if the instruments were primarily intended for internal diagnostic and formative use by schools though whether the evidence derived from the instruments is valid for such purposes would still need to be demonstrated. However, the discourse of policy is evident here in the wording of the question to which policy-applicable answers are being sought: "What kind of learning-to-learn skills does the education system produce?"

In terms of purpose, the current EU project to devise "indicators" of learning to learn is from the same mould. Its origins lie in the aspirations of the leaders of EU states meeting in Lisbon in 2000 which led in time to the European Education Council's support for a programme of work on eight such key competencies, one of which is learning to learn. In the absence of accepted Europe-wide measures of this as yet loosely defined construct, a new working group was set up "to develop new indicators for the monitoring of the development of education and training systems" (Fredriksson & Hoskins, 2007, p. 4). Thus, assessment as a source of performance indicator data has been the explicit driver of this EU project from the outset.

McCormick has argued that defining and developing measures of learning to learn as a way of supplying governments with performance data could distort and damage the construct which the LHTL team have been trying to nurture in the pedagogy of schools in England:

> … in a field where we have trouble defining the concept of L2L, where there are probably few well tried classroom practices for various aspects of L2L, and where we have to struggle to find the instrument that represents whatever we can agree L2L means, we start to improve [education] by measuring. This is the proverbial assessment tail wagging the curriculum dog! (McCormick, 2007, p. 1)

Thus, regardless of its uncertain foundations, the construct of "learning to learn" is being shaped by the need for it to be measurable in ways that will supposedly illuminate the performance of the diverse education systems to be found in the nation states of the EU. Or, put another way, the measures currently being devised by this EU indicators project seem to aim at emphasizing validity for monitoring system performance, and at de-emphasizing validity for identifying individual student learning needs.

12.3.3 Case Study 3: Workplace Learning in the UK

The seminar on workplace learning considered evidence about the nature, scope and ethos of assessment in workplaces, drawing on case studies by Fuller and Unwin (2003) of the Modern Apprenticeship programme in three companies associated with the steel industry, and discussion in two papers by Eraut (2007a, 2007b). One paper focused on the ways in which feedback in different workplace contexts hinders or enhances professional learning and competence and the other on progression in forms of expertise and knowledge over a period of time in different professions.

Fuller and Unwin highlight (p. 408) "the relevance of the institutional arrangements, including the nature of the employment relationship and the formal qualifications required by the programme". The nature of these relationships and the ways in which a workplace deals with the formal requirements for apprentices to develop particular knowledge and competences through a framework of minimum qualification requirements offers some apprentices very "restrictive" environments to "get them through" the formal competences demanded in the qualification, and "expansive" environments that enable apprentices to develop more extensive knowledge and competence.

Understanding the alignment between assessment and learning outcomes in work-place learning is made more complex by the extent to which formal summative requirements are specified tightly or loosely. This takes different forms at different levels of work-based qualifications. For example, the Modern Apprenticeship scheme requires workplaces to enable trainees or workers to achieve tightly specified competence-based qualifications as part of National Vocational Qualifications (NVQs) while an accountant might complete several competence-based qualifications followed by a degree. At different qualification levels, and across different professions and occupations, workplaces vary in having loose frameworks of codified knowledge, skills and notions of progression in expertise, or no codified frameworks at all.

This complexity makes it necessary to understand more about the interplay between informal and formal assessment and the ways in which these are sometimes linked to forms of appraisal and performance review. There is also an interplay between the use of formal, codified knowledge in such systems and the tacit, intuitive forms of knowledge that professionals use often without realizing, but which are crucial to effective performance as part of "capability". These include knowledge embedded in task performance, personal development, team work, the performance of different roles, the application of formal academic knowledge and skills, decision-making and problem-solving.

The work of Eraut and colleagues illuminates some of the subtle and complex ways in which different types of knowledge inter-relate through their studies of five occupational groups – doctors, health scientists, nurses, accountants and engineers. That work shows numerous variables shaping the learning of individuals in workplaces that are very diverse, where the learning and informal and formal assessment cultures that nurses, for example, experience can vary between wards, even in the same hospital (Eraut, 2007a, p. 10). The specification of learning outcomes and forms of assessment, formal and informal, summative and formative, therefore varies enormously across professions and workplaces. Eraut and colleagues' detailed longitudinal analysis of the factors that lead to effective support and mentoring, particularly through good feedback, has implications for assessor training and development in workplaces, both for those designated with formal assessment roles and for those who support colleagues more informally but are, nevertheless, carrying out assessments.

This analysis has several implications for how knowledge is defined, taught and assessed and for how workplaces can foster the intuitive and uncodified knowledge essential to effective practice. First, attempts to capture, codify and then assess informal and tacit uses of knowledge will not necessarily lead to more effective learning in the workplace. The more restricted, formalized and reified the assessment artefacts and forms of knowledge become, and the more they are tied to formal assessments, such as appraisal and performance review, the more likely they are to hamper the sort of conversations and feedback that lead to effective professional learning. On the other hand, if they are just left to chance, essential activities that develop capability, such as induction into the particular learning climates of groups being joined, the mentoring and management of different roles, and day-to-day formative assessment, will not be developed to best effect. Summative assessments are also crucial but perhaps more as snapshots of a professional's learning trajectory rather than as a dominant feature of workplace assessments.

This implies that workplace mentors, assessors and colleagues need to help novices become inducted into the practices of their new occupations so that they can apply tacit and formal knowledge to complex situations as and when they arise. Notions of progression, from novice to expert, and the types of knowledge they use are illuminated through the work of Eraut and colleagues over many years of study. Recent work shows the ways in which feedback can be used more effectively to develop what Eraut refers to as "capability" (rather than competence) as integral to expertise (Eraut, 2007b, p. 4). Developing the skills and processes of effective feedback in different workplaces is crucial for developing capability since the ability to deal effectively with an unfamiliar situation in medicine or engineering, for example, could be vital.

The very obviously situated nature of learning in the workplace, and the complexities of how feedback is used in specific contexts, has implications both for the codification of relevant knowledge and for how the learner's performance is assessed. Eraut and colleagues' work suggests that finding effective ways to align learning outcomes, formal and informal assessment and to codify the right sorts of knowledge without over-specifying them, must be done in the context of each profession or occupation and its relevant stakeholders and interest groups.

12.3.4 Case Study 4: Higher Education in the UK

The seminar on higher education discussed a report on "innovative assessment" across the disciplines (Hounsell et al., 2007) together with two further papers from

Hounsell and colleagues (Hounsell & Anderson, 2008; Hounsell, 2007). A defining feature of the relationship between curriculum and assessment in this sector is that "a distinctive and much-prized characteristic of higher education is that the choice not only of curriculum content and teaching-learning strategies but also of methods of assessment is to a considerable extent devolved" (Hounsell et al., 2007, p. 12). Even the "academic infrastructure" put in place by the UK regulatory body, the Quality Assurance Agency (QAA), emphasizes the fact that its codes of practice, qualification frameworks and subject benchmarks "allow for diversity and innovation within academic programmes". In higher education the regulatory texts have a relatively low profile within the discussion of curriculum and assessment. However, it is crucial to note that this profile varies considerably across disciplines and across institutions, shaped by the learning cultures of disciplinary communities and of institutions. For example, the QAA regulatory texts appear to exert more influence on programme planning and on the assessment of students' work in the post-1992 universities sector than in the pre-1992 sector.

Higher education is one of only two of the case study contexts (vocational education being the other) in which the term "learning outcomes", as used generically by the LOTG, has established currency. Except in a minority of institutions that are content to rely on long-established practices, usually involving responsibility for curriculum design and for assessment resting with the course tutor(s), the specification of "intended learning outcomes" has become integral to the practices of teaching and learning in UK higher education. Among the problems discussed at the ASLO seminar were the difficulty of capturing high quality learning in the language of learning outcomes, with the pitfalls of vagueness/vapidity on the one hand and undue particularity and prescriptiveness on the other.

In this respect the discussion echoed the project's concern about neglect of "significant" outcomes without suggesting ways of resolving dilemmas about both defining and assessing such outcomes. But what was also evident were the pressures on the specification of learning outcomes, typically articulated at institutional level, that were generated by governments' expectations of higher education, for example to demonstrate student employability. Such instrumentalism, communicated by government through its agencies, has similar roots to equivalent influences on the school mathematics curriculum and work-based training and assessment in qualifications such as NVQs.

In spite of the impact of the regulatory framework there is also ample evidence of the staff responsible for course programmes evolving their own interpretations of the "what", "how" and "why" of the learning involved (see, for example, the exploration of "ways of thinking and practising" in two subject areas, biology and history, discussed in Hounsell and Anderson (2008)). However, the goal of many course designers in higher education of "introducing students to the culture of thinking in a specific discipline" (Middendorf & Pace, 2004) may not be compatible either with the aspirations of the diverse student population on first degree courses or with the procedures that universities often adopt for assessing student attainment. While the enculturation approach to course design may move discussion beyond reductive lists of measurable learning outcomes it presents the challenge of valid assessment in a different form – how to judge a student's progress in terms of "connoisseurship" of the subject area.

For most if not all first degree courses in UK universities, the end-of-programme requirement to summarize student performance in a degree classification is a powerful influence on curriculum and pedagogy as well as, more directly, on assessment practices. A picture emerged of assessment in higher education constrained by "delivery" models of teaching and learning. The potential for formative feedback to enhance the quality of learning is undermined by the variability and often poor quality of such feedback as lecturers and their students are typically preoccupied with "what counts" in the reckoning that awards students an end-of-programme degree. In those circumstances, the issue of validity does not appear as an explicit item on the agenda of course designers, disciplinary groups or the institutional committees that have oversight of programme specifications. Instead questions of alignment are buried deep in the interface between course content and assessment, with assumptions about learning and learning theory that are implicit in the formal curriculum and in the associated pedagogy seldom being made explicit.

In contrast to the context in which school mathematics is evolving in England, with the policy texts dominating the discourses, the issue of alignment of curriculum and assessment in UK higher education is being worked through at the local level as the tutors responsible for course units/modules plan their teaching. In the traditional subject-based first degree programme questions about how to assess student learning are more likely to be influenced by departmental colleagues or within-discipline assumptions than by a thorough consideration of the extent to which intended learning outcomes and the evidence elicited by assessment of student performance are aligned. Amid such diversity as is allowed for by responsibility for curriculum and assessment being devolved there are, of course, many exceptions to that generalization. Such exceptions can be found not only among the instances of "innovative" assessment reported by Hounsell et al. (2007) but also in degree programmes where specific content knowledge and skills are required for the programme to be accredited.

12.3.5 Case Study 5: Vocational Education in England

Questions about definitions of outcomes, standards and curriculum content, and their effects on assessment practices in vocational education, arise in a context of numerous failed attempts since the late 1970s to create "parity of esteem" between vocational and academic education, and to encourage young people to see vocational education as a genuine high status alternative to programmes based on traditional subjects.

Assessment based on prescriptive and detailed specifications of learning outcomes, portfolios of achievement, unit-based assessment, locally-devised, teacher-assessed projects and grading based on "learning to learn" skills, has been used partly as a motivating device to encourage young people to gain a credible qualification, partly as an attempt to foster independence as part of "lifelong learning" skills and attitudes and partly as way of reflecting in the curriculum the concerns of employers.

Although these developments have influenced broader education debates about what comprises fair and useful assessment, there is little political, professional or public agreement about curriculum design and content in vocational education, nor about its purpose in relation to the content and outcomes of general education. The combined effect of lack of consensus and ad hoc reforms has been programmes comprising a range of functional, generic and personal skills, attitudes and dispositions and a very uncertain subject base, where diverse bodies compete to have their learning outcomes included (see Ecclestone, 2002; Stanton, 1998).

Learning outcomes in vocational education also reflect competing aims:

- motivating learners who would otherwise not stay on in post-16 education or who are disaffected in Key Stage 4 by responding to and rewarding their expressed interests and notions of relevance
- expanding routes into higher education whilst also making sure that expansion does not lead to over-subscription for limited places
- preparing students for progression into work and job-related NVQs
- encouraging learners to carry on gaining qualifications
- keeping students labelled by defenders of A-levels and GCSEs as "less-able" from "undermining" standards in these qualifications
- convincing learners, teachers, admissions tutors that vocational education has parity of esteem with long-running, higher status academic qualifications
- ameliorating poor levels of achievement in numeracy and literacy through "key skills"
- unifying disparate and confusing post-16 qualification pathways
- satisfying demands from different constituencies, such as employers' representatives or subject associations, to include "essential" content and skills
- having credibility in the school sector which has less experience of mainstream vocational education

A number of studies show these factors affect teaching and assessment practices, ideas about "types" of young people suitable for vocational education, beliefs about their motivation and attitudes to learning.

First, despite political targets to raise levels of participation and achievement, there are large gaps between notions of "choice" and "opportunity" and actual progression. Vocational students often choose progression routes that reflect their images of themselves as "types" of learners suited for different "types" of assessment and while they see themselves as "vocational", many students' vocational aspirations are erratic and vague (see Biesta & Davies, 2006; Davies & Biesta, 2007; Bathmaker, 2003; Torrance et al., 2005; Ecclestone, 2002).

Second, choice is affected by the ways in which learning outcomes and assessment both reflect and reinforce certain "learning identities" and "learning careers", and the creation of self-fulfilling images of learning, progression and appropriate assessment activities. The concept of "learning cultures" illuminates the subtle ways in which students and teachers develop implicit and explicit expectations about teaching, learning and assessment, and how, in turn, these interact with peer norms and relationships, official requirements, institutional ethos and structures and the nature of the relationship between teachers and students (Ecclestone & Pryor, 2003; Ecclestone, 2004).

Third, dispositions and attitudes cannot be isolated from employment prospects, the effects of educational selection and differentiation in a local area, students' social class and cultural background and the educational institutions they choose or are sent to. Images of achievement and failure, and a learning career associated with those images, affect students' and teachers' perceptions about the suitability of a vocational or academic qualification and are rooted in teachers' and students' perceptions about employment and education prospects in local labour markets.

Fourth, ideas about "achievement" and "learning" are influenced by targets to raise attainment of grades, overall pass rates, retention on courses and progression to qualifications at the next level. "Learning" and "achievement" are often synonymous with learning outcomes and criteria prescribed by the awarding body, so that "assessment" is frequently the "delivery of achievement".

Finally, assessment is affected by teachers' images of what students like, need and want. Vocational tutors regard "good assessment" as practical, authentic and relevant activities, work-experience and field trips: there is a widespread view that "these students" do not want or like written assessment, that they are less secure, need more group affinity and should be in a more protected, safe environment. Many vocational teachers see assessment as integral to a strong ethos of personal development that minimizes stress or pressure. Assessment to develop subject knowledge is not prominent in their espoused goals for students, an attitude reinforced by learning outcomes that emphasize generic skills and attitudes rather than subject content. Vocational teachers and students like to work in a lively and relaxed atmosphere that combines group work, teacher input and time to work on assignments individually or in small friendship-based groups. Goals for relevance and real-life application are reinforced by concerns that assessment should engage and retain young people in formal education who are deemed to be demotivated and disengaged.

One effect is a growing tendency to avoid "burdening" vocational students with "too much written work" or with methods that alienate them from formal education. It is now commonplace to elide vocational education with practical activities loosely related to work, so that learning outcomes and assessment are associated with the need to motivate and engage young people. A recent phenomenon is to associate disaffection with "fragile learning identities" and "low self-esteem".

The ad hoc evolution of learning outcomes and assessment methods in vocational education in England over the past 30 years has been a central factor in creating and maintaining certain images and attitudes to learning in vocational education. Difficulty in creating an enduring, high status vocational counterpart to general education, and a stable system of organizations and bodies to implement it, might be countered by a better understanding of:

- how learning outcomes, pedagogy and assessment are inextricably linked
- how they are affected by political imperatives for achieving targets and
- how they are shaped by the learning cultures of different vocational education settings.

12.4 Discussion

Several themes, discussed more fully in Daugherty, Black, Ecclestone, James, & Newton, 2008, recur across the five case studies.

Construct definition – how, and by whom, the constructs involved are defined, interpreted and made real – has emerged as a major issue in each of the contexts. Construct validity has long been a central concern in the field of assessment without the constructs themselves necessarily being critically explored or closely defined. Even if the constructs have been considered at the levels of assessment theory and qualification design, they may not be applied in the day-to-day practice of assessors. At the other end of the curriculum/assessment relationship the constructs informing the design of programmes of learning have in some contexts been strongly contested. What this suggests is a need to clarify the constructs within a domain that inform the development both of the programmes of learning, in principle and in practice, and of the related assessments.

A second theme, *progression,* is crucial to the design and implementation of learning programmes, and in particular for the implementation of assessment for learning. Its relevance to summative assessment depends on the structure of the assessment system. If the only high-stakes summative test is a terminal one, then the desired final outcomes are laid down, the test constructors have to reflect these in as valid a way as they can, and the teachers discern, from study of a syllabus and of examples of the test instruments and procedures, how best to focus their work. Enabling progression is absolutely central to formative assessment but there is evidence in these case studies that summative assessment requirements, driven by pressure for uniformity and for accountability, can constrain teachers and trainers in using their own judgment to nurture progression.

Another theme to emerge across the case study contexts was *the impact of assessment procedures* on the alignment between intended or desirable outcomes from learning and those outcomes which actually emerge. From a measurement perspective, alignment is often conceived quite narrowly – in terms of content validity – where misalignment between an assessment instrument and intended learning outcomes represents a threat to the integrity of inferences from assessment results. However, it can be conceived more broadly too, where misalignment represents a threat to the integrity of learning itself, resonating with the notion of "systemic validity" (Frederiksen & Collins, 1989). The five case study contexts highlighted numerous situations in which the nature of an assessment procedure threatened to disrupt the acquisition of desirable learning outcomes by students. This disruption occurred when assessment procedures led either to the failure to acquire desirable outcomes from learning, or to the acquisition of undesirable outcomes from learning. For both types of disruption potential impacts were attributable either to the design of the assessment instrument or to the nature of the assessment event itself.

A fourth theme to emerge was *system-level accountability as a driver of alignment.* Accountability takes very different forms, has different purposes and stakeholders and has different effects on the interpretation of learning outcomes within each of the contexts reviewed. Two of the case studies in particular – the school mathematics curriculum and the learning to learn indicators – revealed just how influential the political imperatives for system level accountability can be. They can be seen to be determining not only the role of assessment in defining the relevant constructs but also, perhaps more crucially, in shaping how teachers and students then interpret and enact those constructs.

12.5 Conclusion

It became clear in the course of the ASLO seminar series that the language of intended outcomes, alignment and curriculum is embedded in different ways in the assumptions, histories and practices of the different sectors of formal education. It has also been increasingly evident that, in asking whether the inferences drawn from assessments are *aligned* to intended learning outcomes, the project was not using the most appropriate language to express the dynamics of the assessment/curriculum relationship. It is certainly true that "alignment of an assessment with the content standards that it is intended to measure is critical if the assessment is to buttress rather than undermine the standards" (Linn, 2005, p. 95). But "alignment" implies that there is something in place – content standards in the case of the US contexts to which Linn is referring – to which assessments could, at least in principle, be aligned. All the ASLO case studies have exposed a lack of clarity in defining the underlying constructs, whether in terms of content standards or of narrower/broader formulations.

The case study evidence reviewed here has taken the analysis of the relationship between curriculum and assessment beyond the simple notion of explicit outcomes of assessment being in some way aligned to, or congruent with, a pre-specified curriculum. Instead we see a multi-layered process of knowledge being constructed, with numerous influences at work at every level from the national system to the individual learner.

Acknowledgements The authors are grateful for the input from those who presented keynote papers at the ASLO seminars – Jeremy Hodgen, Ulf Fredriksson, Michael Eraut, Dai Hounsell, Kathryn Ecclestone – and for the contributions from all participants in the seminar series. Full reports of each seminar and the names of participants can be found on the project's website at: http://www.tlrp.org/themes/seminar/daugherty/index.html. The authors also wish to acknowledge the contribution of the other members of the Assessment Reform Group – John Gardner, Wynne Harlen, Louise Hayward and Gordon Stobart – who have been involved in the ASLO project from the outset and whose ideas have helped shape this article.

References

Advisory Committee on Mathematics Education (2005). *Assessment in 14-19 mathematics*. London: Royal Society.

Assessment Reform Group (2002). *Assessment for learning: 10 Principles*. Cambridge: University School of Education.

Assessment Reform Group (2006). *The role of teachers in the assessment of learning*. London: University Institute of Education.

Baker., E. (2005). Aligning curriculum, standards and assessments. In C. A. Dwyer (Ed.), *Measurement and research in the accountability era* (pp. 315–335). Mahwah, NJ: Lawrence Erlbaum Associates.

Bathmaker, A. M. (2003). *Learners and learning in GNVQs*, PhD thesis. Coventry: University of Warwick.

Beck, M. D. (2007). Review and other views: 'alignment' as a psychometric issue. *Applied Measurement in Education*, *20*(1), 127–135.

Biesta, G., & Davies, J. (2006). Going to college: aspirations and experiences of vocational education students. Paper from the *ESRC TLRP Project, Transforming Learning Cultures in FE*. Exeter: University of Exeter.

Biggs, J., & Tang, C. (2007). *Teaching for quality learning at university* (3rd ed.). Buckingham: SRHE and Open University Press.

Black, P., Harrison, C., Hodgen, J., & Serret, N. (2006a). *Strengthening teacher assessment practices, learning and evidence*. Paper presented at the 2006 BERA Conference, Cardiff: a report of findings from the first stage of the King's-Oxfordshire Summative Assessment Project (KOSAP).

Black, P., Harrison, C., Hodgen, J., & Serret, N. (2007). *Riding the interface: an exploration of the issues that beset teachers when they strive for assessment systems that are rigorous and formative*. Paper presented at the 2007 BERA conference, London: 2nd report of findings from the King's-Oxfordshire Summative Assessment Project (KOSAP).

Black, P., McCormick, R., James, M., & Pedder, D. (2006b). Learning how to learn and assessment for learning: A theoretical inquiry. *Research Papers in Education*, *21*(2), 119–132.

Boaler, J. (1997). *Experiencing school mathematics: Teaching styles, sex and setting*. Buckingham: Open University Press.

Crooks, T., Kane, M., & Cohen, A. (1996). Threats to the valid use of assessment. *Assessment in Education*, *3*(3), 265–285.

Daugherty, R., Black, P., Ecclestone., K., James, M., & Newton, P. (2008). Alternative perspectives on learning outcomes: Challenges for assessment. *The Curriculum Journal*, *19*(4), 243–254.

Davies, J., & Biesta, G. (2007). Coming to college or getting out of school? The experience of vocational learning of 14- to 16-year-olds in a further education college. *Research Papers in Education*, *22*(1), 23–41.

Deakin Crick, R., Broadfoot, P., & Claxton, G. (2004). Developing an effective lifelong learning inventory: The ELLI project. *Assessment in Education*, *11*(3), 247–272.

Ecclestone, K. (2002). *Learning autonomy in post-compulsory education: The politics and practice of formative assessment*. London: RoutledgeFalmer.

Ecclestone, K. (2004). Learning in a comfort zone: Cultural and social capital in outcome-based assessment regimes. *Assessment in Education*, *11*(1), 30–47.

Ecclestone, K., & Pryor, J. (2003). 'Learning careers' or 'assessment careers'?: The impact of assessment systems on learning. *British Educational Research Journal*, *29*(4), 471–488.

Eraut, M. (2007a). *Feedback and formative assessment in the workplace*, expanded version of a paper for an AERA symposium (2006) on formative assessment in professional education.

Eraut, M. (2007b). *How do we represent lifelong professional learning?*, expanded version of a paper given to an EARLI SIG meeting.

Ernest, P. (2000). Why teach mathematics? In S. Bramall & J. White (Eds.), *Why learn maths?* (pp. 1–14). London: University Institute of Education.

European Centre for the Development of Vocational Training (2008). The shift to learning outcomes. Conceptual, political and practical developments in Europe. Luxembourg: Office for Official Publications of the European Communities. Accessed July 27, 2010, from http://www.cedefop.europa.eu/etv/Upload/Information_resources/Bookshop/494/4079_en.pdf

Frederiksen, J. R., & Collins, A. (1989). A systems approach to education testing. *Educational Researcher*, *18*(9), 27–32.

Fredriksson, U., & Hoskins, B. (2007). Indicators of learning to learn, paper presented to ASLO project seminar, London, March 2007. Accessed July 27, 2010, from http://www.tlrp.org/themes/seminar/daugherty/index.html

Fuller, A., & Unwin, M. (2003). Learning as apprentices in the contemporary UK workplace: Creating and managing expansive and restrictive participation. *Journal of Education and Work*, *16*(4), 407–426.

Gardner, J. (Ed.) (2006). *Assessment and learning*. London: Sage.

Harlen, W. (Ed.) (1994). *Enhancing quality in assessment*. London: Paul Chapman.

Harlen, W. (2007). *Assessment of learning*. London: Sage.

Hounsell, D. (2007). Towards more sustainable feedback to students. In D. Boud & N. Falchikov (Eds.), *Rethinking assessment in higher education, learning for the longer term* (pp. 101–113). London: Routledge.

Hounsell, D., & Anderson, C. (2008). Ways of thinking and practising in biology and history: Disciplinary aspects of teaching and learning environments. In C. Kreber (Ed.), *Teaching and learning in higher education: Within and across the disciplines*. London: Routledge.

Hounsell, D., Blair, S., Falchikov, N., Hounsell, J., Huxham, M., Klampfleitner, M., et al. (2007). *Innovative assessment across the disciplines: An analytical review of the literature* (Review Report and Database). York: Higher Education Academy.

James, M., & Brown, S. (2005). Grasping the nettle: Preliminary analysis and some enduring issues surrounding the improvement of learning outcomes. *The Curriculum Journal*, *16*(1), 7–30.

James, M., McCormick, R., Black, P., Carmichael, P., Drummond, M. -J., Fox, A., et al. (2007). *Improving learning how to learn – classrooms, schools and networks*. London: Routledge.

Linn, R. (2005). Issues in the design of accountability systems. In J. Herman & E. Haertel (Eds.), *Uses and misuses of data for educational accountability and improvement: 104th yearbook of the national society for the study of education* (pp. 78–98). Chicago: NSSE.

McCormick, R. (2007). Learning to learn: reflections on assessment, curriculum and pedagogy, paper presented to ASLO project seminar, London, March 2007. Accessed July 27, 2010, from http://www.tlrp.org/themes/seminar/daugherty/index.html

Messick, S. (1989). Validity. In R. L. Linn (Ed.), *Educational measurement* (pp. 13–103). New York; London: Macmillan & American Council for Education.

Messick, S. (1995). Validity in psychological assessments. *American Psychologist*, *50*(9), 741–749.

Middendorf, J., & Pace, D. (2004). Decoding the disciplines: A model for helping students learn disciplinary ways of thinking. In D. Pace & J. Middendorf (Eds.), *Decoding the disciplines: Helping students learn disciplinary ways of thinking (New directions for teaching and learning, 98)* (pp. 1–12). San Francisco: Jossey-Bass.

Morgan, C., & Watson, A. (2002). The interpretative nature of teachers' assessment of mathematics: Issues of equity. *Journal for Research in Mathematics Education*, *33*(2), 78–110.

Porter, A. C., Smithson, J., Blank, R., & Zeidner, T. (2007). Alignment as a teacher variable. *Applied Measurement in Education*, *20*(1), 27–51.

Qualifications and Curriculum Authority (2006). News release. Qualifications and Curriculum Authority. Accessed July 16, 2007, from http://qca.org.uk/qca_9678.aspx

Schoenfeld, A. (2001). Reflections on an impoverished education. In L. A. Steen (Ed.), *Mathematics and democracy: The case for quantitative literacy* (pp. 49–54). Princeton, NJ: National Council on Education and the Disciplines.

Sfard, A. (1998). On two metaphors for learning and the dangers of choosing just one. *Educational Researcher*, *27*(2), 4–13.

Stanton, G. (1998). Patterns of development. In S. Tomlinson (Ed.), *Education 14-19: Critical perspectives*. London: Athlone Press.

Stobart, G. (2008). *Testing times: The uses and abuses of assessment*. London: Routledge.

Torrance, H., Colley, H., Garratt, D., Jarvis, J., Piper, H., Ecclestone, K., et al. (2005). *The impact of different modes of assessment on achievement and progress in the learning and skills sector*. Learning and Skills Development Agency. Accessed July 16, 2007, from https://www.lsda.org.uk/cims/order.aspx?code=052284&src=XOWEB

Wake, G. (2005). *Functional Mathematics: more than 'Back to Basics'*. Nuffield Review of 14-19 Education and Training: Aims, Learning and Curriculum Series, Discussion Paper 17. London: Nuffield Foundation.

Chapter 13
Developing Assessment for Learning in a Large-Scale Programme

Hak Ping Tam and Yu-Jen Lu

13.1 Introduction

In Taiwan, as in many school systems around the world, most students are assessed on a regular basis, ranging from low-stakes daily classroom quizzes to high-stakes graduation examinations. The purposes of such assessments vary, with some emphasizing formative and others summative outcomes. As a broad generalization, small-scale assessments lend themselves more easily to assessment for learning than large-scale assessments, which are often designed with the intention of acquiring information about performances in ways that facilitate comparisons across large cohorts of students. As Popham (1999) has pointed out, many large-scale educational assessment programs place too much emphasis on the accountability aspect and too little attention on the instructional aspect. As a result, there is an imbalance between the two functions of assessment as practiced in most programs. Popham suggested that large-scale assessment should instead lend itself more towards improving the instructional practices in the classroom, or at least striking a balance between the two aspects. Yet even if one would decide to heed this suggestion, it begs the question as to how one should take on this challenge and actually carry it out in a large-scale environment. Particularly problematic is the issue of extracting separate yet useful feedback to students, teachers and other stakeholders after analyzing huge amounts of test data from the students involved. There is a risk that such an undertaking might prove to be prohibitively expensive, or that the information thus made available might be too superficial to be of any practical use for instruction.

The purpose of this chapter is to provide a brief introduction to just such a large-scale assessment programme in Yilan County of Taiwan – one that has the dual aim of being supportive towards classroom instruction as well as providing policymakers with the requisite information about students' learning status. This assessment

H.P. Tam (✉)
Graduate Institute of Science Education, National Taiwan Normal University, Taipei, Taiwan
e-mail: t45003@ntnu.edu.tw

R. Berry, B. Adamson (eds.), *Assessment Reform in Education*,
Education in the Asia-Pacific Region: Issues, Concerns and Prospects 14,
DOI 10.1007/978-94-007-0729-0_13, © Springer Science+Business Media B.V. 2011

programme can serve as an example of what can be done in terms of assessment reform at a county or even higher level. Based on the Yilan experience, this chapter will suggest, in the subsequent discussion, ways to promote assessment for learning within large-scale testing programs in general. Then we will discuss several issues related to the implementation of this kind of large-scale assessment programme and identify some possible directions for future development.

Yilan is a county on the northeastern coast of Taiwan with a sparsely distributed population of about 460,000 people. Since 2006, the Yilan County has been carrying out a county-wide assessment programme, in accordance with the requirement from the Ministry of Education that local governments should monitor the progress of their students by means of assessment (Ministry of Education, 2003). This chapter will describe the practices in the year 2007 as an example. A guidance committee with two staff was commissioned to oversee the planning of the mathematics assessment programme for the fourth grade. This committee recognized that most assessments performed in schools on a routine basis are achievement oriented. In order to be innovative, they established the ambitious goal at the outset that the assessment for fourth grade mathematics should be designed with the intention of providing useful information to the mathematics teachers, school principals as well as the parents of the participating students.

13.2 The Assessment Framework

In Taiwan, the formal version of the official Grade 1-9 Curriculum Guidelines was introduced in 2003 and was implemented through several stages to cover all grades in primary and junior high schools. Accordingly, the guidance committee decided that the content of the mathematics assessment should be fully aligned with the standards specified in the official curriculum. A committee of 15 local expert mathematics teachers was assembled to compile the assessment framework for the whole county. Each member of the committee had been recognized as an expert teacher in mathematics at the primary school level. Their average experience of teaching mathematics amounted to about 12.2 years.

Since there is a wide array of standards specified in the official curriculum, the first task of the committee was to decide on the content and the cognitive domains for the assessment framework. Their work could be summarized as a three-step procedure. Firstly, the committee studied and analyzed the official mathematics curriculum standards in detail. Additional reference was made to both the Trends in International Mathematics and Science Study 2003 and the US National Assessment of Educational Progress 2005 assessment frameworks. Secondly, the committee had to identify important standards in the curriculum to be tested. Since the county's education officers had decided to allot just one regular class period for the assessment, the committee recognized that only a few curriculum standards could be tested within such a short duration of time, given that there are thirty two curriculum standards that are stipulated for the fourth grade students to learn. In order to identify the appropriate set of standards that would form the basis of the test, the members were asked individually to rate the importance of each standard on a 5-point Likert scale. Those standards with the highest total ratings were prioritized for inclusion in the test. The final criterion for selection lay in the essentiality, interpretability, assessability and the richness of mathematical content associated with the standards as judged by the majority of the committee members. Thirdly, they took practicality into consideration to narrow down on their choices. In view of a limited budget and the vast number of students who would participate in the main survey, they decided that only multiple choices test items would be used to assess the students. The committee further decided to restrict the whole instrument to 30 multiple-choice items so as to fit into the limited accessibility of testing time. Under this constraint, they further trimmed down the scope of the assessment to encompass ten curriculum standards that spanned over 16 fundamental topics.

The committee further resolved that the content domain should include the following five areas: number and computation, quantity and measurement, geometry, algebra, as well as probability and data analysis. For the cognitive domain, conceptual comprehension, procedural knowledge and problem solving were chosen to be the three essential components. The finalised assessment framework is shown in Table 13.1 below.

Table 13.1 The assessment framework for the Yilan County's fourth grade mathematics test

Content domain	
Number and computation	40%
Quantity and measurement	33%
Geometry	13%
Algebra	7%
Probability and data analysis	7%
Cognitive domain	
Conceptual understanding	33%
Procedural knowledge	46%
Problem solving	21%

13.3 Dual Items Design

In order to facilitate a formative aspect in the county-wide assessment, the committee incorporated a special design in its construction of the test instrument. Since the purpose was to obtain rich information of student performances, the committee wanted to avoid constructing a test with a mere compilation of total test scores. Furthermore, the multiple choice item format has a well known weakness in that students can by chance guess the correct answer. If Yilan County would like to find out the actual status of their students with respect to the 16 fundamental mathematical topics, something needed to be done to enrich the multiple choice format. Towards this end, it was decided that two parallel items that tested basically the same concept should be employed for 14 of the topic areas, accounting for a total of 28 items. The remaining two items were not paired due to the limitation of testing time. However, they were both related to interpreting statistical graphs. One important characteristic of this design lies in the fact that the distractors across the dual items correspond to each other. In other words, the distractors were set up such that the same set of misconceptions was being used as options in both items.

The main reason for using this design is to control for chance performance by the students. Obviously, if a certain student displayed the same misconception in the item pair, one could be more confident in identifying the student as holding that misconception. In contrast, if students could consistently get both items correct, there is a high chance that they had already grasped the concept being tested. However, if some students picked the right answer for one item but got the other item wrong, this might indicate that they either did not have a firm understanding of the concept, had misconceptions or had been lucky in guessing a correct answer. One other piece of valuable information would come from those students who displayed different misconceptions across the two items. This probably revealed that they had only a fuzzy understanding of the concept being tested or had been guessing randomly in their responses.

The committee finalized the instrument after four rounds of field testing. The Education Office of the Yilan County decided that in 2007, every fourth grade student in the county should participate in the assessment programme. This amounted to a total of 6,374 fourth grade students from 76 primary schools participating in the mathematics assessment. In order not to impede the regular course of instruction, the assessment was administered in late June of 2007. The test results were analyzed via descriptive statistics, classical test theory and the Rasch modeling approach. They are not reported here due to the limitation of space, and interested readers can refer to Tam and Lu (2008) for more details. It is only mentioned in passing that the test data substantiated very decent reliability coefficients, with KR-20 at 0.88 and split-half at 0.95. Misconceptions about various mathematical topics could be identified. The information was disseminated to the teachers by means of a specially designed report system.

13.4 Online Report System

A tremendous amount of effort was invested to make the test results from the Yilan's assessment programme available to all concerned parties via the internet. The intended list of information recipients included the county's officials, school principals, school mathematics teachers, participating students and their parents as well as the general public. An elaborate online report system was set up so that different amounts of information were made accessible to various parties according to their level of authorization. The purpose behind such an investment is to optimize the applicability of the analysis results so as to facilitate subsequent instructional and/or remedial endeavor (Tam & Lu, 2008). Figure 13.1 displays the front page of the report online system. The school site is password protected and reserved for access by teachers and school officials. The public site is open to any interested parties. Parents can, in addition, use passwords to check the performances of their children. The public site also includes links to webpages on the results of other school subjects being tested. All the webpages are written in Chinese. In this chapter,

Fig. 13.1 The front page of the online report system

the webpages that follow were taken from the report by the Education Department of Yilan County (2008) and translated into English for international readers.

This system allows designated school officials and every fourth grade mathematics teacher to examine the performance of their students at the individual level as well as at the class and school levels. The results of students' performance are organized in various ways for different purposes. For example, there are webpages on students' performance according to the content and cognitive domains as specified in the assessment framework (see Fig. 13.2).

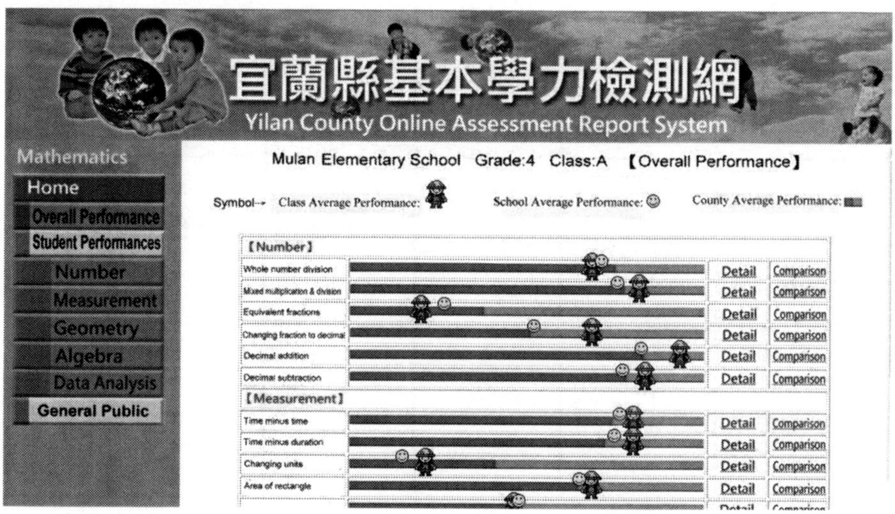

Fig. 13.2 A sample webpage illustrating the overall mean performances for a particular class of students in relation to the school and county averages (NB. The data shown here is for illustrative purpose and is not real data.)

Figure 13.2 shows a sample webpage from the online system for teachers displaying the mean performances for a particular class of students on various topics as compared to the average school and the overall county performances. More detailed results are also presented according to each curriculum standard being tested. Fourth grade teachers can find useful information regarding the types of misconceptions their students might have. There are further links to detailed reports as well as comparisons with the performances of other schools of similar size. Figure 13.3 shows a sample webpage that delineates the distribution of misconceptions across an item pair on a specific topic for a particular class of students. The numbers within each cell indicate the frequency count as well as the percentage of students with the corresponding combination of responses across the item pair. Moving the mouse over any cell would invoke a small pop-up window that reported the seat number of those students who were classified into that cell. In addition, the teachers could click on the hyperlinks of the three misconceptions listed in the headings to read more about their features together with a few suggestions about how to handle them in class.

In addition, school officials could examine their school's performance in comparison to the average performance of all schools across the whole county or the town in which the school is located (see Fig. 13.4). There are webpages that display the average performances of individual school in various subjects. Furthermore, standards setting procedures are used to classify students according to their levels of proficiency in various subjects. In fourth grade mathematics, three categories are used: "effort needed", "met the standard" and "excellent".

Item2 / Item1	Correct	Misconcept A	Misconcept B	Misconcept C	Others
Correct	14 46.67%				
Misconcept A			1 3.33%	3 10.00%	
Misconcept B			9 30.00%		
Misconcept C		2 6.67%			
Others				1 3.33%	

ID: 2,8,11,12,16,20,25,26,31

Fig. 13.3 A sample webpage illustrating the distribution of performances across a dual pair of items with the IDs of students who committed errors typical of misconception B shown

Region	School			City			County		
Value	Effort needed	Met Standard	Excellent	Effort needed	Met Standard	Excellent	Effort needed	Met Standard	Excellent
3rd CHN	16.88%	51.30%	31.82%	26.28%	50.76%	22.97%	35.89%	46.16%	17.95%
4th Math	12.50%	54.17%	33.33%	11.74%	49.08%	39.17%	18.78%	50.02%	31.20%
6th CHN	14.14%	42.42%	43.44%	15.08%	40.78%	44.14%	20.62%	42.39%	36.99%
6th ENG	23.87%	24.90%	51.23%	27.94%	21.97%	50.09%	34.63%	25.04%	40.33%
6th Math	26.23%	38.73%	35.04%	24.97%	43.87%	31.16%	30.18%	44.22%	25.60%

Fig. 13.4 A sample webpage from the online report system for school officials that illustrates the average performances of a school on various topics

A special report card was designed for the dissemination of assessment results to the students and their parents. Figure 13.5 shows a portion of the individualized student report card. The information is relatively easy to interpret and avoids direct referral to grades. The main purpose of this report card is for communication rather

Items	Topics	Performance	Comment	Overall
1	Whole number division	☆☆☆	You did real well in dividing 3-digit numbers by 2-digit numbers.	
2	Mixed multiplication and division	☆☆☆	You did real well in computing mixed multiplication and division problems.	★★
3	Equivalent fractions	☆	You may have mistaken 2/5=2/7, 3/4=3/7. (See misconception 2)	
4	Interchange between decimal and fraction	☆	Please pursue further understanding of the interchange between decimal and fraction. (See misconception 2)	Note from school
5	Decimal addition	☆☆☆	You did real well in addition problems involving 3 decimal places.	
6	Decimal subtraction	☆☆☆	You did real well in subtraction problems involving 2 decimal places.	
7	Time point minus time point	☆☆☆	You did real well in problems involving time point minus time point.	
8	Time point minus duration	☆☆☆	You did real well in problems involving time point minus duration.	
9	Changing units of area	☆	You may need clarification in square centimeter and square meter.	
10	Perimeter of rectangle	☆☆☆	You did real well in items involving perimeter of rectangles.	Comment from parent
11	Area of rectangle	☆	You may have misapplied the area formula. (See misconception 2)	
12	Perpendicularity	☆☆☆	You understand perpendicularity real well.	
13	Parallelism	☆	Please pursue further understanding of what parallel means.	
14	Priority of operations	☆	You may have only one strategy to solve items on priority of operations.	
15	Statistical graph	☆☆☆	You did real well in reading off information from stat. graphs.	
Signatures		Principal	Dean of Studies Teacher	Parent

Fig. 13.5 A sample report card of students' performance with information for students and parents

than for comparison. It is designed to help students to realize which areas they need to strengthen. Nevertheless, parents could have an idea about their children's performance through a 3 white-star rating scale that is used for each of the 15 topics being assessed. The report card also contains a 3 black-star scaling system that represents the overall performance of the student on the whole test. In both scales, top performance is indicated by three stars while poor performance receives only one star. The adoption of the starring system is to promote the diagnostic aspect of the test and attenuate the tendency of parents to compare their children's performances with others. Finally, there are concise verbal descriptions of the students' performances on each topic. Praise for good performance as well as diagnostic suggestions are expressed in a conversational manner.

Given the novelty of the ideas behind the assessment programme together with the intention of maximizing the usability of the assessment results, two workshops were organized for local teachers the attendance of which was mandatory. Instructional procedures were presented during the workshops so as to familiarize the teachers with navigating through the website. The various features of the report system were also explained. After comprehensive demonstrations, a time was set aside for discussions and questions. Important misconceptions were clarified and discussion was initiated with respect to how teachers could best use the test results to plan their remedial activities for these misconceptions as well as other teaching practices. Since the report system is quite elaborate and quite unlike anything instituted in the county before, actual demonstrations of the operations of the system had to be organized for all the fourth grade teachers. Such training sessions were deemed an essential component of the assessment programme by the committee.

13.5 Issues to Consider

The Yilan County's assessment programme represents an attempt at improving the support for classroom instruction by way of providing teachers with diagnostic information about the learning status of their students on important mathematical topics. Another purpose of the assessment is to inform the parents about the learning status of their children. Special effort was invested in compiling an informative report card that aims at providing direct attention to potential misconceptions that a student may have (Sadler, 1989), thereby facilitating remedial education at home. The whole operation demonstrates that assessment for learning is feasible even at the level of a large-scale assessment programme. However, a number of issues and challenges arose in the implementation of the programme.

The adoption of the dual items design is a special feature that helps to render the county's assessment into an assessment for instruction. This idea was not easily accepted at first, since it differs from the experiences encountered by most of the local teachers. It took some time for the idea to precipitate. In Taiwan, most assessments take the form of an achievement test, in which a wide spectrum of topics as listed in the curriculum should be represented. Accordingly, each item can only focus on testing one topic. Thus it appears on the surface that the dual items design represents a waste of resources. Another apparent limitation of the design is the small number of topics (only 16 out of 40 topics) being assessed. Moreover, the timing of the assessment is also an important matter of concern. The choice of June meant that it was conducted close to the end of the school year in Taiwan, given the requirement that it should not interfere with the regular schedule of instruction in schools. As a result, the analysis as well as the compilation of results was carried out during the summer break and the dissemination of results took place at the beginning of the subsequent academic year. Thus contrary to the purpose of formative assessment, borrowed from Scriven's (1967) concept of formative evaluation, the results from the appraisal could not be put to immediate use by the teachers. In this sense, the timing of the operation made it appear more like a summative assessment than a formative one. Two concerns arise here. First, after returning from the summer break, the students may have forgotten part of what they learnt in grade four. Second, in most cases the students will not have the same teachers teaching them mathematics in grade five. It will be less effective if a new teacher has to take care of students' misconceptions in mathematics if he or she has not taught them before. However, this disadvantage has more to do with the administrative constraints that were set by the county office rather than with an inherent flaw in the design.

Another obstacle to successful implementation has to do with reservation, or even skepticism, from some of the teachers because the assessment was initiated by the Education Department of Yilan County and was a top-down operation. Without a sense of ownership, some teachers were suspicious about its real purposes and felt threatened that they would be evaluated by how well their students performed in the county-wide assessment. The low stakes status of the assessment did not help much in desensitizing the apprehension of these teachers. Some of the information presented in the online report system might have actually led the teachers to suspect that they were also being assessed within the operation system. For example, in the online report system, there was information in a graphical display that compared the average performance of each class with respect to the average performances of all the fourth grade classes within the same school and also with respect to the average across the whole county. Some teachers might have interpreted this information as a way of comparing their effectiveness with other mathematics teachers within the same school or within the same county. Likewise, school principals might reason along the same lines and become anxious about the performance of their schools with respect to the other schools in the county.

A further undesirable outcome is that it may initiate a tendency for some teachers to teach to the test. At first, this may seem unlikely as the assessment is a low stakes test in Yilan. Yet from another angle, the likelihood is actually not negligible because all the items were made accessible to the teachers after the assessment. Moreover, the misconceptions associated with each option were also explained and displayed in the online report system. As a result, there is ample opportunity for some conscientious teachers to prepare similar items and then teach them to their students rather than focusing on the mathematical concepts. Nevertheless, it is still too early to tell whether this will happen in Yilan, since the current assessment programme and the report system were set up only quite recently. Follow-up observations are essential in this regard.

The decision to disseminate the results through a report card that is specially designed for the parents and the students could also be regarded as controversial. On the one hand, the feedback was seen as valuable for the parents and students, who can take advantage of the information provided and try to improve in their knowledge. On the other hand, it could be argued that the results might have an adverse impact. For example, the results might become a source of unnecessary competition among the students (Black & Wiliam, 1998a, 1998b), and the report card might turn into a source of over-concern for the parents towards the performance of their children. Although the report card included diagnostic statements with explicit suggestions so as to attenuate the tendency by parents to compare their children's performance with others', the practice of using stars to indicate the level of student performance in the assessment programme can still be regarded as a kind of grading system.

13.6 Future Directions for Improvement

This chapter will close by suggesting some possible future directions for enhancing the assessment programme of Yilan County. First and foremost, it is suggested that the reservations and concerns of various stakeholders towards the programme should be taken seriously and addressed. The active participation of teachers in the project should be encouraged. One way of increasing the level of teacher's involvement in the data dissemination phase of the assessment is to open up various channels through which expert teachers can share effective ways of handling the listed misconceptions by fourth grade students. Also, mutual communication should be established and measures should be undertaken to alleviate their worries that the programme serves as an implicit way to perform teacher evaluation. More consideration needs to be devoted towards devising a meaningful grading system as well as an informative report system, so that the intentions of the programme can be more easily appreciated by teachers, school principals, students, parents and education officials. A useful reference on grading and reporting is discussed in the article by Brookhart (1999), even though it is basically written for pre-service teachers. The section on setting meaning for grades can also have implication for large-scale assessments. Meanwhile, a more extensive study should be conducted to evaluate the success of the whole assessment programme, especially in relation to how well the stakeholders perceive the efficiency and the effectiveness of the programme. The educational impact that has been generated should also be gauged whenever possible.

In terms of the technical design of the assessment, some adjustments might be required. The suitability of using Rasch modeling to analyze the data should be reconsidered. Because of the special dual item structure adopted in the formal instrument, the relationship between the item pair would very likely violate the local independence assumption required by item response theory. It is suggested that more advanced techniques, such as the testlet response theory (Wainer, Bradlow, & Wang, 2007), that can handle this violation should be adopted to re-analyze the 2007 data as well as the data in the years to come. Another technical matter concerns the establishment of formal standard setting procedures for the assessment programme. Currently, there is a three black-star system on the report cards that reflects the overall performances of the participating students. However, this system was set up by consensus among members of the administrative team rather than by using more rigorous methods. It is suggested that the current system should be removed from the report cards in the future. In other words, only the performance level with respect to each mathematical topic should be provided to each student. This would be more in tune with the purpose of assessment for learning and instruction. On the other hand, should the overall performance decision be deemed essential, formal benchmarks corresponding to the basic, proficient and advanced level of performances should be established using appropriate standard setting procedures. Meanwhile, education officers in the county can set up goals for their students' attainment in mathematics with respect to these standards. For example, they can establish the goal that 80% of all students in the county should reach the proficiency level. These standards can then provide incentives and directions for improvement should the students' performances fall short of this goal. Also, these goals can illuminate the need for adjustment on the existing educational policies or practices at the school or even at the county level. In sum, the intention of these standards would be to bring about academic success to as many students as possible.

Administratively and pedagogically speaking, the timing of assessment is an important consideration. It would probably be better to carry out the assessment at a date well before the end of the school year so that the teachers have ample opportunity to modify their teaching plans and incorporate the diagnostic information into their instructional practices. Since in many cases, the fourth grade mathematics teachers may be different from the fifth grade teachers, an earlier date can avoid the embarrassing situation of requesting the upper grade teachers to deal with the misconceptions of students accrued under the tutorship of other teachers (Black & Wiliam, 1998b).

While the innovative use of assessment for learning in the large-scale programme outlined in this chapter has shown promising signs of success, it currently is only administered in fourth grade mathematics. Implementing it in other subject areas and at other grade levels in the future might create new sets of challenges. Such expansion, while seemingly desirable, does pose another danger – that the programme will become a victim of its own success. More large-scale assessments might be viewed as desirable, or even the norm, thereby resulting in more intrusion on instruction and demands on more time for testing. As a result, the scope for using small-scale formative assessment in regular classrooms – which, it could be argued, is more desirable than anything large-scale assessment can offer (Sadler, 1989) – might be diminished.

Howard Wainer (2007) argues that, while there has already been much progress in the field of psychometrics, further developments should concentrate on getting "the bang out of the buck" from tests rather than on test theory. The assessment programme that took place in Yilan represents an attempt along this line of thinking by endeavouring to make the assessment more useful to both teachers and students. Of course, there is no quick fix in educational matters and many challenges still remain. However, the attempt to transcend the traditional role of large-scale assessment towards that of assessment for learning and instruction represents one small step of assessment reform in Yilan.

Disclaimer The opinions expressed in this paper are those of the authors and do not necessarily represent the position of the Education Department of the Yilan County.

References

Black, P. J., & Wiliam, D. (1998a). Assessment and classroom learning. *Assessment in Education, 5*(1), 7–74.

Black, P. J., & Wiliam, D. (1998b). Inside the black box: Raising standards through educational assessment. *Phi Delta Kaplan, 80*, 139–144.

Brookhart, S. M. (1999). Teaching about communicating assessment results and grading. *Educational Measurement: Issues and Practice, 18*(1), 6–13.

Education Department of Yilan County (2008). *2008 Yilan county assessment: Report in language arts and mathematics*. Yilan, Taiwan: Education Department.

Ministry of Education (2003). *General grade 1–9 curriculum guidelines for elementary and junior high school education – Area of mathematics learning*. Taipei, Taiwan: Author (in Chinese).

Popham, W. J. (1999). Where large scale educational assessment is heading and why it shouldn't. *Educational Measurement: Issues and Practice, 18*(3), 13–17.

Sadler, D. R. (1989). Formative assessment and the design of instructional systems. *Instructional Science, 18*, 119–144.

Scriven, M. (1967). The methodology of evaluation. In R. W. Tyler, R. W. Gange, & M. Scriven (Eds.), *Perspectives of curriculum evaluation*. Chicago: Rand McNally.

Tam, H. P., & Lu, Y. J. (2008). *Assessment of students' performance in mathematics at the county level – The Yilan County's approach*. Paper presented at the eleventh International Council of Mathematical Education in Monterrey, Mexico.

Wainer, H. (2007). A psychometric cicada: Educational measurement returns. *Educational Researcher, 36*(8), 485–486.

Wainer, H., Bradlow, E. T., & Wang, X. (2007). *Testlet response theory and its applications*. New York: Cambridge University Press.

Chapter 14
Embedding Assessment for Learning

Bob Adamson

14.1 The Values of Assessment for Learning

The Assessment for Learning (AfL) advocacy movement that grew over the past two decades was a reaction by educational researchers and practitioners to what they perceived to be an over-emphasis on other purposes of assessment, most notably atomistic testing of student performance as part of an ethos of school accountability and selection. In many educational contexts, assessment was treated as an event that occurs at the end of a school year in order to assign grades for purposes of certification or promoting students to the next level. Assessment was used for measuring success rather than to bring about that success (Berry, 2005). Critics argued that assessment in education largely focused on the retention of knowledge and tended to perpetuate a culture of rote-learning. The high-stakes, summative nature of many assessments was seen to be eroding the formative use of assessment, leading to a distortion of the link between assessment, teaching and learning.

Policy-makers embraced the idea of AfL when it linked to their views of society's needs and governmental goals. For instance, the emphasis on developing learner autonomy in AfL ties in with the "global futures" curricular orientation that suggests that the economy will need workers who are innovative, creative, flexible, able to think critically and solve problems independently, and committed to lifelong learning (Kennedy & Lee, 2008). The devolution of decision-making responsibility to teachers and students inherent in AfL matches the general trend of instituting decentralized school-based management systems. The use of AfL in countries that ranked highly in international comparisons also persuaded some education ministries of its value – although others took a step in the other direction by strengthening their standards-based testing systems.

AfL is, on the surface, a simple and attractive idea – that students' learning can be enhanced by information garnered in the assessment process. This is an idea

B. Adamson (✉)
Department of International Education and Lifelong Learning, Hong Kong Institute of Education, Tai Po, Hong Kong
e-mail: badamson@ied.edu.hk

R. Berry, B. Adamson (eds.), *Assessment Reform in Education*,
Education in the Asia-Pacific Region: Issues, Concerns and Prospects 14,
DOI 10.1007/978-94-007-0729-0_14,

that – again, on the surface – would appeal to all stakeholders as contributing to their vision of an effective education system. Enhanced learning would result in a higher qualified workforce and better standings in international comparison tables; in better opportunities for social advancement, and in happier experiences of schooling. However, as this book demonstrates, the reality is far more complicated. Fitting the philosophy of AfL into the multiple goals of education policy in ways that move beyond rhetorical flourishes and in forms that match the culture of individual classrooms presents a number of challenges, some of which will be briefly addressed in this chapter.

14.2 Adopting AfL

The characteristics of AfL commonly found in the assessment reform policies in this volume can be summarized as follows:

- the close relationship between assessment and learning is highlighted, and assessment is viewed as a bridge linking teaching and learning;
- assessment strategies and tasks are designed to facilitate teaching and learning;
- whole-person development and the use of multifaceted assessment strategies and different kinds of assessment tasks are advocated in order to acknowledge and cater for variations in student development and learning approaches;
- learner autonomy, a key element of life-long learning, is encouraged by designing and incorporating self- and peer-assessment in the teaching and learning activities, so that students can be empowered by taking advantage of these self-regulating assessment activities;
- assessment is seen as providing the means to understand where the student is in his or her personal progress, and to diagnose difficulties students may be facing in their learning;
- rubrics are to be designed so as to facilitate judgments of the data collected through alternative assessment strategies;
- test results are to be interpreted with a view to informing teaching and learning;
- timely and comprehensive feedback is to be provided on the extent to which the students are achieving the goals and objectives of their learning and to form the basis for the creation of opportunities for students to act upon the constructive suggestions given by their teachers or their peers.

While the philosophy of AfL in very general terms might be seen as uncontroversial, these characteristics call for a realignment in contextual dynamics that might not enthuse all stakeholders. AfL empowers teachers and students, and renders the classroom (real or virtual) into a locus for assessments that are potentially high-stakes, if classroom-based assessments contribute to decisions about selection and/or accreditation. The conception of AfL is one that focuses on finding where students are in their learning progression, identifying any difficulties students may be having in the learning, and providing directions to them in the steps to be taken to enhance learning (Berry, 2008). This shift raises concerns of those who argue for a completely level playing field as the basis for such decisions, on the grounds that the judgments of teachers and students in the AfL process increases subjectivity in an area in which objectivity is valued as an indicator of fairness. Teachers who prefer a didactic pedagogical style might feel uncomfortable with the move towards incorporating assessment by students, seeing it as a lessening of their authority or the devolution of important pedagogical functions to people who are unqualified to assume them. The kind of detailed information to direct future learning that AfL would produce might be seen as indigestible by potential employers, government ministers or other stakeholders who want data presented in a simplified format to facilitate decision-making. These concerns need to be addressed if the values of AfL are to become embedded in educational practices.

Where AfL has been a reform initiative, results to date have not been as favourable as advocates had hoped, for a variety of reasons. Aligning AfL with teaching and learning is highly complex and multidimensional, as Daugherty et al. (see Chapter 12) point out. It is clear, too, that AfL will founder if teachers are not adequately and systematically prepared (e.g., Gardner et al., see Chapter 8; Chow and Leung, see Chapter 10; Berry, see Chapter 4). Continuous professional development for teachers needs to be well planned and sustained, and teachers need to be supported by policy-makers, researchers and other agencies. It is also crucial that teachers develop a sense of ownership and agency, and feel comfortable that they have the requisite knowledge and skills to carry out AfL effectively (e.g., Gardner et al., see Chapter 8; Tam and Lu, see Chapter 13; Berry, see Chapter 4). Moreover, it is not just the teachers who require professional development – students require on-going training and support in carrying out self- and peer-assessment (Chow and Leung, see Chapter 10). Problems also arose in terms of the quality of feedback (Hargreaves, see Chapter 9), which is a key component of the AfL initiative. Even when thoroughly prepared and carefully phrased, feedback does not produce the desired results without attention to the social dynamics of the classroom. Students have to truly value the feedback they receive before they act upon it.

Several authors in this book (e.g., Chow and Leung, Chapter 10; Berry, see Chapter 7) have suggested that the continuing prioritization of success in high-stakes examinations have constrained the implementation of AfL, particularly in cultures that have a long tradition of formal, standardized examinations. Several (e.g., Chow and Leung, see Chapter 10; Flaitz, see Chapter 3; Tam and Lu, see Chapter 13) have pointed out the need for contextual sensitivity in the adoption of AfL.

14.3 Linking Policy with Practice

Previous experience of educational initiatives introduced at the policy level show that they are reconfigured by examination authorities and educational publishers (at the resourced level), school principals (at the adoption level), and teachers and students (at the implementation level) to address local concerns (Adamson, Kwan, & Chan, 2000), resulting in hybrids that often distort the original goals and frustrate

1. Reform in context A
2. Generalisation & internationalisation
3. Appropriation in context B_1 (policy level)
4. Appropriation in context B_2 (resourced level)
5. Appropriation in context B_3 (adopted level)
6. Appropriation in context B_4 (implemented level)

Synthesis and adaptation

Fig. 14.1 Typical process of policy-making and implementation

efforts to bring about significant change (Fig. 14.1). This model of change is essentially a top-down model, with policy-makers eyeing the intentions of the reform rather than the context of implementation.

An alternative approach is a bottom-up model, which addresses educational concerns that arise at the chalkface. However, this approach tends to ignore the social, economic and political macro-context in which policy-makers (and funders) operate.

Pragmatism is required – a bottom-up-top-down process – so that policies attend to macro-, meso- and micro-level issues, are realistic in what they set out to achieve and engage all stakeholders from the outset (Fullan & Stiegelbauer, 1991; Fullan, 1993). Such a pragmatic approach is shown in Fig. 14.2. It takes as the point of departure the existing cultural contexts of the classroom in which the initiative is to be implemented, rather than the systemic level. Teachers are important gatekeepers of educational reform and therefore their capacity for action requires important consideration when determining the scope of the initiative. Once this has been done, then the needs of other stakeholders can be incorporated in the policy. The notion of "capacity for action" corresponds to the Vygotskyan zone of proximal development and the implementation of an initiative such as AfL can be construed and supported as a learning opportunity.

Pragmatism does not equate to laissez-faire. Change must occur at more than just the rhetorical level; there must be systemic change. For instance, a major stumbling block to the effective embedding of AfL in many systems is the presence

1. Assess features of the policy in context A
2. Align compatible features of the policy in context A with salient features of:

   appropriation sub-context B_4 (implemented level) (priority)

   appropriation sub-context B_3 (adopted level)

   appropriation sub-context B_2 (resourced level)

   appropriation sub-context B_1 (policy level)

Synthesis and adaptation

Fig. 14.2 Pragmatic process of policy-making and implementation

of high-stakes examinations. The high-stakes nature of these examinations holds implications not just for students but also for teachers, schools, parents and others, and AfL will be undermined unless it too becomes high-stakes. This requires a commitment to quality assurance so that there is societal confidence in the processes and outcomes. Whether formal or informal, holistic or atomistic, self-, peer- or teacher-assessed, AfL needs to be implemented in a rigorous, valid and reliable manner.

The compromise regarding assessment reforms that can be constructed in different settings will vary according to the political, economic and pedagogical dynamics of the policy-making process, and the weight accorded to the voices of various stakeholders. Consensus-building might start with the philosophy of assessment. As argued at the beginning of this chapter, the notion of assessment as a facilitator of learning would likely to be supported by all stakeholders. The next step would involve an examination of the current context and of the possibilities for enhancing this role of assessment as a facilitator of learning within that context. A radical overhaul of the intended practices would be likely to be beyond the capacity for action of the implementers and the system itself; what would be more feasible is a measured and realistic series of changes that the implementers and the system could be reasonably expected to cope with, given the support mechanisms and resources available.

This pragmatic approach might mean that, in some contexts, not all of the characteristics of AfL identified above would be strongly evident in early manifestations of the initiative. For instance, in the context in which teacher-centred pedagogy is the preferred norm, self- and peer-assessment might not be emphasized initially – it could be introduced gradually as the capacity for such action permits. Nonetheless, whatever manifestation of AfL is deemed appropriate for a given context, it must retain its integrity and coherence, in terms of both philosophy and practice, in order to preserve its credibility. The pragmatism needs to be principled (Kumaravadivelu, 2006).

The flexibility for integration and accommodation offered by a principled pragmatic approach can assuage the concerns of stakeholders at other levels. As noted earlier, prospective employers, college admissions officers and government ministers have very pressing needs that require assessment data in formats that might be very different from the kind of information that is valued in AfL. The creative use of technology demonstrated in the Yilin County project in Taiwan described in Tam and Lu in Chapter 13 is an example of principled pragmatism, permitting the presentation of data in a variety of ways according to different needs.

14.4 Conclusion

Assessment policy needs to be an intricate compromise, as assessment performs a variety of functions, some of which strain to be mutually compatible. The pedagogical function that lies at the heart of AfL is not easily aligned with the socio-economic and political functions of schooling when these strongly emphasize assessment of atomistic learning. Integration and accommodation is required to ensure that there is space for all of the different functions of assessment (which, as noted in Chapter 1 include grading, selection, diagnosis, mastery, guidance and prediction) without falling into the trap of assessing becoming a substitute for learning. The alignment of these functions can be centred on the notion of learning – the common goal that all stakeholders wish to see enhanced. Embedding AfL would occur through a process of synthesis, not wholesale replacement of existing practices. Assessment would be multidimensional and conducted through different modalities; the range of purposes that it serves would be integrated as far as possible. Through greater integration with teaching and learning, assessment would become less visible yet more pervasive; it would become less of an end and more of a means. The process of synthesis would be construed as a learning process for all stakeholders, and this learning needs to be scaffolded. Professional development for teachers is vital, and, if students are going to be involved in self- and peer-assessment, then they also need to be trained appropriately through exemplars, practice and moderation. Likewise school principals, parents, government officials, employers and other stakeholders need to be properly prepared for the roles they are to play, in order to maintain the integrity of the initiative.

However, "learning" itself is a slippery and multifaceted concept, so further integration and accommodation of different views is necessary. The contexts in which learning takes place also vary considerably, and the realities of these contexts have to be built into any construction of a policy – indeed, as argued above, they would need to be given prioritized consideration. All this requires on-going and purposeful dialogue between policy-makers, researchers, teachers and other stakeholders.

Even if assessment policy is context-sensitive, integrative and accommodating, there is no guarantee that it will be implemented successfully. Assessment reforms need to be systemically coherent, properly resourced and, above all, attentive to the human dimensions. As Fullan (1993) notes, reform is a journey, not a map. It is, in itself, a learning experience. If an education system wishes to adopt AfL, then it needs to do so with caution and flexibility. The words of Michael Sadler, a leading figure in the development of comparative education, are apposite:

> We cannot wander at pleasure among the educational systems of the world, like a child strolling through a garden, and pick off a flower from one bush and some leaves from another, and then expect that if we stick what we have gathered into the soil at home, we shall have a living plant. (Sadler, 1900, reprinted 1964, p. 310)

References

Adamson, B., Kwan, T., & Chan, K. K. (Eds.) (2000). *Changing the curriculum: The impact of reform on primary schooling in Hong Kong*. Hong Kong: Hong Kong University Press.

Berry, R. (2005). Entwining feedback, self and peer assessment. *Academic Exchange Quarterly*, *9*(3), 225–229.

Berry, R. (2008). *Assessment for learning*. Hong Kong: Hong Kong University Press.

Fullan, M. (1993). *Change forces: Probing the depths of educational reforms*. London: Routledge/Falmer Press.

Fullan, M., & Stiegelbauer, S. (1991). *The new meaning of educational change*. London: Cassell.
Kennedy, K. J., & Lee, J. C. K. (2008). *The changing role of schools in Asian societies - schools for the knowledge society*. London/New York: Routledge.
Kumaravadivelu, B. (2006). *Understanding language teaching: From method to post-method*. Mahwah, NJ: Lawrence Erlbaum Associates.
Sadler, M. (1900). How far can we learn anything of practical value from the study of foreign systems of education? Reprinted 1964. *Comparative Education Review*, *7*(3), 307–314.

Author Index

R. Berry, B. Adamson (eds.), *Assessment Reform in Education*,
Education in the Asia-Pacific Region: Issues, Concerns and Prospects 14,
DOI 10.1007/978-94-007-0729-0, © Springer Science+Business Media B.V. 2011

Subject Index

Lightning Source UK Ltd.
Milton Keynes UK
175462UK00006B/15/P

9 789400 707283